Acknowledgments

The authors would like to thank their spouses, Kathryn DesLauriers and Maggie Morrissey, for their patience during the many hours spent researching material.

Norm Brisson would also like to especially thank his son Nick for encouragement and technical assistance. This support was invaluable when he was able to recover a first draft of the book that was believed to be irretrievably lost, thereby saving scores of hours of work.

Mitch Morrissey would like to acknowledge the people in the Denver district attorney's office who provided guidance, support, and entertainment during his career as a prosecutor. In particular, Norm Early and Bill Ritter personified leadership and created an office nationally recognized for its innovative and effective approaches to justice.

Finally, without the help of Deanna Cook who swooped in to review, edit, and encourage, this book would never have been finished.

Dedication

This book is dedicated to my parents:

My father, Michael F. Morrissey, an incredible trial lawyer and unforgettable character.

My mother, Eileen Singer Morrissey, who raised and inspired six rambunctious children. - Mitchell R. Morrissey

And to my parents:
Norman F. Brisson and Mildred P. Brisson who gave up much in order to care for their nine children - Norman J. Brisson

Sources

This book draws from a variety of data sources, including newspaper articles, books, court decisions, and personal experience.

Note on the Authors

Mitch Morrissey worked in the Denver district attorney's office for more than 30 years, including three terms as the elected district attorney (2005 to 2017). He is an international expert on the use of DNA technology in criminal prosecutions and exonerating innocent people. After retiring from the district attorney's office, he co-founded United Data Connect, a company that helps solve cold cases using DNA and genetic genealogy. Mitch is a fourth-generation Colorado native.

Norm Brisson worked as the legal administrator in both the Denver city attorney's office, the Denver district attorney's office, and the Colorado governor's office. He taught at the University of Colorado Denver for more than 30 years. He retired as the court administrator at Lakewood Municipal Court. Originally from upstate New York, he has lived in Denver since 1978.

Table of Contents

Introduction

This book presents a brief profile of each of the district attorneys as well as some of the notable cases they handled during their terms of office in Denver. An overview on Denver's early history is presented first, followed by a chapter on the tenure of each of the 29 district attorneys who have served in this elected office. Chapter 1 begins in 1869 with Vincent Markham—before Colorado achieved statehood—and chapter 29 concludes in 2021 with Beth McCann. Similar crime themes run throughout the eras of Denver's history, including domestic violence, organized crime, corruption, and difficulties with law enforcement connecting with the community.

The district attorney has been an elected official since Colorado statehood in 1876. During the territorial period, district attorneys served two-year terms. After statehood, terms were extended to three years until 1902, when state statute created four-year terms for prosecutors. Term limits established in 1996 reduced district attorneys to two four-year terms, although Denver voters increased term limits in 2012 to allow the Denver district attorney to serve three full terms. The district attorneys were never career prosecutors in the early years. Of thc 29 district attorneys covered in this book, 20 served one term and 9 served two or more.

Early Denver

Prior to the arrival of Europeans, Denver was a lightly settled area, mostly inhabited by the Arapaho, Cheyenne, and Ute tribes.[1] The first significant white settlement occurred in 1859 with the discovery of gold at the confluence of Cherry Creek and the Platte River.

Denver (circa 1870 – 1880), courtesy of Denver Public Library Special Collections X-23177

By 1860, the number of settlers grew, and Denver was large enough to be considered a town. Located in the far western end of the Kansas Territory. Government in the area was sporadic and weak. With the nearest cities of any note hundreds of miles away, early Denver prosecutors had significant ground to cover. Arapahoe County of 1868 had boundary lines of 30 miles by 160 miles, embracing most of the present state of Colorado from the Kansas line on the east to within twelve miles of the base of the Rocky Mountains on the west—about the location of present Sheridan Boulevard. The county's 4,800 square miles was approximately the size of the state of Connecticut. Recognizing the need for more structure in the rapidly growing area, the United States Congress created, and President James Buchanan signed into law, legislation creating the Colorado Territory in 1861. The Organic Act established the territorial and local government in Colorado and created the structure of municipalities and courts as well as 17 counties and three judicial districts.

---

[1] Louvaris, Elenie. "Early Auraria: Native Peoples." University of Colorado Denver. https://clas.ucdenver.edu/historical-dialogues/Early%20Auraria%3A%20Native%20Peoples.

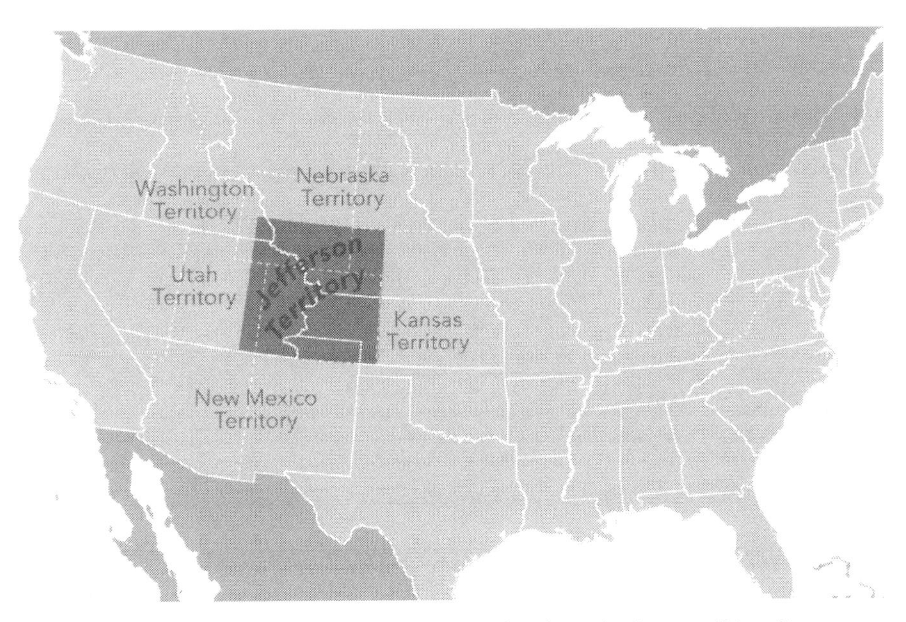

"Colorado" in 1859, map in the public domain from Wikipedia

The early settlers in what would become Colorado created the extralegal and unrecognized "Territory of Jefferson," which existed from 1859 until 1861 when the officially recognized "Territory of Colorado" was created. This territory continued from 1861 until the state of Colorado was created in 1876.

Denver grew slowly at first. In 1860, there were 4,749 people calling the city home. Over the next 10 years, by one count, the population increased by a mere ten people.[2] Though the city was no larger than a medium-sized town, the number of people passing through Denver was great—a hundred thousand or more from 1860 through 1870. Many of these itinerants were single men looking for quick riches in the Colorado mountain mining camps. They frequently brought to the young town drunkenness, disorder, and fights. Assaults and even murders in the new city were common. The difficulty of dealing with this level of violence was reflected in the succession of men hired as marshals in the town: six men served in that post in the two years between December 1859 and December 1861. One early crime control method was to hold public hangings after quick trials. From 1859 to 1860, "People's Courts" held 14 homicide trials in Denver, resulting in six hangings. A typical case of 1860 was described as follows: Thomas Freeman's body, "covered with gunshot wounds and bruises, was found floating in a stream. The People's Court gathered witnesses, who gave testimony during a two-day trial, and the court convicted Patrick Waters. A little before 3 p.m. on the third day, the sheriff, deputy sheriff, and a

[2] "History of Denver." *Wikipedia.* https://en.wikipedia.org/wiki/History_of_Denver.

posse escorted Waters to the gallows. He spent a few moments in prayer, confessed his guilt, and was launched into eternity—the fall broke his neck instantly and ended his sufferings."[3]

People's Courts were not the only way disputes were managed. "Vigilance Committees" also meted out "justice," seldom with public trials and often dispensing extreme punishment. One example occurred on September 1, 1860, when suspected horse thief Black Hawk was caught. After a secret and speedy trial by the "Committee of Safety," he was hanged. During his trial he confessed to being part of a ring of horse thieves and he implicated two others: John Shear and a local lawyer, A.C. Ford. Shear was quickly apprehended and executed. Ford left Denver by stagecoach when he heard he was named as part of the gang. The stage was stopped a short distance from Denver, and Ford was summarily shot. His body was found riddled with buckshot, with a note pinned on it that said, "Executed by the Vigilance Committee."[4]

The first murder trial in Denver occurred in 1859, about 10 years before Vincent Markham was sworn in as the first district attorney of the city. The murder itself occurred outside the city limits, but within the jurisdiction of the district. On April 8, 1859, John Stuffle was tried for killing his brother-in-law, Arthur Binegraff, while stealing $10 in gold from him. Two days previously, Stuffle put a bullet in Binegraff's head, stole his gold dust and hid his body behind a log near the juncture of Clear Creek and Ralston Creek. Stuffle then proceeded to Denver and started spending the gold dust at local saloons. After Binegraff's body was discovered by his family, Stuffle was confronted and confessed to the killing. The People's Court trial was presided over by Seymour W. Wagoner. It was an orderly trial in which Stuffle repeated his confession to the jury. Stuffle was found guilty of murder and sentenced to death. The next day before a crowd of about a thousand people, Stuffle was hanged on a Cottonwood tree near 10th and McGaa Streets.[5]

---

[3] Diane Kania and Alan Hartman. 1993. *The Bench and the Bar: A Centennial View of Denver's Legal History*, p 20.
[4] *Rocky Mountain News*, September 5, 1860, p 2, and October 29, 1860, p 2.
[5] Ben Herman and Hannah Bretz. 2008. "The First Horse Thief Vigilante Justice and Lynching in Golden." Golden Cemetery Research Project.

Marshal David J. Cook, photo from *Hands Up; or Thirty-Five Years of Detective Life in the Mountains and on the Plains,* published in 1897

Hangings were popular public events. In 1866, under Marshal David J. Cook, two men, Franklin Foster and Henry Stone, were hanged in front of a crowd estimated at 3,000—well more than half the population of Denver at that time. Foster and Stone were convicted of killing two men about 100 miles east of the city.[6] In yet another lynching, a group of 90–100 vigilantes stopped a police wagon just as it was crossing a bridge over Cherry Creek. Inside the wagon was the notorious criminal Sam Dougan, aka Sanfourd Dougan (or Dugan). The crowd lynched Dougan at Cherry Street, midway between 4th and 5th streets.[7] Dougan had murdered a man near Denver in 1865 but had escaped punishment at that time. In 1868, he and Ed Franklin robbed a man at gunpoint. Denver lawmen chased them to nearby Golden, Colorado, where Franklin was shot dead resisting arrest. Miles Hill, a local who had befriended Franklin and Dougan, perhaps unaware of their criminal activities, was also killed in the gunfight. Dougan escaped and made a run for Wyoming but was apprehended within a few days at Fort Russell after he stole a mail carrier's horse. He was returned to Denver by Marshal David Cook. Cook later said in his memoir, *Hands Up; or Thirty-Five Years of Detective Life in the Mountains and on the Plains*, that he would gladly have prevented the lynching "but it was useless for [lawmen] to fly in the face of an entire community, which had been outraged and which was aroused not so much to vengeance as to the necessity of protecting itself against the rough element of the

[6] *Rocky Mountain News*, May 17, 1866, p 1.

[7] Thomas Correa. 2019. *The American Cowboy Chronicles Old West Myths & Legends: The Honest Truth*. Page Publishing, Chapter 10, "Lynching of Dugan"; David Cook. 1897. *Hands Up; Or Thirty-Five Years of Detective Life in the Mountains and on the Plains*, p 54–56.

plains."[8] Vincent Markham took office as district attorney the year following this extra-judicial killing but took no action to prosecute any of the participants, even though many were widely known.

Fatal fight in Golden, Colorado, between Officers Cook and Goff on one side, and Sanfourd Dougan and Miles Hill on the other, from *Hands Up; or Thirty-Five Years of Detective Life in the Mountains and on the Plains* by David J. Cook published in 1897

[8] David Cook. 1897. *Hands Up; or Thirty-Five Years of Detective Life in the Mountains and on the Plains.* pp 42–47 and 54–56.

Lynching of Sam Dougan in 1868, courtesy of Denver Public Library Special Collections Z-5786

Franklin had been involved with a gang of outlaws lead by L.H. Musgrove. Musgrove himself was lynched by a Denver mob on November 23, 1868, a week earlier than Dougan. According to Cook, Musgrove shot and killed at least four men before his arrival in Denver. On July 27, 1886, after Colorado became a state, Andrew Green became the last legal public hanging; he was convicted of murdering a streetcar driver during a robbery.[9] The hanging was presided over by undersheriff John Chivington, infamous as the commander at the Sand Creek massacre, and was witnessed by 10,000 to 15,000 Denver citizens. Subsequent executions were carried out behind the walls of the state prison.

Not all crime in the area was so dramatic. In the mid-1850s, Denver was plagued by a group of misfits known as the "Bummers" who would steal clothes off clotheslines, take items

[9] Stephen J. Leonard and Thomas Noel. 1990. *Denver: Mining Camp to Metropolis*. University Press of Colorado, Niwot, CO.

from farmers' wagons, and steal from marketplaces. On January 30, 1860, the citizens of Denver finally had enough after a group of hunters was robbed of the wild turkeys they had brought to Denver to sell. Suspicion immediately focused on the Bummers, sparking the "Turkey War." A citizens' committee determined the guilty parties, but the Bummers armed themselves and fought back, threatening residents and on at least two occasions shooting at and wounding those attempting to hold the Bummers accountable. One report of events had Town Marshal "Noisy Tom" Pollock killing one of the Bummers by cracking him over the head with a rifle during a street altercation over the thefts. After another citizens' meeting, it was determined the Bummers either had to leave town or they would be lynched. Gang members must have realized the community was serious because they quickly departed for parts unknown, thus ending the Turkey War. This incident, together with the proliferation of lynchings and general mayhem of the times, illustrated the need for organized government in the area—including a prosecutor's office.[10]

One odd criminal episode took place in Denver in 1864, before a formal justice system was in place. On February 13, the first of three recorded robberies of the Denver Mint in its 150-year history occurred.[11] Mint employee James Clark stuffed his pockets with $37,000 in gold bars and treasury notes and left work. At that time, the mint was located at 16th and Market Streets in Denver. "The gold bars were so heavy that Clark began dropping them about one mile away in what is now Cheesman Park." Clark was able to get to Pueblo County before being captured, six days after the robbery. His horse was gone, and Clark was sobbing when the posse caught up to him. The captors recovered $32,580 in gold but $4,500 was never found. After his arrest, Clark was returned to Denver, where he escaped from jail. Recaptured just north of Denver, he was tried by a People's Court and banished from the city, a lenient punishment, perhaps because Clark was well known and liked by the community.

---

[10] "Denver City Turkey War," posted on January 17, 2017, by Jvl.Bell; Stanley W. Zamonsky and Teddy Keller. 1961. *The Fifty-Niners: A Denver Diary*, pp 73-75; *Rocky Mountain News*, February 8, 1860, p 2.
[11] "Mint Robbery—The Wall Street of the Rockies." https://readtheplaque.com/plaque/mint-robbery.

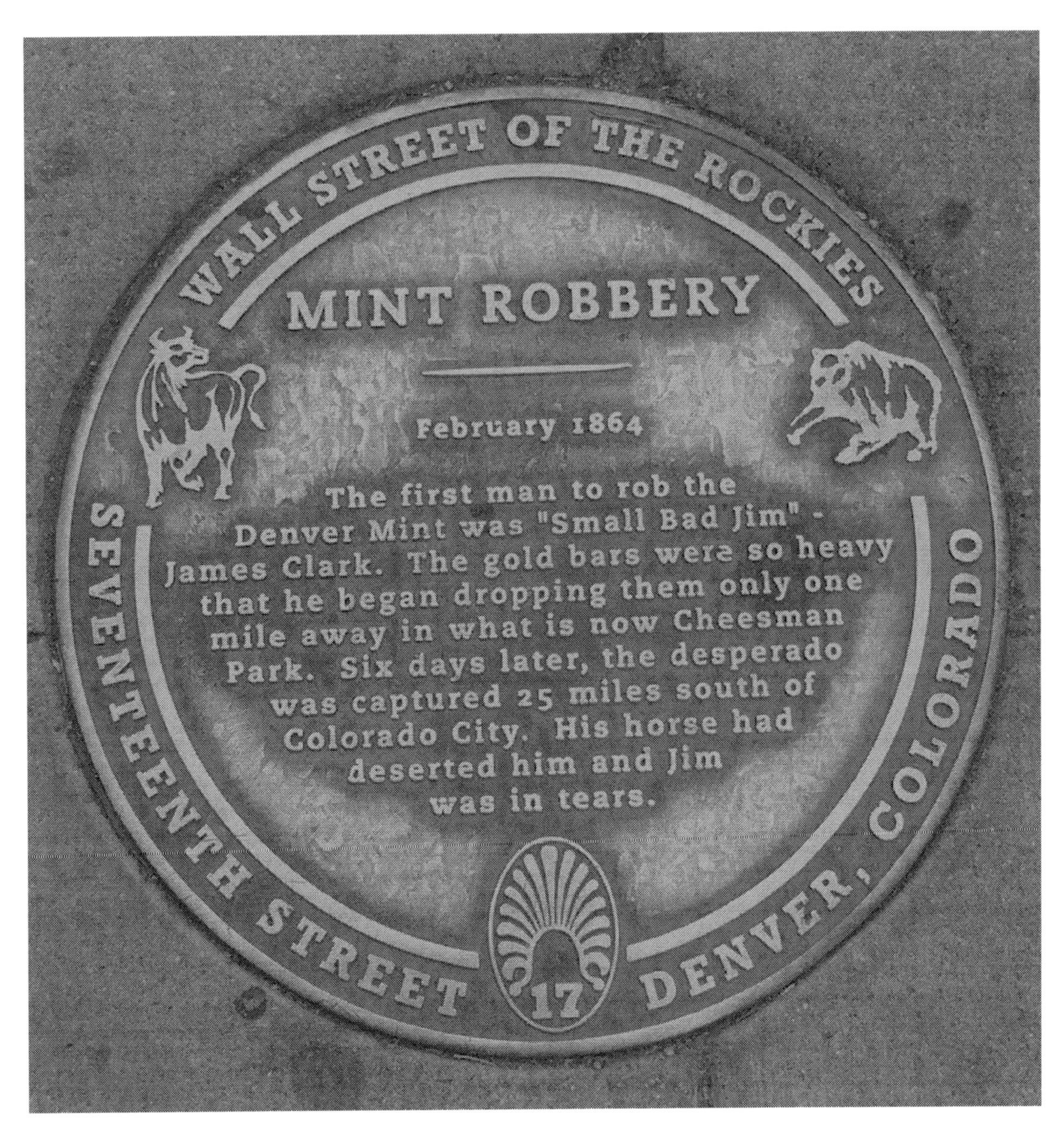

Seventeenth Street plaque, photo from https://readtheplaque.com/plaque/mint-robbery

The Clark and Gruber Mint Building. The building served as both bank and mint. The minting function of the building was sold to the U.S. government in 1863, although no U.S. coins were ever minted at this facility. A second mint building was built nearby in 1870. Photo courtesy of Denver Public Library Western History "View of the Clark, Gruber, and Co. Building" Special Collections XL-6199.

Denver's first attempts to organize a formal criminal justice system occurred during this early period of growth. In large measure due to the efforts of William Byers, the first publisher of the *Rocky Mountain News*, by 1862, "Denver had a jail, a marshal, and six policemen, plus ordinances outlawing crimes against persons and property and a law against discharging firearms in the city limits."[12] Byers explained, "Recent events in and around this city have shown the great necessity that exist for some kind of government and laws. Crime has long stalked throughout the land, but never until within the last two months has all its hideousness been presented to the eye of day."[13] The first jail for the city was built in 1861 in the alley between Market and Blake Streets. It was a rough affair built of logs; soon after its construction, it burned and had to be rebuilt.

[12] Lyle Dorsett. 1977. *The Queen City: A History of Denver*. Pruett Publishing Company. Boulder, CO. p 9.
[13] *Rocky Mountain News*, as quoted in *The Bench and the Bar*, p 19.

Denver City Jail, photo from History Colorado

The first prison in the Colorado Territory was built in Cañon City in 1871. One story, perhaps apocryphal, was that the legislature gave Cañon City its choice of either a university or a prison. Cañon City chose the prison, and the city has been home to the Colorado State Penitentiary since.

Colorado, the Centennial State, was admitted to the union in 1876, one hundred years after the signing of the Declaration of Independence. Denver became the permanent capital in 1877. Golden and Colorado City each served as the state capital for short periods of time before the state legislature decided on Denver. The State Constitution of 1876 added a judicial district to deal with the growing population, bringing the number of districts to four. In 1881, state redistricting created seven judicial districts, which jumped to 13 in 1891. Legislation in 1902 established a new county of Denver, separating it from Arapahoe County and making Denver an autonomous city, county, and the Second Judicial District. Further changes occurred over the years, leading up to the present 22 judicial districts as created in 1965.

Denver's early prosecutors worked as the district attorney part-time and usually maintained a separate private legal practice. Funding for the office budget, including staff salaries, came from the fines and fees levied against criminal defendants, a clear potential for a conflict of interest as prosecutors might be inclined to misuse the law to increase revenue to pay their own salaries. The first prosecutors also worked solo. Like the city, the Denver district attorney's office grew slowly. As late as the mid-1960s, the office consisted of 35 employees. By the late 1990s there were 65 prosecutors and approximately 200 total employees. Denver has always been a city of newcomers, of the 29 elected district attorneys in Denver between 1869 and the present, only six have been Denver natives.

Denver's prosecutors had varied careers after leaving office. Most district attorneys returned to private practice after a stint in the public sector; some became businesspeople, authors, and publishers. For others, public service became their career, going on to serve as judges, Colorado Supreme Court justices, U.S. congresspeople, U.S. senators, and Colorado governors.

Denver's District Attorneys

1869–2021

1. Vincent D. Markham (1869–1871)

VINCENT D. MARKHAM
1869–1871

Vincent D. Markham was Denver's first district attorney. He was born on his family's plantation in Chesterfield County, Virginia, on February 11, 1829. At the age of 13, he entered William and Mary College, graduating in 1848. The next few years he studied law and was admitted to practice in Virginia in 1854. In 1858, he went west to Kansas, where he was elected to the legislature in 1860. In 1862 he moved to Denver and was elected county attorney of Arapahoe County in 1866. Life in Denver at the time was not particularly pleasant or easy. There were no railroads connecting Denver to any other communities and, except for the telegraph, communication was maintained under very tedious and laborious conditions. Often the Indigenous people threatened the road to the river—completely isolating the community. There was little development of resources except in the gold regions of Gilpin County. At the time Markham arrived in Denver, many people were leaving Colorado for Montana. In 1868, he became the first district attorney for the Second Judicial District of Colorado which then included Denver. The first of three district attorneys who served when Colorado was still a territory, Markham held office from 1869 to 1871.[14]

While still Arapahoe County attorney, Markham handled an 1867 case of stolen horses. Marshal David Cook pursued William Hilligoss and George Britt into Kansas Territory after they took two horses from a corral in Denver. Although Markham was able to obtain a three-year sentence for both criminals, they escaped from prison—never to be seen by Colorado territorial authorities again.[15]

Also prior to becoming district attorney, Markham prosecuted George Corman for the hatchet murder of August Gallinger. On December 15, 1866, Gallinger—aka "Cheap John"—was murdered in his store on the corner of 12th and Blake Streets in Denver. Gallinger was a popular street peddler who did a thriving business. He lived alone in a room over his store where he was attacked by George Corman, a neighbor and well-known thief and pimp. Corman struck Gallinger in the head with a hatchet, fracturing his skull. City Marshal Cook and one of his officers were in the area and responded to Gallinger's room after hearing a strange sound. As

---

[14] "District Attorneys of Weld County." Weld County Government. https://history.weldgov.com/county_150/justice/district_attorneys.
[15] David Cook. 1897. *Hands Up; or Thirty-Five Years of Detective Life in the Mountains and on the Plains*, p 187–191.

they entered the room, they heard Corman fleeing down the back stairs. They found Gallinger bleeding profusely from a large gash in his head. He was alive but unable to speak coherently. Gallinger died without ever being able to describe his attacker. Cook searched the area and found footprints leading to Corman's home, where he lived with a prostitute named Foster. Officers found the bloody hatchet in the yard of Corman's house. When investigators interviewed Corman's neighbor, Mrs. Kerwin, she indicated that she had overheard Corman admit to the attack through the thin wall that separated their bedrooms. Corman told Foster that he "hit the damned old Jew and hit him hard." She heard Corman explain that he got no money because the marshals arrived so quickly. He also said that he buried his bloody shirt in the backyard. Cook's men dug up the yard and recovered the bloody shirt. Corman was charged with murder and future DA Markham prosecuted the case in 1867. The jury could not reach a unanimous verdict, however, and a mistrial was declared. At that time District Court only had one session per year in January. The retrial was scheduled for the next year. By the time of the new trial, Mrs. Kerwin had died and Markham could not go forward. In 1868, the case against Corman was dismissed and he moved to Georgetown, Colorado. A few years later Corman accidentally blew himself up when he dropped a canister of nitroglycerin in a tunnel outside of Georgetown.[16]

[16] David Cook. 1897. *Hands Up; or Thirty-Five Years of Detective Life in the Mountains and on the Plains*, pp 383–386.

Markham started the law firm of Markham, Patterson and Thomas, which became one of the most successful firms in Colorado for many years. One of the partners, Thomas Patterson, was the editor of the *Rocky Mountain News*, later serving in the U.S. House of Representatives and the U.S. Senate. In addition to its legal work, the firm also built the Markham hotel, named in honor of their senior partner. The hotel survived in Denver for almost 100 years until it was demolished under urban renewal in the 1960s.

Senator Patterson, Courtesy of the U.S. Senate Historical Office. The Markham Hotel at 17th and Lawrence Streets, postcard view in the public domain

After his time as DA, Markham lectured on the Law of Contracts as one of the inaugural faculty at the University of Colorado at Boulder law school.[17] Markhan continued his career as a judge and was quoted giving his friend Judge George Q. Richmond the following advice, "If you are drinking, never let your client smell your breath."[18] Markham died of bronchitis after an operation for tongue cancer on May 31, 1895, in Denver. On June 15, 1895, the *Arizona Weekly Citizen* wrote: *"Denver Republican* editorially says of the distinguished jurist: By the death of Judge Vincent D. Markham, Colorado has lost one of its most distinguished and honorable citizens.*"*[19] He was buried in the Fairmount Cemetery with his wife who had died two years earlier. Since he had no children, Markham put a clause in his will ordering his executors to choose an appropriate monument to honor him and his wife, Mary. The monument also needed

[17] Aaron Gove et al. 1894. *The Colorado Law School Journal*, Volume 10, p 105.
[18] *The Colorado Magazine*, Volume 1, November 1923, p 150.
[19] "The Good Samaritan." 2015. gravelyspeaking.com/2015/05/07/the-good-samaritan.

to display their values: "Humanity and charity are our religion." The commission to build the monument went to William Greenlee, who owned and operated the Denver Marble and Granite Company. The statue atop of the monument depicts "the Good Samaritan" giving aid to the man who had been robbed and beaten on the road from Jerusalem to Jericho.[20]

Markham's monument depicting "the Good Samaritan," photo in the public domain

2. Merrick A. Rogers (1871–1875)

Merrick A. Rogers
1871–1875

Merrick A. Rogers was born on December 28, 1838, in Dexter, New York and raised in Illinois. At age 19 he started working in a law office. He moved to Denver and worked in mining until 1861. He served in the First Regiment of the Colorado Infantry where he held the position of Quartermaster Sergeant of his company. He was a scout on the frontiers of the New Mexico Territory, Texas, and the Indian Territory. His unit was instrumental in defeating a confederate army of Texans invading New Mexico under General Henry Hopkins Sibley. Rogers's regiment marched a remarkable 92 miles in 36 hours to engage and defeat the rebels at Apache Canyon and Glorieta Pass. The Confederates, who had hoped to take

---

20 Annette Stott. 2013. "The Vincent and Mary Markham Monument." Yale Center for the Study of Material & Visual Cultures of Religion. https://mavcor.yale.edu/conversations/object-narratives/vincent-and-mary-markham-monument.

over the valuable Colorado gold and silver mines, were forced to retreat to Texas. After service in garrisons across the west, Rogers and his unit were mustered out in late 1865.[21]

In July 1867, Rogers resumed the study of law and became an attorney. After just one year as a practicing lawyer, he was elected district attorney, serving two terms for the Second Judicial District. One of the first cases handled by Rogers was the murder trial of Charles Bennett. Bennett was convicted and became the first murderer to be sentenced to the Colorado Territorial Prison. During Bennett's transport to Cañon City, the train on which he was riding was delayed, forcing the now elected Arapahoe County Sheriff, David Cook, to rent a wagon to transport Bennett and two other prisoners safely to prison. Bennett was pardoned and released from prison in 1879.[22]

Colorado Territorial Prison in Cañon City, Fremont County Heritage Commission[23]

[21] "District Attorneys of Weld County." Weld County Government. https://history.weldgov.com/county_150/justice/district_attorneys.
[22] Trac Harmon. 2011. *Old Max Turns 140*. Pueblo Chiefdom, June 13, 2011.
[23] Fremont County Heritage Commission. "CC-01." https://fremontheritage.com/cc-01-colorado-territorial-prison-1871-1876-colorado-state-penitentiary-1877-1979-colorado-territorial-correctional-facility-1979/.

Even 150 years ago, justice could be nuanced. On October 6, 1871, three-year-old Emelie Cole and her five-year-old brother William died from strychnine poisoning. The children were in the care of washerwoman Johanna Bottig at her home on G Street, below Wewatta Street in Denver. Bottig reportedly fed the Cole children and two of her own children pieces of a jelly cake and a pear. All the children complained about the taste of the cake and spit it out. The Cole children became ill, started vomiting, and having spasms. Bottig summoned doctors but Emelie died as the doctors arrived. Treatment was started on William, but he died during the night. Bottig's children did not get ill. The investigation determined that the cake was laced with strychnine. Bottig claimed that she found the cake and pears on her table, but because she ran a boarding house, boarders often left things on the table. She said she thought nothing of giving the food to the children. A local bakery indicated that James Boyce and Arthur Anderson had purchased the cake earlier that morning. Boyce had previously been a boarder at Bottig's house, and Anderson brought his washing to Bottig, often leaving it on the table. Rogers brought the case to the grand jury. They refused to indict Bottig but did indict Boyce and Anderson for the murder of the children. Rogers took the two to trial, but both were acquitted. The jury members reported that there were too many alternative suspects.[24]

Having a formal justice system did not always ensure it was used. In the spring of 1872, a Canadian crook named Bill White came to Denver. He teamed up with "Handsome" Larnigan, taking up residence at the Broadwell House on Larimer Street. White pretended to be an invalid. One night a room in the hotel was burglarized, and $300 in cash as well as a watch valued at more than $700 were stolen—a significant haul in 1872. White and Larnigan were arrested, but Rogers determined that the crimes could not be proven against the two and they were released. Warned to leave town, they moved to Pueblo. However, White took up the invalid scam again in Pueblo, and once again there were several thefts in the hotel where White stayed. White fled back to Denver, and he was arrested and transported back to Pueblo—where an angry mob lynched him.[25]

---

[24] "Who Poisoned the Cole Children." *Daily Register Call*, October 29, 1871, p 4.

[25] David Cook, 1897. *Hands Up; or Thirty-Five Years of Detective Life in the Mountains and on the Plains*, p 231–234.

Lynching of Bill White at Pueblo, from *Hands Up; or Thirty-Five Years of Detective Life in the Mountains and on the Plains* by David J. Cook published in 1897, p 380

DA Rogers worked to maintain the rule of law. In 1872, L.P. Griswold moved to Denver and established a "Vigilance Committee." Griswold had been a member of such a group in Laramie, Wyoming, prior to moving to Denver. Shortly after its formation, the Committee determined that James O'Neal was guilty of a crime serious enough to merit being lynched. It was subsequently discovered, however, that O'Neal was innocent. Griswold was the real murderer—Rogers arrested Griswold and charged him with murder. Believing he stood no chance if brought to trial, Griswold attempted an escape and was killed while doing so.[26]

Also in 1872, Theodore Miears (or Meyers) was a ranch hand working for Annabelle Newton. On August 10, he shot and killed fellow ranch hand George Bonacina over Bonacina's failure to repay a $25 loan. Miears then went to the ranch house and shot and wounded Newton. Miears fled the ranch, believing Newton was dead. Newton was able to get to Denver the next day and reported the crime to Sheriff David Cook. Cook investigated the crime scene, caught Miears in Woodbury, Colorado, and returned him to Denver—where Rogers charged Miears

[26] "Hanging of James O'Neal at Brown's Bridge," *Rocky Mountain News*, July 12, 1870, p 4.

with first-degree murder and attempted murder. At trial, the defense argued alternately that the crime lacked premeditation and that it was in self-defense. Neither strategy worked. Miears was convicted and hanged on January 24, 1873, in front of 3,000 people.[27] Prior to his execution, Miears gave a full confession to reporters, albeit with extenuating circumstances.[28]

Rogers was elected to the state senate in 1878, and in 1889, he was appointed as the second and last judge of the Superior Court of the City of Denver. In 1901, Rogers committed suicide in Steamboat Springs by lighting the fuse of an explosive stick of "giant powder" (dynamite) with his cigar and lying down on the stick.[29]

3. Christian S. Eyster (1875–1877)

Christian S. Eyster was born on May 19, 1814, in Chambersburg, Pennsylvania. Eyster attended Wesleyan University in Connecticut, leaving in 1833. He practiced law in Pittsburgh from 1837 to 1840 and was the acting district attorney of Allegheny County, Pennsylvania from 1840 to 1846. Eyster served as a member of the Pennsylvania Legislature from 1853 to 1855. Before the Civil War he practiced law with William H. Seward, Secretary of State to Abraham Lincoln and Andrew Johnson. Eyster was a well-read lawyer with a large practice, but when his office was destroyed in the burning of Chambersburg during the Civil War, he decided that he preferred to become a judge in the U.S. territories rather than rebuild his office. U.S. Senator Thaddeus made the recommendation for the judgeship. Appointed to the Colorado Territorial bench by President Andrew Johnson, Eyster was an associate justice from 1866 to 1871. Eyster was elected district attorney for the Second Judicial District of Colorado, and served in that capacity for two years, until 1877.[30] He was the last Denver district attorney under Colorado Territorial government.

One of the first cases handled by Eyster involved a disputed killing that resulted in an acquittal. On June 5, 1875, Clarence Chubbuck and John Phillips got into an argument over the

---

[27] David Cook. 1897. *Hands Up; or Thirty-Five Years of Detective Life in the Mountains and on the Plains*, p 147–162.
[28] *Rocky Mountain News,* January 24, 1873.
[29] "Suicide of Judge Rogers, One of Steamboat's Esteemed Citizens Takes the Giant Power Route," Steamboat Pilot. November 27, 1901, p 1.
[30] James K. Logan. 1911. *The Federal Courts of the Tenth Circuits: A History*, Volumes 62–63, p 44. Wesleyan University, Alumni Record, p 612.

ownership of a steer during a cattle roundup near Lake Loveland. During the exchange, Chubbuck struck Phillips with a snake whip and drove him out of the camp. Phillips returned the next day and again pressed his ownership claim. As Chubbuck approached Phillips with his whip in hand, Phillips shot him. Chubbuck died the next day, saying that the shooting was all his fault. Notwithstanding Chubbuck's dying statement, the grand jury indicted Phillips, and Eyster took the case to trial. Future Denver DA Ledru Rhodes effectively defended Phillips in trial, with a speedy acquittal from the jury.[31]

Another case investigated by Eyster involved the famous outlaw and sometime lawman John Henry "Doc" Holliday. As the story goes, Holliday worked as a faro dealer at Babbitt's House in Denver in November 1875. At the time, it was illegal to carry firearms in Denver, though many people ignored the law. Holliday carried only a knife. One night an angry gambler named Bud Ryan pulled out a gun at Holliday's faro table. Doc leaped at Ryan, overpowered him, and cut him with the knife. Even though Holliday fled town immediately after the incident, Eyster refused to file charges against him, considering his actions as self-defense.[32] A biography of Doc Holliday by a family member challenges this story, saying that although he did indeed work as a faro dealer at that time and in that saloon, Doc never had any run-ins with the law. She blamed gambler and gunslinger William Barclay "Bat" Masterson with perpetuating this Wild West tale.[33]

---

[31] Weekly Courier, January 20, 1911, p 6; Las Animas Leader, V3 No. 3, June 25, 1875, p 2; and Denver Daily Times, July 23, 1875, p 4.

[32] "More about Doc Holiday of Spalding County," http://sites.rootsweb.com/~gaspald3/more_about_doc_holliday.htm.

[33] Karen Holliday Tanner. 1983. *Doc Holliday: A Family Portrait*, University of Oklahoma Press, Norman.

John Henry (Doc) Holliday, as he appeared in the early 1880s, photo courtesy of Denver Public Library Special Collections : Z-8850

Eyster failed to file charges in another well-documented incident involving a famous and connected citizen when charges clearly would have been justified. On April 5, 1876, editor and owner of the *Rocky Mountain News* William Byers was going home for lunch at 13th and Bannock Street when he was confronted by his mistress, Hattie Sancomb. (The Byers-Evans House, now a museum, still stands at the 13th and Bannock location.) Byers had recently ended their long-term love affair. Sancomb accosted Byers on the street near his home and produced a pistol. Byers's wife, Elizabeth, saw the altercation from the house, jumped into a horse drawn coach, and rescued her husband. Sancomb fired twice at Byers but missed. When Sancomb approached the Byers' home she was convinced to leave by Byers's son. His "convincing" was enhanced by the fact that he was holding a shotgun at the time. Police arrested Sancomb a block away. It was rumored that Eyster never charged Sancomb because Byers was interested in running for office and wanted to keep the affair quiet. His plans to keep the incident under wraps and his political ambitions both took a hit when another newspaper editor in Golden printed the entire story.[34]

William Byers, founder of the *Rocky Mountain News*, photo in the public domain

Denver's first recorded mass murder occurred during Eyster's term. On October 21, 1875, four bodies were found in a basement room at 634 Lawrence Street. The victims—itinerant Italian musicians and scissor-grinders—were new to Denver and consisted of a father, his two sons, and a nephew. They had been savagely killed, their throats slit and their bodies mutilated. The incident became known as the "Italian Murders." Philomeno Gallotti, the mastermind of the murders, was a local gang leader who had started his criminal life in Italy before immigrating to Denver. A strong odor from the building led to the discovery of the killings several days after the murders. In the interim, Gallotti and accomplices left town, most heading for Mexico. Deputies for Marshal Cook captured Gallotti and two other gang members in Taos, New Mexico, after tracking them from Cañon City to Pueblo to Trinidad and Fort Garland. In total, nine individuals

[34] Kerry Klun. 2011. "Historic Homes of Denver: People Who Shaped Denver's History – William Byers and the Divorcee," https://activerain.com/blogsview/2161200/historic-homes-of-denver--people-who-shaped-denver-s-history---william-byers-and-the-divorcee.

were implicated and arrested for the murders. The evidence and their own confessions indicated that this band would surely be hung. Attorneys for the accused Gallotti, Valentine, Campagne, and Ballotti, however, found a loophole in the law that allowed them to avoid a death sentence. The law called for death by hanging if the defendant were found guilty by a jury. Because Gallotti, Valentine, Campagne, and Ballotti had pleaded guilty without a jury trial, there was no mechanism to empanel a jury to determine if they should get the death penalty, so they were sentenced to life.[35] Two other defendants, Anatta and Allessandri entered pleas to voluntary manslaughter and received 10 years each. The defendant Deodotta was acquitted on the charge of being an accessory, and the others went free. Gallotti, the leader of the cut-throat band, was pardoned in 1885, leaving immediately for his native Italy. According to reports, however, he died on his journey. Ballotti died in prison on December 20, 1887. Campagne was pardoned out on June 29, 1888, and Valentine was released by Governor Waite on August 5, 1895.

Illustration of the "Italian Murders" from *Hands Up; or Thirty-Five Years of Detective Life in the Mountains and on the Plains*, published 1897, p 18

[35] The Colorado Supreme Court addressed the ruling in another case, and the life sentences were upheld. The Colorado legislature changed the law and closed this loophole in 1881.

The Italian Mob, circa 1876, photo courtesy of Denver Police Museum

Eyster died of paralysis at his home in Fruita, Colorado, on November 6, 1886.[36] Former DA Markham remembered Eyster fondly: as "a true and faithful friend, generous to a fault." The Colorado Supreme Court read on the record a resolution about Eyster,

> "Resolved, That in the death of Judge Christian S. Eyster the bar of Colorado has lost one of its most honest, honorable and conscientious members; and Colorado and society one of its noblest ornaments of generousness, humanity and charity."[37]

---

[36] Montezuma Millrun, November 13, 1886, p 2.

[37] William Beck. 1889. *Cases Argued and Determined in the Supreme Court of the State of Colorado*, Volume 12, the In Memoriam Section, Callahan and Company, p XXV.

4. David B. Graham (1877–1882)

DAVID B. GRAHAM 1876-1882

David B. Graham was one of the first practicing attorneys in Denver and the first Denver district attorney elected after Colorado gained statehood. Graham served as district attorney for six years, two full terms. This duration of service was not repeated for almost 50 years, until Earl Wettengel served from 1929 to 1936. Graham was born February 17, 1846. He graduated from Duff's College in Pittsburgh, Pennsylvania. He served in Company 1 of the 211th Pennsylvania volunteers during the Civil War, seeing action at Petersburgh and Richmond. After the war, Graham attended Westminster College in Wilmington, Pennsylvania. Upon graduation, he became the principal of a small school in Pennsylvania before enrolling in law school in Albany, New York. He moved to Denver in 1871, opened a practice, and was elected district attorney as a Republican in 1876. The Second Judicial District at that time was composed of Arapahoe, Douglas, Elbert, Larimer, and Weld counties—a huge geographical area. Graham was reelected in 1879.[38]

Graham oversaw several cases of note as the city's top criminal prosecutor. On August 13, 1879, the *Rocky Mountain News* reported Graham's prosecution of one George Stratton, accused of murdering Daniel Farr. The prosecution of a case was much less involved in those days than it is now. The entire case, from opening statements to the jury deliberations and verdict, was completed in one day.[39]

Graham was the district attorney during the anti-Chinese riots in Denver. These began on the afternoon of Halloween, 1880. There are several accounts about how the riots began—the most plausible explanation is that the riots started as the result of an attack on two Chinese citizens by a group of drunken whites. But the rumor that night was that two Chinese shot at a couple of railroad workers in a poolroom altercation. Although no one was injured in the alleged shooting, rumors quickly spread that a "Chinaman" shot a white man. Mobs numbering up to 2,000 people attacked Chinese businesses and any Chinese person unfortunate enough to be caught in lower downtown.

---

[38] "District Attorneys of Weld County." Weld County Government. https://history.weldgov.com/county_150/justice/district_attorneys.

[39] "Murder in Denver," Daily Register Call, January 15, 1879, p 4; "Found Guilty," Colorado Weekly Chieftain, February 13, 1879, p 4.

A cartoon depiction of Denver's anti-Chinese riot of 1880 printed in the November 20 issue of Frank Leslie's *Illustrated Newspaper*. Source: Library of Congress

Former city marshal David Cook—now the head of the Rocky Mountain Detective Association—deputized 125 citizens to supplement the eight regular city police officers on duty when the rioting started. One Chinese man, Sing Lee (Look Young in some references), was lynched. The mayhem was over in a little more than one day, but the Chinese community never recovered from the devastation to their homes and businesses. Several thugs were arrested, but no convictions resulted.[40]

Some of the least reputable citizens of Denver distinguished themselves by showing a humane and courageous spirit in face of the anti-Chinese mob. One of them was gunfighter and gambler Jim Moon. Moon single-handedly opposed a portion of the mob. Facing the crowd, he demanded in strong language to know what they wanted. When there was no response from the crowd, Moon declared: “This Chinaman is an inoffensive man, and you shan’t touch him, not a ------- one of you.” His comment was enforced by the “mute elegance of a leveled revolver”; the mob turned abruptly away, being afraid “to face the music.”[41]

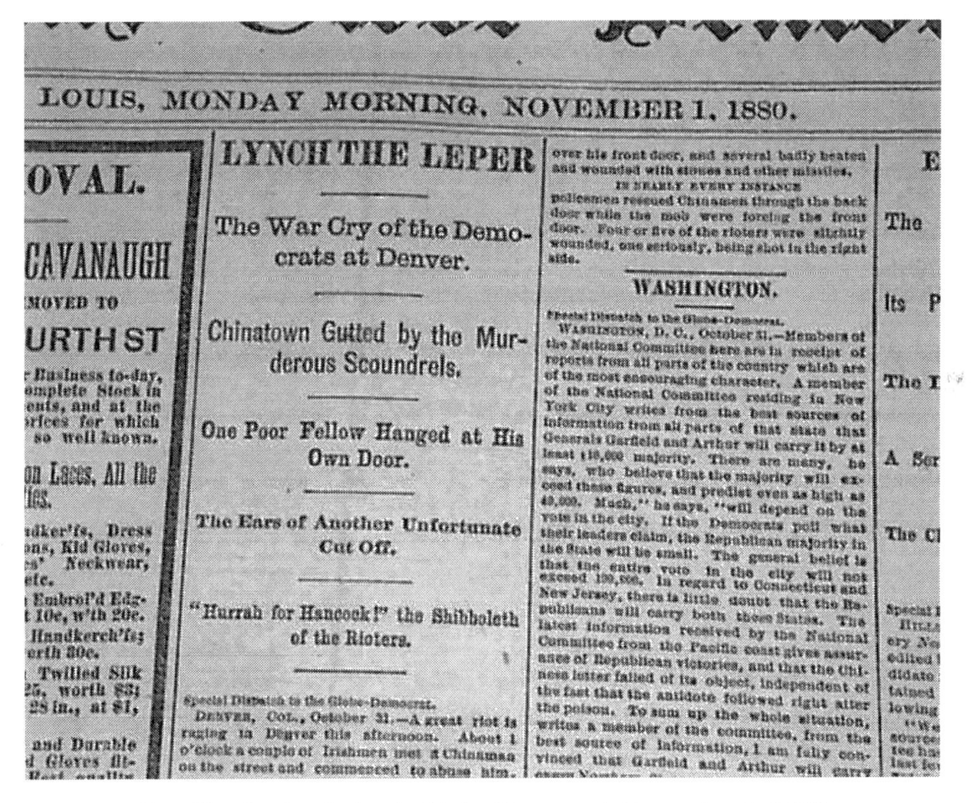
LOUIS, MONDAY MORNING, NOVEMBER 1, 1880.

OVAL.

CAVANAUGH

MOVED TO

URTH ST

Business to-day, omplete Stock in ents, and at the prices for which so well known.

on Laces, All the ies.

dker'fs, Dress ons, Kid Gloves, s' Neckwear, etc.

Embroi'd Edg- t 10c, w'th 20c. Handkerch'fs; orth 30c. Twilled Silk 25, worth $3; 28 in., at $1,

and Durable d Gloves fit-

LYNCH THE LEPER

The War Cry of the Democrats at Denver.

Chinatown Gutted by the Murderous Scoundrels.

One Poor Fellow Hanged at His Own Door.

The Ears of Another Unfortunate Cut Off.

“Hurrah for Hancock!” the Shibboleth of the Rioters.

Special Dispatch to the Globe-Democrat.

DENVER, COL., October 31.—A great riot is raging in Denver this afternoon. About 1 o'clock a couple of Irishmen met a Chinaman on the street and commenced to abuse him.

over his front door, and several badly beaten and wounded with stones and other missiles.

IN NEARLY EVERY INSTANCE

policemen rescued Chinamen through the back door while the mob were forcing the front door. Four or five of the rioters were slightly wounded, one seriously, being shot in the right side.

WASHINGTON.

Special Dispatch to the Globe-Democrat.

WASHINGTON, D. C., October 31.—Members of the National Committee here are in receipt of reports from all parts of the country which are of the most encouraging character. A member of the National Committee residing in New York City writes from the best sources of information from all parts of that State that Generals Garfield and Arthur will carry it by at least 10,000 majority. There are many, he says, who believe that the majority will exceed these figures, and predict even as high as 40,000. Much," he says, "will depend on the vote in the city. If the Democrats poll what their leaders claim, the Republican majority in the State will be small. The general belief is that the entire vote in the city will not exceed 190,000. In regard to Connecticut and New Jersey, there is little doubt that the Republicans will carry both these States. The latest information received by the National Committee from the Pacific coast gives assurance of Republican victories, and that the Chinese letter failed of its object, independent of the fact that the antidote followed right after the poison. To sum up the whole situation, writes a member of the committee, from the best source of information, I am fully convinced that Garfield and Arthur will carry

Headline in the St. Louis Globe Democrat, November 1, 1880

Sometimes, the community decided that justice was best dealt with on the street. That was the situation in 1881 when Graham brought Clay Wilson to trial for killing the notorious gambler James Moon, the one-time hero in the 1880 anti-Chinese riots. On June 16, 1881, Moon

[40] Roy T. Wortman. 1965. “Denver’s Anti-Chinese Riot, 1880.” *The Colorado Magazine* XLII/4.
[41] *The Colorado Magazine - History Colorado* v42 N4 Fall 1965, p 283.

was the manager of the Arcade Saloon and Gambling House on Larimer Street, and Wilson was employed as a faro dealer. Moon believed that Wilson was developing a romantic relationship with Moon's wife Emma and threatened to kill Wilson. As a result of the threat, Wilson armed himself with a .45 Colt revolver when he went to the Arcade. Moon entered the saloon that morning and immediately threatened Wilson. Wilson shot Moon who collapsed, suffering four gunshot wounds. Graham charged Wilson with murder.[42] When the jury got the case, however, it took them only 20 minutes of deliberation to find Wilson not guilty. The citizens felt Wilson did the community a favor by ridding it of a violent bully with a history of beating and killing.[43]

Within days of the acquittal, a woman came to Wilson's room in the middle of the night. When Wilson refused to open the door, the woman pulled a revolver and sent a bullet through it. Wilson was not injured, and the woman was never identified—but she apparently was not happy with the outcome of the trial.

Gunfighter and gambler, James Moon, *The Colorado Magazine* XLII/4 1965 p 283

[42] Gunnison Daily News-Democrat, V1 No.81, September 22, 1881, p 1.
[43] "Gambler Jim Moon Killed in Denver." *Aspen Daily Times*, Aug. 2, 1956, p 2; *Dolores News*, June 25, 1881, p 1.

The Arcade Saloon on Larimer Street where Moon was killed, circa 1890
Courtesy of Denver Public Library Special Collections, X-25715

As much as the justice system was evolving at this point in Denver's history, it was still very much in its infancy. For example, shortly after midnight on March 30, 1882, a group of men took accused cattle thieves W.T. Phebus and Jay McGrew from the Denver Jail and hanged them nearby. Although the Cattle Growers' Protective Association was suspected of organizing the two lynchings, authorities were never able to identify any of the participants, and no one was ever charged with the crimes.[44]

DA Graham spent a short period in private practice after he left the district attorney's office, and then was elected to the District Court bench. As judge, one of Graham's more notable rulings related to the 1894 "City Hall War." The conflict illustrated the resentment that Denverites felt about the Colorado governor appointing certain city positions. In this confrontation, Judge Graham issued a restraining order to stop Governor Davis Waite's appointees to the Denver Fire Commission and Denver Excise Commission from taking office. When the governor could not get the judge to modify his order, Waite called out the First Regiment of the Colorado Infantry and the Chaffee Light Artillery of the Colorado National Guard to physically enter Denver City Hall and remove the two incumbent commissioners so his appointees could move in. The city police force and a large contingent of armed deputy sheriffs

---

[44] *Macon Telegraph*, April 1, 1882.

protected City Hall. More than 200 men with handguns, rifles, and dynamite faced off against the militia armed with howitzers and heavy guns. The Colorado Supreme Court eventually ruled against the incumbent city officials, and a court order accomplished what the governor had attempted through arms.

The Mob at City Hall Denver, Denver Public Library Special Collections X-22122

Colorado State Militia Marching to Denver City Hall 1894, photo from Denver Public Library Special Collections X-22116

5. Herman E. Luthe (1883–1885)

Herman E. Luthe was another of Denver's first practicing attorneys, starting his practice in 1872. Luthe was born in Columbia County, Kinderhook, New York, on January 27, 1847. When he was three years old, his family moved to Beaver Dam, Wisconsin, where Luthe pursued literary studies and graduated from Wayland University in 1867. He then began the study of law, was admitted to the bar, and began to practice in Beaver Dam in 1869. In the fall of 1870, he moved to Denver, Colorado Territory, traveling in a covered wagon. He became a member of the Denver bar and held the office of police magistrate for two years before being elected a member of the state legislature in 1878. In 1883, he was elected district attorney for the Second Judicial District.[45] One of Luthe's first hires as an assistant district attorney was John Shafroth, who went on to a career as a U.S. congressman, U.S. senator, and Colorado governor.

Luthe prosecuted the first case held in the Arapahoe County Courthouse which was located on 16th and Tremont streets in Denver. (The origin of the downtown, "Court Place street name.) It was a three-story building when it opened; a fourth story was added in 1893. A statue of Lady Justice originally stood atop the dome of the courthouse. Below the dome eight griffin sculptures faced out in all directions. The Courthouse, known as the "Grand Old Courthouse" was razed as an unemployment relief project in 1934 at the height of the depression.[46] Attorneys from the district attorney's office tried criminal cases at the Arapahoe County Courthouse until the West Side Courthouse, located at Speer and Kalamath Street, was opened in 1921. The West Side Courthouse still stands and today is the Hispanic Heritage Center.

---

[45] "District Attorneys of Weld County." Weld County Government. https://history.weldgov.com/county_150/justice/district_attorneys

[46] *Denverite*. 2017. "A Denver relic for sale on eBay conjures memories of the city's resistance to change." https://denverite.com/2017/07/15/a-historic-denver-relic-for-sale-on-ebay-conjures-memories-of-denvers-resistance-to-change/.

Old Arapahoe County Courthouse in the area bounded by 15th and 16th Streets/Tremont and Court Place in the City of Denver, circa 1900. Photo from the New York Public Library.[47]

West Side Courthouse, photo courtesy of History Colorado. The building served for many decades as the primary municipal court for the City of Denver as well as a state district court. It housed the Denver district attorney's office until 1984.

[47] New York Public Library Digital Collection. "Courthouse, Denver, Colo." Detroit Publishing Company Postcards. https://digitalcollections.nypl.org/items/510d47d9-a0f5-a3d9-e040-e00a18064a99.

John Franklin Shafroth, Denver assistant district attorney, U.S. representative, U.S. senator, and then governor of Colorado, photo in the public domain

Between September 1883 and December 1884, Luthe tried fourteen people for murder before District Court Judge Victor A. Elliott in Denver. Of the fourteen, he obtained 11 convictions. Judge Elliott was the father of future Denver DA Willis V. Elliott.

Although Denver's criminal justice system has changed considerably from the days of Herman Luthe, some parts of the system are all too familiar. For example, getting convictions on cases of domestic violence has always been problematic. On October 23, 1883, O.J. Haller murdered his estranged wife, Alice Haller, and Samuel H. Morris. The two were lodging at the same house at the corner of 19th and Arapahoe Streets in Denver. Haller had not lived with his wife for some time but continued to come to the house to see his two children and to abuse his wife. No sexual relations were believed to have existed between Morris and Mrs. Haller, but they planned to marry if she could get a divorce. Haller was insanely jealous of his estranged wife and hid in the coal house in the rear of the house in order to kill Morris; he then ran into the house and shot his wife dead. Luthe charged Haller with two counts of first-degree murder, but the jury found Haller not guilty by reason of emotional insanity.[48]

In December 1883, young prizefighter Harley B. McCoy was drinking at the Free and Easy Saloon at 21st and Market Streets in Denver when he got into an argument with reputed prostitute Lottie Perry. McCoy struck Perry, knocking her to the floor. Benjamin F. King

[48] *Fairplay Flume*, October 25, 1883, p 5.

interceded and left with Perry in a carriage. When the two arrived at Preston's boarding house, where Perry resided, they found McCoy waiting for them with a revolver. McCoy ordered King out of the buggy, but before the man could comply, the boy who was driving the buggy whipped the horses and they started away. McCoy fired at the carriage as it pulled away, and a bullet passed through the cushions of the back seat and struck King in the side. Luthe charged McCoy with murderous assault. He was convicted and sentenced to a year imprisonment in the Arapahoe County Jail.[49] Several years later, the same McCoy went to prison on a life sentence for the murder of Denver Police Captain Charles Hawley after gunning him down outside the Windsor Hotel. McCoy received a pardon from Governor Charles Thomas, however, after serving less than 10 years of his life sentence—McCoy had previously worked for Governor Thomas's political machine in Denver.[50] McCoy was killed in a train wreck nine months after being released from prison.

Earlier in 1883, Luthe prosecuted William Walker for murder in the killing of Chinese laundryman Sam You. In the trial the prosecution attempted to prove the defendant had time to deliberate before shooting the victim. Testimony established that Walker told a boardinghouse keeper earlier in the day that before the day was over, he would, "kill some son of a bitch." The woman tried to convince the defendant to leave his gun at home but he refused. The defendant, in his own testimony, stated that he struck the victim during a billing dispute after the victim told him to leave his laundry business. The defense contended that when You retaliated by hitting Walker with a stick, Walker shot and killed You in a fit of rage. His attorney maintained that Walker was too drunk to form intent and he should not be found guilty of murder. The jury agreed and found him guilty of manslaughter. Many citizens in Denver still held strong anti-Chinese sentiments at the time of Walker's trial, and the lenient verdict may have been a result of those feelings.

In 1884, future Denver mayor Robert Speer ran for the office of city clerk. The election was rife with fraud and ballot stuffing. After winning the election, Speer and several of his associates went to the city offices and banged on the door of the incumbent city clerk, demanding to be let in. When the clerk refused to open the door, Speer and his group took the

---

[49] *Carbonate Chronicle*, December 22, 1883, p 5.
[50] *Daily Journal* (Telluride), June 22, 1900, p 1.

door off its hinges, beat the clerk unconscious, and then threw him into Larimer Street.[51] Neither Speer nor any of the other participants were charged or prosecuted by Luthe for the incident.

Luthe was also the district attorney when Herman Webster Mudgett, better known as Dr. Henry Howard (H.H.) Holmes, married Georgiana Yoke in Denver while still married to Myrta Belknap, thus committing the crime of bigamy. Mudgett/Holmes was one of the first confirmed serial killers in America. While operating the World's Fair Hotel in 1893 in Chicago, Holmes was credibly determined to have killed nine people (although he confessed to 27 murders). Holmes was convicted and executed in 1896 in Philadelphia for yet another murder. Bigamy was a crime in Colorado, but by the time it became clear to Luthe that Holmes had multiple wives, he was already charged with murder in Philadelphia.[52] Holmes's story was told in the best-selling book, *Devil in the White City* by Erik Larsen.

Herman Webster Mudgett, better known as H.H. Holmes, in his 1895 mug shot, photo in the public domain.

[51] *Fairplay Flume*, May 15, 1884, p 1.

[52] Colorado Statewide Marriage Index, 1853-2006, Henry M. Howard and Georgiana Yoke, January 17, 1894, Denver, Colorado, United States; citing p 16256, State Archives, Denver; FHL microfilm 1,690,090.

Josephine Moody Luthe, photo in the public domain

Luthe's wife, Josephine, was an accomplished attorney in her own right. She was the second woman in Colorado to be admitted to the Colorado bar and was arguing criminal cases to all male juries in Denver before women had yet achieved the right to vote. She was also a gifted artist, Chair of the Art Department at Coe College in Cedar Rapids, Iowa, and a vocalist. As a delegate to the Silver Convention in Washington, D.C. in 1892 she delivered a widely admired address on "free coinage."[53] Free coinage advocated for the unlimited minting of silver coins in the belief it would improve the economic lot of the common man.

Herman Luthe died on November 25, 1931, at age 84.[54]

6. Ledru R. Rhodes (1886–1889)

Ledru R. Rhodes became the district attorney for the Second Judicial District after defeating Isaac Stevens. Rhodes was a prominent Larimer County attorney when elected. At that time, the Second Judicial District consisted of Arapahoe, Weld, and Larimer Counties. Rhodes was born in Licking County, Ohio, on February 12, 1849. He left school at age 15 and was teaching school in his home state of Ohio by age 16. He never attended law school but was admitted to the Iowa bar in 1870 after working in a law office in Marengo, Iowa. He moved to Ft. Collins, Colorado in 1872 and opened a law practice there a year later. While working as a private attorney, he successfully defended a man charged with murder. He

[53] William C. Sprague. 1893. *The Law Student's Helper*, V1, No.1, p 138.
[54] "Herman E. Luthe." 2021. *Find a Grave*. https://www.findagrave.com/memorial/123838555/herman-e_-luthe.

was elected city attorney in Fort Collins in 1874 and a Colorado state senator in 1877. In 1885 he was elected Denver district attorney.[55]

One of his early significant cases as district attorney was a murder trial. On the night of May 19, 1886, Andrew Green shot and killed streetcar driver Joseph Whitnah. A special grand jury was impaneled and indicted Green. The danger of a lynching convinced Rhodes to act quickly. At trial on June 22, 1886, a jury found Green guilty and he was sentenced to hang. On June 27, the scaffold was erected on a bend of Cherry Creek, about midway between the Broadway and Colfax Avenue bridges. An estimated 10,000 to 15,000 people witnessed the free, public execution that day.[56]

Killing of streetcar driver Whitnah by Green from *Hands Up; Or Thirty-Five Years of Detective Life in the Mountains and on the Plains* by David J. Cook published in 1897, p 51

[55] Ansel Watrous. 1911. *History of Larimer County, Colorado*; "District Attorneys of Weld County." Weld County Government. https://history.weldgov.com/county_150/justice/district_attorneys.

[56] *Hands Up; Or Thirty-Five Years of Detective Life in the Mountains and on the Plains* by David J. Cook, pp 48–56; *Herald Democrat*, July 28, 1886, p 1.

Andrew Green, drawing in the public domain

Hanging of Andrew Green in the bend of the Cherry Creek July 27, 1886, from *Hands Up; Or Thirty-Five Years of Detective Life in the Mountains and on the Plains* by David J. Cook published in 1897, p 54

Another important case during Rhodes's tenure related to abortion care. On March 28, 1887, Minnie Davy's father arrived in Denver from his home in Iroquois, Canada, intending to kill his daughter's former lover Elwood N. Jenkins.[57] Minnie Davy had died from sceptic peritonitis after she received an abortion performed by Dr. U.S. Clark in Denver.[58] Jenkins had allegedly seduced Davy and then arranged for the operation to end the pregnancy. Jenkins and Clarke were both indicted by Rhodes on murder charges on April 22, 1887. Rhodes and F.W. Hankey prosecuted the cases. Senator Thomas Patterson defended Jenkins, and famed defense attorney Edward Caypless defended Dr. Clarke. The courtroom was crowded; in those days, hundreds would try to watch whenever cases were heard. Clarke went to trial first and was found guilty of murder by a jury that deliberated for only two hours. He was sentenced to life in prison. Jenkins was acquitted of the charges in a second trial. Davy's father did not carry out his plan and never got his revenge.[59]

Rhodes also prosecuted famous Old West character William Barclay "Bat" Masterson for assault after Masterson hit Lou Spencer across the face with a pistol. Masterson had attended Spencer's acting performance in a Denver theatre. After the play, Spencer confronted Masterson for being a little too cozy with Spencer's wife while both were in the audience. Spencer and Masterson were both charged, fined, and released. Three days later, Spencer's wife filed for divorce. Rumors circulated, never confirmed, that she eloped with Masterson.[60]

[57] *Aspen Daily Times*, March 29, 1887, p 1.
[58] *Gunnison Review-Press*, March 29, 1887, p 1.
[59] *Montezuma Millrun*, May 28, 1887, p 1; Aspen Daily Chronicle, March 19, 1889, p 1.
[60] *Rocky Mountain News*, September 22, 1886.

Bat Masterson, photo in the public domain

Masterson came to the attention of the district attorney again on November 14, 1887, when Charles E. Henry murdered Effie Moore, a song and dance actress. Henry shot Moore in the Palace Theatre on 15th and Blake Streets. The Palace Theatre was at the time owned by Bat Masterson and had been the location of several violent crimes over the years. Henry met Moore as she was coming off stage; they went to a theatre box where he shot her twice. DA Rhodes charged Henry with first-degree murder. At trial Henry claimed that Moore had promised to marry him, but he found out that she was already married. He admitted to the shooting but claimed to be an innocent boy duped by a siren for his money. The jury acquitted Henry of all charges, showing again how difficult it was to successfully prosecute cases relating to violence against women. Henry moved to Dallas, Texas, where he shot and killed another young woman under similar circumstances. He was acquitted of that murder as well.[61]

[61] *The Times Picayune*, April 19, 1892; *The Galveston Daily News,* June 19, 1892; *Kansas City Times*, November 17, 1887; *Rocky Mountain News* April 23, 1892; *National Police Gazette*, December 3, 1887, *Rocky Mountain News*, November 15, 1887; *Columbus Daily Enquirer*, November 18, 1887.

Left: Charles Henry gunning down Effie Moore; Right: Charles Henry
Drawing and photo in the public domain

Yet another murder occurred at the Palace Theatre during Rhodes's tenure. In November 1888, local blacksmith R.D. Vaughn was killed during a general melee in the theatre. It was agreed by all witnesses that Vaughn was trying to break up a fight when he was shot by Palace bartender Peter Anderson. Rhodes charged Anderson with murder "with felonious intent," but a Denver jury believed Anderson's claim of self-defense (saying that Vaughn attacked him with a board), and Anderson was acquitted.[62]

[62] *Daily Mail.* "Rocky Mountain Rippers." August 7, 2019. https://www.dailymail.co.uk/news/article-7331689/amp/Rocky-Mountain-Rippers-forgotten-stories-Denvers-cold-blooded-prostitute-pimp-killers.html

Palace Theatre circa 1870, Denver Public Library Special Collections X-24703

Rhodes was also district attorney when the notorious "House of Mirrors" was built at 1942 Market Street, one of many enticements all along the street that was renowned for vice. The original owner of the "Palace of Sin" was Madam Jennie Rogers, who reportedly built the brothel with funds provided by the Denver police chief, who had blackmailed a businessman.[63] When completed, the House of Mirrors was one of the finest and most extravagant houses of prostitution in the west, featuring 22 "boarders." The architect of the building, William Quale, also designed West High School. Featuring mirrors on every wall, the building was constructed specifically to be a bordello, which is a testament to the immense financial success enjoyed by

[63] "A Brief Walk Along Denver's Notorious Market Street," November 26, 2018. History Colorado. https://www.historycolorado.org/story/going-places/2018/11/26/brief-walk-along-denvers-notorious-market-street.

Jennie Rogers.[64] The famous Mattie Silks, the "Queen of the Tenderloin, bought the House of Mirrors in 1911 and continued the tradition of entertaining politicians and cowboys until the government closed it down in 1915. During a time of limited opportunities for women, the entrepreneurial skills and powerful personalities of Jennie Rogers and Mattie Silks provided excellent incomes not only for themselves but also for all the women who worked in their establishments.

Jennie Rogers (left) and Mattie Silks (right), Fred M. Mazzulla Collection, 10037401 and 10026978

Rhodes owned and published two newspapers, *The Courier* and the *Larimer County Democrat*. He was active in the Larimer County Democratic Party as well as the Democratic Party in Utah for the dozen years he lived there after his term as district attorney. As a private attorney, Rhodes specialized in water law. While in the state senate, he sponsored a bill that allowed the purchase of land for Denver's City Park and the appropriation for the Agricultural College at Ft. Collins, now Colorado State University. Rhodes was one of the founders of the City of Fort Collins—he had come to Fort Collins in 1872, married a local girl, Elspeth Cowen, and built the third brick house in the city, located at 255 North College Avenue. In the early 1900s the family of the silent movie star Harold Lloyd occupied the house. The Rhodes house was the oldest existing brick house in Fort Collins until its demolition in 1990.[65] Rhodes also

---

[64] "The House of Mirrors." Clio Foundation. https://www.theclio.com/entry/24593.
[65] Fort Collins Images. 2018. "The L.R. Rhodes' House and a Hint of Harold Lloyd." https://fortcollinsimages.wordpress.com/2018/02/25/the-l-r-rhodes-house-and-a-hint-of-harold-lloyd/.

authored a book in 1909 entitled, *Circumstantial Evidence,* which presented an early argument for the theory of intelligent design.

Rhodes died in Fort Collins on May 14, 1919, at age 70.

7. Isaac Stevens (1889–1891)

ISAAC N. STEVENS
1889–1891

Isaac Stevens was one of the most prominent and successful early attorneys in the new city of Denver, with a long and prolific public life spanning more than 35 years. He was born in Newark, Ohio on November 1, 1858. His father was a successful physician, and his mother was the grandniece of the naval hero Commodore Perry. Stevens started his professional career as a schoolteacher at the age of 17, and never attended law school. Like his predecessor in the district attorney's post, Stevens was admitted to the bar after working for a law firm. He moved from Burlington, Iowa, to Denver in 1880 immediately after being admitted to the bar.

Stevens was active in Colorado real estate transactions on his own behalf in the early 1880s, while also handling divorce cases. Stevens was prominent in Republican politics and was appointed assistant U.S. attorney for Colorado by President Chester A. Arthur in 1884. He was elected district attorney for the Second Judicial District in 1888. During his tenure, Stevens tried 26 murder cases, with convictions in 23.

Stevens's three-year term was known for several significant prosecutions, including the high-profile murder trial of Dr. Thomas Thatcher Graves of Providence, Rhode Island for the killing of Mrs. Josephine Barnaby. The case received national media attention. Mrs. Barnaby, a wealthy widow, was passing through Denver on a trip from California to her home in Rhode Island. While staying with a friend in Denver, she took a potion from a bottle she received in the mail. She thought the elixir was either medicine from her doctor, Dr. Graves, who had been treating her for a long-standing illness, or whiskey from an east coast friend. Regardless of what she thought was contained in the "gift" bottle, within three days of ingesting the contents, Mrs. Barnaby was dead. An autopsy suggested arsenic poisoning. Barnaby's family hired detectives from the recently created Pinkerton Detective Agency, which still actively solves crimes today. (Pinkerton was an intelligence agency during the Civil War that established the first criminal database, was the first company to hire a female detective, and was a forerunner for the Secret Service.[66]) Along with the Pinkerton detectives, Stevens thoroughly investigated the case. Stevens himself traveled to eight states, examining evidence, and interviewing witnesses. This was an incredible undertaking in an age when travel was by horse or train and took days or weeks to complete. Stevens's investigation revealed that Dr. Graves, who had graduated first in his class at Harvard, held great emotional sway over his patient. He had convinced her to make him her financial advisor and even the beneficiary of her will. Stevens put together a case, using only circumstantial evidence, which showed motive and opportunity. The trial resulted in conviction and the death penalty for Dr. Graves on the first ballot of the jury. A technical error resulted in the Colorado Supreme Court granting the defendant a new trial, but the doctor committed suicide by ingesting arsenic before he could be re-tried. His suicide note purportedly stated, "Please don't hold any autopsy on my remains. The cause of death may be rendered as follows: Died of persecution; worn out; exhausted."[67]

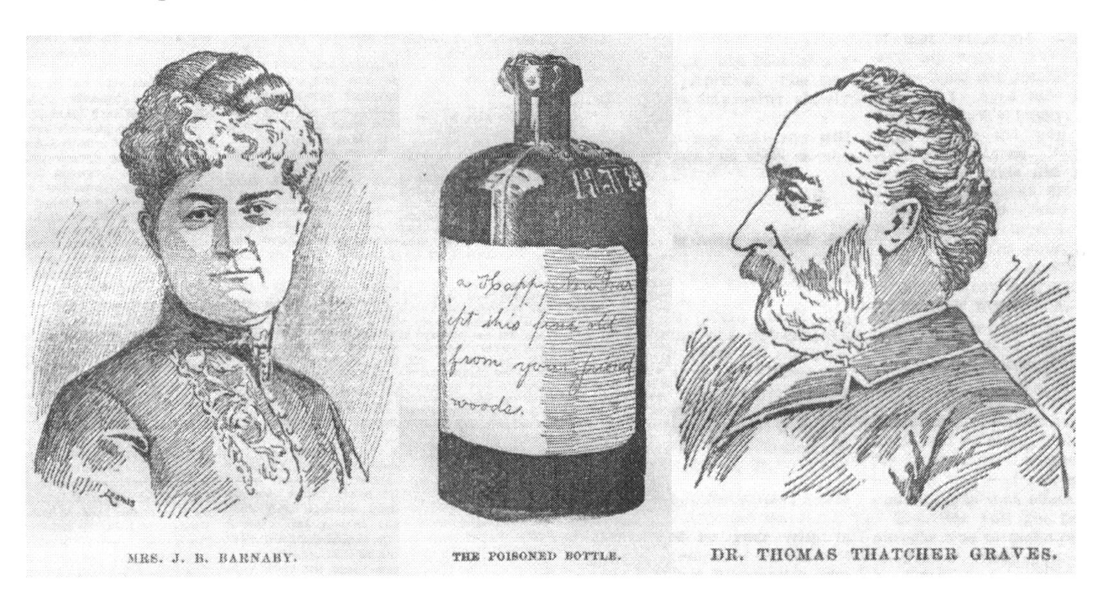

MRS. J. B. BARNABY. THE POISONED BOTTLE. DR. THOMAS THATCHER GRAVES.

[66] "Our Story." 2021. Pinkerton Consulting & Investigations. https://pinkerton.com/our-story/history.
[67] Martin Day. 1892. *Murder by Mail.* As discussed in New England Historical Society article, "Dr. T. Thatcher Graves and the Rhode Island Mail Order Murder." https://www.newenglandhistoricalsociety.com/dr-t-thatcher-graves-rhode-island-mail-order-murder/.

Illustrations from *Murder by Mail* by Martin C. Day, 1892

Author and journalist Rudyard Kipling provided an outsider's view of the Queen City of the Plains at the time Stevens was district attorney. Kipling stopped briefly in Denver as part of his trip across America in 1889 and described coming down from the mountains into Denver as a "journey with every available brake on and frequent shrieks, until [they] reached a level plain and later the city of Denver." Although he did not spend much time in Denver on his way to Omaha, he found that "the pulse of the town was too much like the rushing mighty wind in the Rocky Mountain tunnel." He got a taste for the seamier side of Denver when complete strangers tried to get him to invest in mines that were actually built on inaccessible cliffs. Kipling was also put off when a strange woman urged that he should supply her with strong drink. He noted that he "had almost forgotten that such attacks were possible in any land"[68]

[68] Rudyard Kipling. 1899. *The Works of Rudyard Kipling*. Century Company, p 135–136.

Rudyard Kipling, photo in the public domain, Wikimedia Commons

Stevens was the Denver district attorney when the city recorded its first police officer line of duty deaths; three officers were killed during Stevens's tenure.[69] Denver police officer John C. Phillips was shot and killed on July 16, 1889, when he questioned a suspected burglar. Without warning, the suspect pulled out a concealed pistol and shot the officer. Phillips returned fire but did not strike the shooter. Phillips made it to a call box to report the incident but died from his wounds. The killer was never caught.[70] The second officer killed was Charles Wanless. On September 18, 1890, Wanless was shot while responding to a disturbance at a boarding house. The drunk causing the disturbance shot the officer as he entered the house. Wanless returned fire, seriously wounding the suspect. The individual was tried and convicted of second-degree murder and sentenced to 10 years imprisonment.[71] The third officer to die during Stevens's term was Captain Charles Hawley on January 16, 1891. Captain Hawley and another officer were attacked by two men who shot both officers; Captain Hawley died from his wounds. One of the suspects involved in the shooting, Harley McCoy, was caught and sentenced to life in prison. He was paroled after serving a little more than 9 years of his sentence.[72]

---

[69] Denver Police Department: Officer Down Memorial Page. https://www.odmp.org/officer/10637-police-officer-john-c-phillips; https://www.odmp.org/officer/13822-police-officer-charles-f-wanless; https://www.odmp.org/officer/6245-captain-charles-a-hawley.

[70] Denver Police Department: Officer Down Memorial Page. https://www.odmp.org/officer/10637-police-officer-john-c-phillips.

[71] *Rocky Mountain News*, September 19, 1890.

Denver police officers John C. Phillips, Charles Wanless, and Captain Charles Hawley, photos courtesy of the Denver Police Museum

City Detective Charles Hawley (later Captain Hawley and one of the early law enforcement officers killed in the line of duty) handled an early "make my day" case—a Colorado law that permits people to use deadly force against intruders—during Stevens's tenure as district attorney. On January 12, 1889, Mrs. John Berkey shot a man in the process of burglarizing her home on Sherman Street. Mrs. Berkey had spotted two suspicious men in the vicinity of her home the night before, so she decided to sleep with a handgun in her bedroom. That night, Mrs. Berkey confronted one burglar and shot him. He was able to escape with the help of an accomplice whom Mrs. Berkey threatened to shoot as well. Blood on the windowsill confirmed that the homeowner did indeed wound the burglar, who was never located and therefore never prosecuted.[73]

Another 1889 case during Stevens's tenure illustrates how legal priorities and social morality evolve and change. On April 15, 16-year-old Lizzie Leichsenring, the daughter of a prominent westside German, attempted suicide by taking rat poison because her father would not allow her to marry Thomas O'Brien. The prompt action of doctors saved her life. Stevens charged O'Brien with seduction of the teenager. On July 12, 1889, O'Brien was convicted and sentenced to prison not to exceed 10 years. O'Brien appealed to the Colorado Supreme Court, and in 1892 his conviction was overturned. O'Brien was granted a new trial, but the case was not tried again.[74]

This time in Denver's history is also interesting in terms of corruption. Prior to 1891, a fee system in Colorado was used to pay the district attorneys throughout the state. Instead of

---

[72] *Georgetown Courier*, Volume XXIV. Number 10, June 30, 1900. p 3.
[73] *Aspen Weekly Chronicle*, January 4, 1889, p 1.
[74] *Aspen Daily Chronicle*, May 25, 1889, p 1.

receiving salary, the chief prosecutor in a judicial district was paid from the fees generated by criminal cases; a lawyer could make decent money as a prosecutor. The fee system could lead to abuses where the district attorney would file charges just to generate fees. There were also allegations that certain prosecutors around the state would dismiss cases in exchange for fee payments by those accused of crimes. Stevens was in office when the Colorado legislature started to eliminate the fee system through statutory changes. There was never any indication that Stevens filed or dismissed cases purely to collect a fee.

Stevens prosecuted several individuals involved in Denver corruption, including Deputy Denver Auditor George Raymond and Deputy Denver Treasurer James P. Hadley. During their terms in office, which ended in April of 1891, the men changed the amounts owed on city payment warrants and pocketed the excess amount the city paid on those warrants. In one instance, the amount owed was $3.50, and Raymond and Hadley changed the warrant to read $303.50. They then put the warrant through the system and stole the $300 overcharge. Stevens brought the cases to a grand jury and indicted both individuals on 12 counts of forgery and conspiracy. After a 10-day trial, the jury convicted Hadley and Raymond, and the court sentenced them to five years of hard labor in prison. On appeal, the court reversed the convictions on a technicality, finding that the original warrants were defective before they were altered, and therefore the defendants were not guilty of forgery because the original warrants were void. Raymond and Hadley were able to get away with stealing thousands of dollars of taxpayers' funds with no consequences.[75]

Stevens also indicted former Denver Police Chief Henry Brady on June 11, 1889, for accepting protection money from the leader of the Denver Chinese gamblers, Chin Poo, while Brady was serving as police chief. The newly elected Mayor Wolfe Londoner had fired Brady only a couple of months earlier, believing that Brady was operating the police force as a political machine, as well as blackmailing prostitutes. At trial, Chin Poo, who was accused of funneling protection money to Chief Brady, claimed he was a legitimate business owner, with a "restaurant for whites" as well as "clean, and well-aired opium rooms."[76] Chin Poo testified that the money was from the laundrymen and not gamblers; that he gave it to a Lieutenant O'Connor, not Brady;

[75] *Colorado Daily Chieftain*, April 3, 1892, p 1.
[76] *The Aspen Weekly Chronicle*, July 15, 1889, p 1.

and that it was a political contribution, not protection money. Stevens's office did what it could, but the jury returned a not guilty verdict in less than 15 minutes.

Former Denver Police Chief Henry Brady, photo from the Denver Public Library Special Collections X-29676

Later that summer, Stevens indicted the now former Denver Police Lieutenant O'Connor, along with two others, James Marshal and Charles Connors, for attempted robbery of a Denver and Rio Grande train. O'Connor had been fired from the police department and was running a saloon. An undercover detective for the Denver and Rio Grande railroad testified at trial that he and the others planned the robbery over a game of cards at the saloon Connors owned at 18th and Lawrence Streets in Denver. The trio, defended by former Denver DA Ledru R. Rhodes, denied any knowledge of the plot. In the first trial, the jury was unable to reach a verdict. The men were convicted at a second trial and sentenced to one to two years in prison.[77]

[77] *Aspen Daily Chronicle*, July 13, 1889, p 1.

Circa 1895 group of Denver Police and Fire Chiefs: back row, left to right: Police Chief Daniel Mays; Fire Chief George Duggan; Police Chief John L. Russell; Senator Charles S. Thomas; Police Chief Henry Brady; Police Chief Hamilton Armstrong; Police Chief A.W. Kellogg. Officers seated in the front row, left to right: Fire Chief Phil Trounstine; Fire Chief William E. Roberts; Police Chief John Farley; Fire Chief Joseph L. Bailey; Police Chief and Sheriff David Cook; Police Chief and Sheriff William A. Smith; Police Chief and Sheriff James Lomery. Photo from the Denver Public Library Special Collections X-29676.

In another case involving a Denver police chief, Stevens charged Chief of Detectives William H. Loar, as well as Detectives George Watrous, William Crocker, and William Ingersoll. On October 14, 1890, a man named Daniel Sinks appeared before the Arapahoe County grand jury in Denver, to confess to burglaries. Instead of confessing, Sinks told the grand jurors that he had been taken to the detectives' quarters where detectives Watrous, Crocker, and C.E. Clark struck him repeatedly, knocking him down and kicking him to force a confession. Sinks was injured badly enough to be taken to the hospital. The jurors visited the room where the beating took place and saw walls that still had blood splatters. Investigating further, the grand jury heard from Benjamin F. Smiley, who had confessed to robbery after being beaten by Watrous, Crocker, and Ingersoll. Richard Hughes, another accused burglar, told the grand jury that he had been intimidated by tales of Sinks's treatment into making a "confession" to matters he knew nothing about. Charges against Chief Loar were dismissed but Stevens personally prosecuted Watrous and Crocker on the assault charges. Chief Loar told the newspapers that the charges were a political move by Stevens and that his men would be acquitted. The jury returned a verdict against Watrous of assault and against Crocker for assault and battery received a fine of $70 and one day in jail. Crocker was fined $35. Loar was acquitted. Watrous, Crocker, and Chief Loar all resigned from the police department.[78]

Police Chief William H. Loar, Detective George Watrous, and Detective William Crocker, photos courtesy of Denver Police Museum

After leaving the district attorney's office, Stevens served as county attorney for Arapahoe County, which at that time included the city of Denver. As Arapahoe County Republican Chairman in 1892, Stevens opposed the American Protective Association (APA), a nativist organization aligned with the national Republican party. The APA sought the removal of Catholics in government service; the organization had as much political power as the Ku Klux Klan did in Colorado in the 1920s. At its apex, the APA had more than 10,000 Colorado supporters and opposing it took a good deal of political courage.

[78] *Colorado Daily Chieftain*, October 10, 1890, p 1.

THE PAPAL OCTOPUS.

Romanism is a Monster, with arms of Satanic power and strength, reaching to the very ends of the earth, the arm of superstition crushing the American child, that of subversion crushing the American Flag, that of bigotry crushing the American Public School, that of ignorance crushing the credulous dupe, that of corruption crushing the law of the land, that of greed grasping public moneys, that of tyranny destroying freedom of conscience, freedom of speech, freedom of the press, all over the world—*per totam orbem terrarum.*

Illustration by Jeremiah J. Crowley in *The Pope: Chief of White Slavers, High Priest of Intrigue*[79]
This image represents a common nativist portrayal of Catholics in the late 1800s.

Stevens left the Denver area in 1900 to become the editor of the *Colorado Springs Gazette*. Showing minimal modesty, the newspaper reported that its new editor, who had purchased much of the newspaper's stock, "will not rest nor continue to be a deadhead in any enterprise. He will set to work with vigor and intelligence in his chosen line and lift the Gazette to the dignity and consequence of a state rather than a local paper. To this work he will bring

[79] Jeremiah J. Crowley. 1913. *The Pope: Chief of White Slavers, High Priest of Intrigue.* Aurora, Mo., Menace Pub. Co.

wide practical experience in public affairs, unsurpassed knowledge of Colorado politics and a deftness that cannot safely be underestimated."[80]

The *Denver Times*, in noting Stevens's departure from the Denver political scene reported that his, "friends and enemies alike, for he had both in this city," would miss him. Stevens was a national figure in the Silver Republican movement, which supported the country using a silver standard. This issue split the Republican Party in Colorado in the late 19th century. Stevens was also a western founder of the Progressive or Bull Moose Party—the party of Teddy Roosevelt.[81]

Stevens maintained a legal practice in Denver for a short while after he took over the *Gazette*. In March 1900, he filed a brief on behalf of the Colorado Athletic Association against the police board to restrain the board from interfering with prizefights the association held. However, he quickly withdrew his appearance in this case as well as other legal matters in Denver to concentrate on his new endeavor in Colorado Springs. Stevens successfully published the *Colorado Springs Gazette* and went on to publish the *Pueblo Chieftain* as well. In 1910 Stevens ran unsuccessfully for a seat in the U.S. House of Representatives against incumbent Democrat Edward Taylor Stevens then returned to Denver politics full time and served as city attorney from 1913 to 1915 under the short-lived commission form of government.

One of Stevens' more incongruous accomplishments was his role in the introduction of sugar beets in Colorado. Stevens and an associate investigated sugar beet growing in Nebraska and determined that Colorado growing conditions were better. They ordered seeds from the Department of Agriculture in Washington, D.C. for an experimental plot. From this experiment, Colorado's sugar beet industry developed.

Stevens was an early advocate of women's suffrage. In 1893, he campaigned and fundraised across the state to support granting women the vote. After Colorado became the first state to enact women's suffrage by popular vote, Stevens continued the campaign for women's voting in several eastern states. He ran for the U.S. Senate in 1895, losing by only one vote (at the time U.S. senators were elected by the state legislature). Stevens wrote three books after leaving office: *The Liberators: A Story of Future American Politics* (1908), *An American Suffragette* (1911), and *What is Love* (1918).

---

[80] *Denver Evening Post*, February 2, 1900.
[81] *The Colorado Magazine* XLIII/2 1966, p 102.

Stevens died in Philadelphia on February 11, 1920, where he had lived the last six years of his life.

8. Robert Wilbur Steele (1892–1895)

R. W. STEELE
1892–1894

Robert Wilbur Steele had a long and successful career in Denver, serving as Denver district attorney, Denver County Court judge, and chief justice of the Colorado Supreme Court. Steele's father and grandfather were both physicians. His father, Dr. Henry Steele, was one of the founders of the Colorado Medical Society and served as the first dean of the medical department of the University of Denver. Robert Steele was born in Lebanon, Ohio, on November 14, 1857. His family moved to Colorado to improve young Robert's health when he was 13 years old. Steele was one of seven students in the first graduating class of Denver High School in 1877. After graduation, he played left field on a semi-professional baseball team known as the Brown Stockings while getting involved in politics. He attended the law department of the Columbian University, predecessor of George Washington University in Washington, D.C., and was admitted to the Colorado Bar in 1881. He spent three years as clerk of the Arapahoe County Court before going into private practice in 1884 in partnership with future Denver DA Booth Malone. His practice specialized in land law, and he amassed a small fortune representing the Atchison, Topeka, and Santa Fe Railroad and acquiring property along the train's route. He lost much of this fortune during the Silver Crash of 1893. Even though he suffered significant financial losses from the crash, he refused to file bankruptcy and spent the rest of his life paying back money he owed from this setback. Steele was active in Republican politics and was elected district attorney of the Second Judicial District as a Republican in 1891, taking office in January 1892.[82]

Steele remained Denver's district attorney for only two years before being appointed to a vacancy on the Arapahoe County bench. In 1895 he was elected to a full term in the same position, and in the fall of 1900 he was elected as a justice of the Colorado Supreme Court. Justice Steele supported Benjamin Lindsey, the renowned and controversial judge, as his successor on the County Court bench, thus starting Lindsey's judicial career. (Ironically, when Judge Lindsey was removed from office in 1927, Steele's son, Robert W. Steele Jr., would replace Lindsey on the Juvenile Court.) Steele served as chief justice of the Supreme Court from 1907 until his death in 1910 at the age of 53. In honor of the jurist, Governor John Shafroth

[82] Walter Lawson. 1913. *Robert Wilbur Steele, Defender of Liberty*. Carson-Harper Company, Denver, Colorado. Chapter 4; *Wilder Los Angeles Herald*, October 1910, p 3.

ordered flags flown at half-mast for four weeks, and Colorado government offices were closed while the body of the Chief Justice lay in state at the Capitol. To recognize his service to the court, a stained-glass window portraying him as Chief Justice was placed above the bench in the courtroom of the Supreme Court in the State Capitol Building. In addition, Steele Elementary School was named in his honor; it still stands at 320 S. Marion Street in Denver.

Supreme Court Chambers in the Colorado State Capitol, image from Wikipedia

The same year that Steele was elected district attorney, he participated in the purchase of a gold mine in the mountains above Cripple Creek, Colorado. The mine, Forest Queen, was jointly owned by brothers and Denver underworld bosses Sam and Lou Blonger. Stevens was part owner, along with another Denver district attorney employee Neil Dennsion. Although no allegations of improper conduct on the part of Steele or Dennison were ever made, the optics of the elected district attorney being the business partner of a notorious criminal would certainly have raised concerns if known publicly.[83] In another business dealing of 1892, Steele was notified by the land commissioner in Washington, D.C. that his homestead entry had been

[83] July 22, 1892. Mining deed transfer from Robert W. Steele, W. Neil Dennison, Jonn E. Phillips, L.H. Blonger and S.H. Bonger to Oscar W. Jackson "...all right, title and interest...in and to the Forest Queen..." recorded El Paso County July 26, 1892, book 153, page 36; August 3, 1892, Agreement (typed and notarized); an agreement formalizing the arrangement where OWJ pursues the Patent, the other pay their fair shares of any expenses and listing the following undivided interests: Robert W. Steele 1/10, W. Neil Dennison 1/5, John E Phillips1/5, L.H. Blonger 1/5 and S.H. Blonger 1/5.

approved. Steele was able to obtain land near Denver for free because it had been abandoned by the settlers who had previously claimed it under the original railroad land grants. Steele filed his claim for the land, established his residence there, and made the improvements required by the land grant. His homestead covered 160 acres, extending south from Exposition Street to Mississippi Street west to Fairmount Cemetery. At the time, the Steele ranch was conservatively estimated to be worth $100,000. As comparison, the average salary for a bricklayer in the United States in 1890 was about $3/day[84] and a $100,000 would be equivalent to $3 million.

Elected in 1893, Colorado Governor Davis Waite attempted to end vice in Denver. He ordered the city's bars, brothels, and gambling houses closed. The entrepreneurial but nefarious Jefferson Randolph "Soapy" Smith figured out how to take advantage of customers who had just been scammed in his gambling houses by threatening to arrest them for violating the vice laws, using his deputy sheriff's badge. They were offered an alternative to depart without being charged and without their cash. Because the victims dd not file complaints with the police, Steele never filed fraud or theft charges against Smith.[85]

The popular local image of "Soapy" Smith in Denver history is of a quaint con artist who swindled the gullible with his soap bar scam. In reality, Smith was a violent street thug. On October 11, 1892, an argument between "Troublesome Tom" Cady and Jim "Gambler" Jordan led to a shootout on Larimer Street at Murphy's Exchange bar, locally known as "The Slaughterhouse." On this date, the saloon lived up to its nickname. The argument that led to the shooting had occurred in a different bar; Cady was arrested after striking Jordan in the head with his cane. Cady was an associate of Smith's, and when word reached Smith that Cady had been arrested, Smith bonded Cady out of jail. Then the two of them, along with a couple of additional gunslingers, went looking for Jordan. They found him in Murphy's Exchange drinking with Cort Thomson. John Murphy was behind the bar, and Smith's gun was quickly drawn and cocked. Cady pulled a sword from his cane and made for Jordan. Two shots were fired, killing Clifton Sparks, who reportedly was not involved in the dispute. Jim Jordan, John Murphy, and Cort Thomson were all arrested. Smith and Cady escaped but turned themselves in the following day. No one could agree on an accurate account of the conflict. Steele charged Cady and Jordan with

---

[84] Walter Lawson. 1913. *Robert Wilbur Steele, Defender of Liberty*. Carson-Harper Company, Denver, Colorado. Chapter 4; *Wilder Los Angeles Herald*, October 1910, p 55–57.

[85] "Soapy Smith." Genealogy Trails. http://genealogytrails.com/tex/bigbend/upton/soapy_smith.html; Jeff Smith. 2009. *Alias Soapy Smith: The Life and Death of a Scoundrel.* Klondike Research, p 321.

first-degree murder, but both were acquitted at trial. Smith was also charged but found not guilty by District Court Judge Burns.[86]

One Denver police officer was killed in the line of duty during Steele's time in office. Denver Special Policeman Gustave Gisin was killed on January 24, 1892, while negotiating with Thomas A. Jordan, a drunk ex-employee of the Grant smelter factory, who had been fired the day before. Jordan had returned to the smelter looking for his supervisor. Gisin, who had been advised of Jordan's threats, entered the building but Jordan stopped him at gunpoint. Officer Gisin tried to reason with Jordan. Unfortunately, his efforts were unsuccessful and Jordan shot the police officer at close range in the chest. After running from the facility, the suspect was captured. Gisin died the following day with his family by his side.[87] The suspect was arrested, tried for first-degree murder, and hanged on May 11, 1895. At the time of his death, Gisin was 60 years old and had been in the department for eight years. Jordan's defense at trial was insanity, but the evidence showed that he purchased the murder weapon after he was fired. After his guilty verdict and death sentence, Jordan became "pale as death and fell all to pieces as he was being led back to the jail."[88] Prior to being hanged, Jordan was a "trembling shaking wretch, who, when the hour for the expiation for his crime was at hand, had to be carried to the few steps to the execution house" in Cañon City.[89]

Even 120 years ago, prosecutors had discretion on whom and when to prosecute. For example, on April 19, 1893, 16-year-old Michael Sweeney shot his stepfather, Patrick Flaherty, on the stairway of Flaherty's boarding house at 1730 Larimer Street. At the time, Flaherty was in custody for beating his wife, and was being taken to jail by a Denver police officer. As they passed Mrs. Flaherty, the drunken Flaherty swung his arm loose and punched her in the face with his fist. The woman fell to the ground, and her husband hit her again. Her son grabbed his stepfather's revolver, which the boy had hidden away to keep the drunken man from using it to harm his mother. The teenager rushed through the crowd with the revolver, and when he reached the top of the stairs, he took aim and shot his stepfather. The bullet struck Flaherty in the small of the back. The boy made no attempt to escape and was arrested after Flaherty was sent to the

---

[86] https://soapysmiths.blogspot.com/2011/08/did-soapy-smith-murder-gambler-cliff.html; *Herald Democrat*, April 30, 1893, p 1; *The Aspen Times*, May 12, 1895, p 1.
[87] Denver Police Department: Officer Down Memorial Page https://www.odmp.org/officer/22004-special-policeman-gustave-gisin.
[88] *The Herald Democrat,* April 30, 1893, p 1.
[89] "Arapahoe County, Colorado Genealogy Trails. Genealogytrails.com/colo/arapahoe/news_crimes.html.

county hospital. Sweeney confessed to the shooting, saying that he was driven to desperation by the man's inhumane treatment of his mother. Flaherty's wound was not fatal.[90] DA Steele refused to charge Sweeney, probably in the belief that a jury would think that Flaherty had it coming.

This time period during Steele's tenure saw animosity between the Arapahoe County Sheriff's office and the Denver Police Department take a deadly turn. On October 5, 1894, Denver police officer Robert Boykin shot and killed Milton Smith, an Arapahoe County deputy sheriff, at the corner of 20th and Market Streets in Denver. Boykin claimed that Smith had pulled a revolver on him while he was attempting to stop a fight between Smith and his mistress. Immediately after the shooting, Boykin surrendered to Chief Hamilton Armstrong, who was a witness to the whole affair. Smith was Black, and soon stories about the killing began circulating in the Black population of Denver. They claimed that when Smith drew his weapon, Boykin and another officer began clubbing him, while four other Denver officers watched from across the street without intervening. DA Steele charged Boykin with first-degree murder. The police officer was convicted of second-degree murder and sentenced to 10 years in prison. He appealed his conviction to the Colorado Supreme Court, and they reversed it based on improper descriptions in court of the law of self-defense. The Court indicated that it was a matter of regret that the case needed to be sent back for a new trial—they found Boykin's story "improbable" in that to save his own life, he was compelled to take Smith's life, particularly when he and a fellow police officer clubbed the deceased, with four other policemen visible and within easy call just across the street. The prosecution was unable to go forward with a second trial[91] and on July 23, 1897, Judge Russell of Durango (brought in because of potential conflict with Denver judges) dismissed the charge of murder against Boykin. After his release, Boykin became a gunman in the employ of the Rocky Mountain Fuel company, hired to breakup labor strikes.[92]

On a lighter note, Judge Steele was known for his love of animals. At a time when horses were beasts of burden and were often treated no better, Steele was credited with establishing a "traffic squad" that ensured horses in the city were humanely treated. He was also an animal humane officer with powers to intervene if he witnessed animal cruelty. As a Denver County Court judge, Steele once sentenced a defendant, Christopher Mack, to six months in jail for

[90] *The West Side Citizen*, v 5, Number 22, April 14, 1893, p 1.
[91] Boykin v. People, 22 Colo. 496. 1896.
[92] *The Lafayette Leader,* vol. viii Number 37, October 18, 1912, p 1.

drunkenly beating a horse to death.[93] Steele also felt a particular compassion toward children. In 1895, the H.K. Milford Company of Philadelphia started production and testing of diphtheria antitoxin in the United States. Diphtheria was one of the leading causes of death among children. When the anti-toxin treatment for diphtheria became available, County Court Judge Steele contributed $100 to bring the first portion of the new remedy to Denver, for use by City Health Commissioner Dr. William Munn.[94]

Steele died on October 12, 1910. Steele Elementary School on Marion Parkway in Denver is named after him today. He was the father of Robert Steele Jr., a legendary Denver District Court judge who sat on the District Court bench a record 38 years.

Plaque at Steele Elementary School honoring Judge Steele

[93] Walter Lawson. 1913. *Robert Wilbur Steele, Defender of Liberty*. Carson-Harper Company, Denver, Colorado. Chapter 4; *Wilder Los Angeles Herald*, October 1910, p 81.
[94] Walter Lawson. 1913. *Robert Wilbur Steele, Defender of Liberty*. Carson-Harper Company, Denver, Colorado. Chapter 4; *Wilder Los Angeles Herald*, October 1910, p 86–87.

9. Greeley Webster Whitford (1895–1896)

Greeley Webster Whitford was born June 6, 1856, in Rockville, Indiana. His father was the county superintendent of schools but died when Whitford was just two years old. Whitford's brother-in-law was Iowa U.S. senator Jmes Harlan, father-in-law of Robert Lincoln, President Lincoln's son. Whitford attended Iowa Wesleyan College and studied law in the office of an Iowa attorney. He was admitted to the Iowa bar in 1882. As a young attorney, Whitford moved to Whatcom (now Bellingham), Washington Territory, where he was postmaster. He came to Denver in 1887 to join his brother, already practicing law here.[95]

Whitford was associated through his law practice with former Denver city attorney, one-term governor, and U.S. senator John Shafroth as well as Denver mayor Platt Rogers. In 1889, Whitford was named assistant city attorney, followed by an appointment as assistant district attorney. In November 1894, he was elected district attorney as a Republican. He was in this post for only two years before being named U.S. attorney for Colorado by President McKinley.[96] He served in that position for four years, then resumed his private law practice with his brother. Whitford was elected to the Colorado Supreme Court and served from 1921 to 1931, the last four years as Chief Justice. Whitford was voted out of office after referring to popular Governor W. H. Adams as "an old buzzard." Whitford died in 1940.[97]

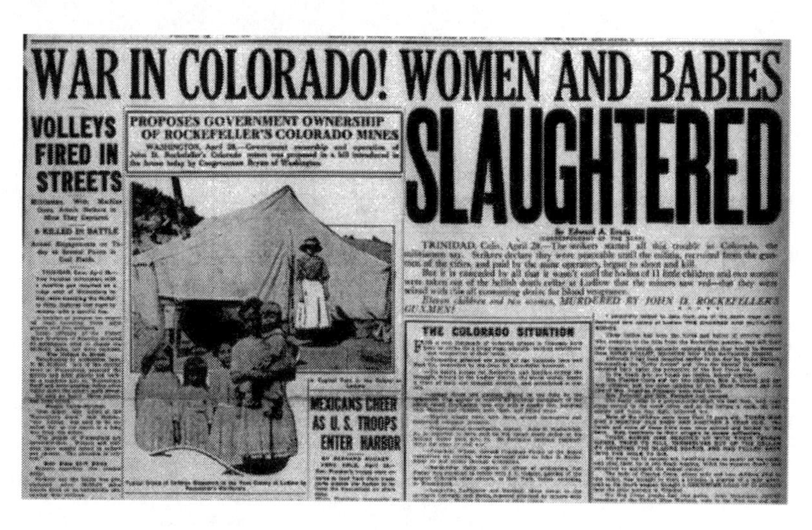
WAR IN COLORADO! WOMEN AND BABIES SLAUGHTERED

VOLLEYS FIRED IN STREETS

PROPOSES GOVERNMENT OWNERSHIP OF ROCKEFELLER'S COLORADO MINES

THE COLORADO SITUATION

MEXICANS CHEER AS U. S. TROOPS ENTER HARBOR

Colorado Coalfield War and the Ludlow Massacre, part of the labor troubles in Colorado at the turn of the last century. Photo from *The Seattle Star*, April 28, 1914.

[95] *Bench and Bar of Colorado*. 1917. Bench and Bar Publishing Co, p 186.

[96] *Colorado Daily Chieftain*, April 16, 1897, p 2.

[97] Obituary of Greeley Webster Whitford, *The Spokesman-Review*, May 7, 1940.

One criticism leveled against Whitford during his term as district attorney was that he spent taxpayers' money lavishly. County commissioners felt that Whitford could have run the office for half the $15,200 he spent in 1896 for his staff of six assistants and the district attorney. Assistants at that time were paid $2,000 and $3,000 annually.

Two Denver police officers died during Whitford's time in office.[98] Detective Alpheus Moore was shot on March 19, 1895—the fifth line-of-duty death of a Denver policeman. Detective Moore was in the process of trying to recapture one of three suspects who had just escaped his custody. The detective fired two shots at one of the fleeing suspects who returned fire, hitting the officer in the groin, which caused severe bleeding and internal injuries. Detective Moore died in the hospital the next day after surgeons amputated his leg. Detectives caught up with the other two arrestees, "Old Bob" and Edward Cooper, alias "Blackey." They confessed that they were with James McDonald, alias "Los Angeles," and said McDonald shot Moore. "Los Angeles" James McDonald was arrested, tried, and acquitted.[99]

Detective Alpheus Moore (left) and wanted handbill for James McDonald (right), Courtesy of the Denver Police Department

On February 6, 1896, while walking their beat, Denver Police Officer Wendell Smith was shot and killed, and Officer Calvin R. Rowland was severely wounded in the early morning hours. The officers caught a burglar in the act of breaking into a house/grocery store at the corner of Colfax Avenue and Josephine Street. When the officers were making the arrest, the burglar

---

[98] Denver Police Department: Officer Down Memorial Page, https://www.odmp.org/officer/9537-detective-alpheus-j-moore.

[99] *Greeley Tribune*, April 18, 1895, p 6.

opened fire. Whitford was never able to charge anyone for the murder or attempted murder because the case was never solved.[100]

Traffic accidents occurred even before motor vehicles were on the road. One of Whitford's early prosecutions was such a traffic matter. On July 5, 1895, a peddler, H. Albert, drove his horse-drawn two-seated surrey into Mary Wallace, who was driving a horse-drawn buggy on the Twelfth Street bridge in Denver. Albert was attempting to avoid a tramway car and collided with Wallace's buggy, wrecking it, and throwing the occupants to the road. After the accident, Wallace demanded that she be reimbursed for the destruction of the family carriage. Albert denied that he was responsible and attempted to drive off. He was stopped by a Denver health officer who placed Albert under arrest. Whitford prosecuted Albert for careless driving; he was convicted, and Judge Webber assessed a fine of $10 and costs.[101]

Carriage accident in the Victorian Era. Jane Austin's London[102]

The criminal justice system often interacts with mentally ill individuals and has long recognized that there are crimes that can be attributed to the diminished ability or understanding of the perpetrator. Addiction or mental illness, therefore, are often considered when filing decisions are made. Before insights into brain function and effective mental health advocates, however, society responded to the special needs of the mentally ill by establishing asylums

[100] Denver Police Department: Officer Down Memorial Page. https://www.odmp.org/officer/22003-special-policeman-wendell-p-smith.
[101] Denver Post, July 6, 1895.
[102] Louise Allen WordPress. 2016. "Jane Austen's London." https://janeaustenslondon.com/2016/02/05/curricle-crashes-and-dennet-disasters-the-dangers-of-the-regency-road/.

designed to care for, and segregate, people who committed crimes while unable to distinguish right from wrong. Then as now, some criminals feigned insanity to game the system; of course, some individuals were clearly legally insane. The challenge for police and prosecutors was to distinguish between the two.

On November 6, 1895, T.J. Whitlock entered Solomon's Pawn Shop at 413 Larimer Street and asked to be shown some revolvers. He selected a weapon and then asked for some cartridges. Before anyone could stop him, Whitlock began flourishing the weapon around the store. Chin Fung, a customer in the store, was shot when he was suddenly selected as a target by Whitlock. Denver Police Sergeant Inman, hearing the gunfire, rushed into the store and seized Whitlock, yanking the gun from his grasp. A few days after the incident, Fung died from his wounds and DA Whitford charged Whitlock with first-degree murder. The jury found Whitlock guilty of second-degree murder, but District Court Judge Carpenter granted him a new trial. The second jury had little difficulty finding Whitlock insane. After the trial, Whitlock told the court that he would rather hang or go to the penitentiary than to an asylum. But he was nevertheless sent to the asylum as a dangerous lunatic. His statements were no bluff. He refused to eat while at the asylum and died of starvation.[103]

Even more than a century ago, police shootings could be controversial. On February 26, 1896, another incident occurred at Solomon's Pawn Shop, this time resulting in the prosecution of a Denver officer. Denver Police Captain Wilson Swain was outside on Larimer Street when he heard a shot near the Solomon establishment. Yelling at bystanders to clear the area, Swain ran toward the pawnshop with his .45-caliber revolver drawn. He took cover at the shop and saw John Fitzgerald attempting to load a .45-caliber bullet into a .44-caliber revolver he had just taken from the pawnshop. A clerk had fired off a round to signal Swain when he saw Fitzgerald take the gun. Although Fitzgerald was not threatening anyone at the time, Swain shot him. Before he died, Fitzgerald told police he stole the gun to kill himself and Swain had saved him the trouble. Whitford charged Swain with murder, but a judge dismissed the charges after two days of testimony. Denver's Irish community was outraged with Swain's exoneration and felt that he should have at least suffered a manslaughter conviction. Swain had a reputation for having his gun ready for the "most trivial matters." The protests grew and on March 15, 1896,

---

[103] *Colorado Daily Chieftain*, November 13, 1885, p 5.

Swain resigned from the Denver Police Department. He subsequently moved to Washington state, where he joined a private detective agency.[104]

In 1906, Whitford was elected to the office of Denver District Judge and served on the bench for six years, during which time he figured prominently in several cases involving Colorado's historic labor troubles. His rulings enraged labor leaders, who called for his impeachment and marched en masse around the Capitol. While serving on the Colorado Supreme Court, one of Whitford's notable decisions was his vote to disbar Denver Juvenile Court judge Henry Lindsey.[105] Lindsey was a legendary and controversial figure in Colorado's legal community. He was the first Juvenile Court judge in the state, a vocal critic of Mayor Speer, and an advocate for women's rights. The relationship between Whitford and Lindsey became so heated that years later in 1933 when Lindsey appealed to be reinstated to the Colorado Bar, the Colorado Supreme Court based its denial solely on Lindsey's refusal to apologize for the public comments he made about the Colorado Supreme Court and about Judge Whitford in particular.

10. Samuel Disney Creighton Hays (1897)

S. D. C. HAYS
1897

Samuel Disney Creighton Hays was born on September 30,1856 in Mercer County, Illinois. His father was a county judge in Mercer County. Raised on a prairie farm, Hays attended public schools and went to Monmouth College. After graduating, Hays taught school for two years in his hometown. In 1878, he returned to Monmouth College to study law and finished his legal education in Chicago, where he was admitted to the bar in 1880. Two years later, Hays returned home to Mercer County, and in 1884 was elected state's attorney. He served as state's attorney until 1888, and in 1891 moved to Denver to continue the practice of law. In 1895, Hays became a deputy serving under Denver DA Greeley W. Whitford. When Whitford was appointed U.S. attorney in 1897, Hays was appointed Denver district attorney by the five District Court judges. Hays's time in office was short, however; he ran for a full term as district attorney in the next election but was defeated.

Despite a short time as district attorney, Hays' year in office had several interesting cases. For example, prostitute Annie Tresize had a long history of keeping Colorado prosecutors busy. She first went to prison in 1894 for shooting two men in Gunnison, Colorado. Tresize shot one of

[104] *Colorado Daily Chieftain*, February 27, 1886, p 1; March 3, 1886, p 8; and March 12, 1886, p 8.
[105] *Steamboat Pilot*, December 13, 1929, p 8, and June 16, 1933, p 4.

the men through the arm, and the bullet hit and killed the second man. She went to prison for involuntary manslaughter for two years. Upon her release she went to Colorado Springs and then Denver. In Denver she was charged by DA Whitford with vagrancy in 1896. Vagrancy was a catchall charge sometimes used to clear the streets of undesirables. In 1897, Tresize attacked her landlord on Market Street with a knife, and DA Hays charged her with assault. She received a one-year suspended sentence because of her poor health. Unfortunately, her reprieve did not last long. That same year Hays again charged her—this time she was convicted of larceny and sentenced to three years in prison. At sentencing the judge said, "we will put you out of the way where you won't annoy people anymore." Tresize bowed and threw the judge a "rather angry kiss."[106]

In October of that year, hotel guests of the dingy Colorado rooming house at 1634 Larimer Street heard a pistol shot in the middle of the night. The hotel night clerk found Federico (aka Frederick) Chavez Sanchez sitting on the bed with a smoking revolver in his hand. Sanchez reported that a robber had entered his room, and in the ensuing gun battle one of the robber's bullets had killed Sanchez's wife, Jennie Warren Sanchez. In a subsequent statement, he said that in the excitement he accidentally discharged his own revolver, killing his wife. His 19-year-old wife had been an orphan with no immediate family. She had placed an advertisement in a matrimonial paper—the "Tinder" of the time—which was answered by Sanchez, who described himself as a "Spaniard of royal blood." After a courtship by mail, they were married August 22, 1897, in Illinois. Sanchez brought his young wife to Denver and took out $11,000 in life insurance; an equivalent insurance policy in today's dollars would be close to $350,000. Dr. Leavitt of Denver examined Jennie and advised New York Life Insurance Company not to insure her because he believed her husband was just trying to get money. Nevertheless, the policy was accepted.

[106] Sheila O'Hare and Alphild Dick. 2012. *Wicked Denver: Mile-High Misdeeds and Malfeasance*, Arcadia Publishing, Charleston, S.C.

Frederick Sanchez (left) and Jennie Warren (right). Illustrations from the Herald Democrat, December 3, 1897, p 7

DA Hays charged Sanchez with first-degree murder. In trial, the prosecution showed that Sanchez had planned the murder for nearly a year. A friend of Sanchez testified that a few days before the killing Sanchez had boasted that he "would have $10,000 in a few weeks." The evidence also showed that Sanchez was running out of money; the couple had moved from the expensive Windsor Hotel to the cheaper Columbine Hotel, finally ending up at the Colorado, a rooming house. Sanchez had originally left his hometown after shooting a young woman in a fit of jealousy. She survived, and Sanchez's father—the sheriff of Los Lunas, New Mexico—gave him money to leave the state until things quieted down. He came to Denver in the summer of 1897 and spent most of his time and money in Meskow's Saloon on Larimer Street.

After hearing contradictory experts testify about somnambulism and epilepsy, the jury found Sanchez guilty of first-degree murder; he was sentenced by Judge George W. Allen to life in prison. When he was sentenced, Sanchez sneered that he "would be out of prison in ten years." Members of the jury were sorry that the death penalty in Colorado had been abolished, holding that Sanchez's crime was cold-blooded.[107]

From the time of his sentence, members of Sanchez's wealthy New Mexico family attempted to use their money and influence to get him released. In November of 1906, Sanchez

---

107 *The Leavenworth Post,* July 4, 1906, p 1.

received clemency from the board of pardons, but before Governor Jesse Fuller McDonald could approve the release, newspapers across the country, including all the Denver newspapers, expressed outrage. In an open letter to Governor McDonald and others, the *Denver Post* made the following protest against any pardon or parole:

> "... It desires to call your attention especially to the fiendish ingenuity, cunning and planning of this man Sanchez in the murder of his girl wife. It is not strange that he should have selected an obscure orphan girl to marry? Did he not select this orphan girl for the reason that in murdering her he would not be held personally responsible by any of her blood relations? Did he not plan that there should be no brothers, no father, to avenge the murder of his helpless girl? Did he not anticipate doing the very thing that he is now doing, and which you are helping him to do seek a pardon with no relations to protest against this granting? Wasn't he cunning enough, even nine years ago, to anticipate in the murder of this little girl, the condition that exists today? Follow his criminal planning and observe its extraordinary scheming. First he selects and marries an orphan girl. Second he has her life insured for $11,000 for his benefit. Third he brings her to the state of Colorado, where there is no capital punishment. Do you see how he was protecting himself all along, taking the minimum amount of chance on his own to him precious neck? ..."[108]

The *Durango Democrat* described Sanchez's release as "the payment of a political debt by the pardon of a bloody-handed murderer, the murderer of a pure young girl he had influenced to be his wife that he might insure her life, kill her and get the insurance is the latest act to be credited to the Republicans of Colorado. The pardon of Frederick Sanchez was promised before election as a bid for the Mexican vote, and Chairman Vivian recommended the pardon."[109]

The parole board claimed they relied on a letter from the trial judge. Judge Allen had said n his letter to the board that "the evidence introduced on behalf of the state was unsatisfactory to establish a case of first-degree murder. Sanchez was very incoherent at the trial and I think the verdict of murder in the first degree was too severe, but no motion for new trial was made by Sanchez and under the verdict I had to sentence him for life." Sanchez was released from prison and as a condition of his release had to remain in Colorado for the remainder of his sentence.[110]

Hays continued to practice law until 1898 when President McKinley appointed him as a major and paymaster in the Spanish-American war. He was honorably discharged in 1899 and resumed the practice of law. In 1906, Hays was elected county commissioner of the City and

---

[108] Quote from the *Denver Post* as included in the Albuquerque Citizen, November 21, 1906, p 5.
[109] Durango Democrat, November 21, 1906.
[110] Herald Democrat, December 3, 1897, p 7; Aspen Democrat, November 25, 1906, p 1.

County of Denver and in 1908 became chairman. Hays retired from the active practice of law to become attorney for the Grand Fraternity Insurance Company, of which he was vice president until his death. Hayes left Denver in 1911 and moved to Philadelphia, where he died on July 30, 1915, at the age of fifty-nine.[111]

11. Booth Malone (1897–1901)

Booth Malone was born in a log cabin in Benton County, Mississippi, in 1854. His father died when Booth was four years old and his mother moved the family to Chicago at the outbreak of the Civil War. Malone attended Chicago public schools and Beloit College in Wisconsin. He graduated from Albany, New York, Law School. After law school, he returned to Beloit where he served as superintendent of schools and president of the school board. He was also city attorney in Beloit for six years and mayor for an additional two years. He was elected district attorney for three terms in Rock County, Wisconsin, from 1885 to 1891. He moved to Denver in 1891 to join the law practice of his brother and Robert Steele; the latter soon left the firm to become Denver district attorney in 1892 and Malone joined the DA's office as a deputy shortly thereafter. Malone was elected district attorney himself as the Republican candidate in 1897. Malone was considered an outstanding prosecutor. The *Denver Times* reported that he obtained convictions in 39 of the 47 murder cases handled by his office during his four-year tenure.[112]

Malone's most famous case was the prosecution of a fellow member of the bar, William "Plug Hat" Anderson, for the double shooting of *Denver Post* owners Harry Tammen and Frederick Bonfils. The case involved another Colorado celebrity: Alferd Packer, the only man in America to be convicted of cannibalism.

After Alferd Packer was convicted, the *Denver Post* ran a series of articles alleging he had been wrongly convicted and incarcerated. William "Plug Hat" Anderson was a private attorney who contacted Packer with a scheme to win his release. Before he traveled to Cañon City to meet with the inmate, Anderson met with Polly Pry, the *Post* columnist who was writing the Packer series. She suggested Anderson meet with Tammen and Bonfils to discuss his ideas

---

[111] Aledo Times Record, August 12, 1915, #1 and #2.
[112] Wilbur Fisk Stone. *History of Colorado*, The S.J. Clarke Publishing Company 1918, V II, pp 184–186.

for Packer's appeal. Anderson did this and thought he had secured the interest of Tammen and Bonfils in his plan. They in turn recommended that he meet with Isaac Stevens, attorney for the *Post* (and a former Denver DA). Instead, Anderson went to Cañon City, skipping the appointment with Tammen, Bonfils, and Stevens. While at the prison, Anderson met with Packer. Anderson asked for and received $25 from Packer, supposedly to offset the costs of pursuing Packer's case. The basis of Anderson's appeal was that Packer's crime occurred on federal land but state authorities, without proper jurisdiction, conducted the trial and obtained conviction.

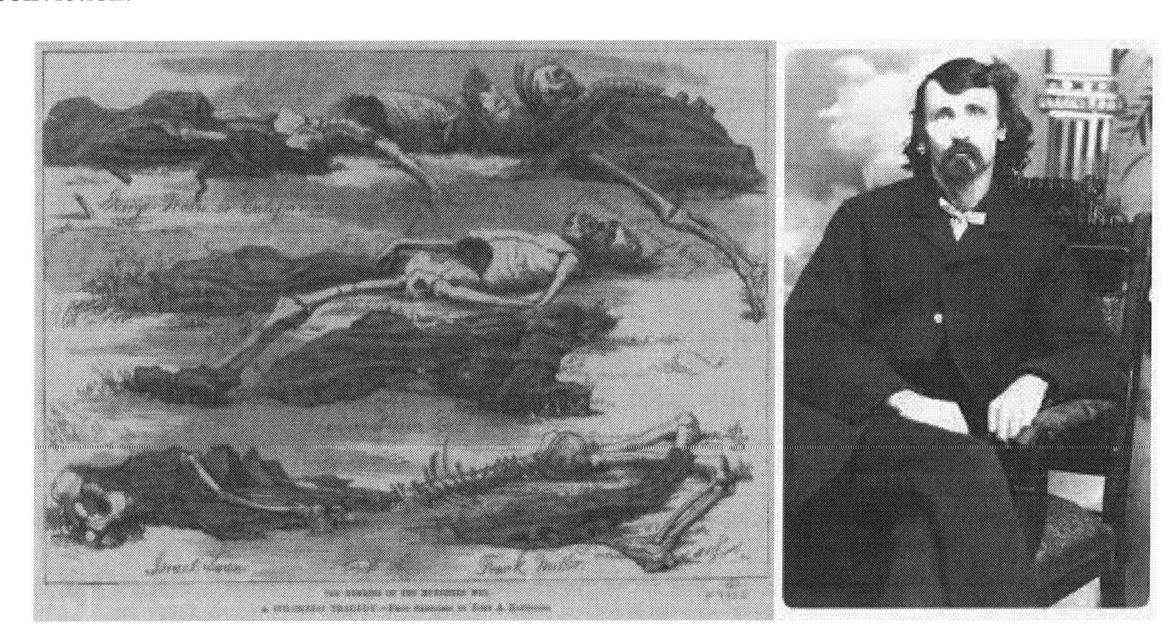

Left: The skeletons and partially clothed remains of the miners murdered by Packer. Sketch by John Randolph, published in an article about Alferd Packer in "Harper's Weekly" (credit: Wikicommons).

Right: Alferd Packer, the only person in the United States convicted of cannibalism. Photo in the public domain.

Polly Pry met Anderson when he returned to Denver on the Cañon City train. Pry presented Anderson with a letter that Packer had telegraphed explaining that Packer no longer wished Anderson to represent him. Anderson arranged to meet with Tammen and Bonfils the next day. The meeting was brief. The two *Post* editors accused Anderson of being a bunco man and of cheating Packer. Tammen told Anderson, "In my opinion, you are a cheapskate and a liar, and I want nothing more to do with you." After Tammen's insults, Bonfils struck Anderson in the face. Bonfils claimed that Anderson made threatening moves toward them. Bonfils and Tammen claimed that only Bonfils struck Anderson and that they then accompanied him out of their office. Anderson claimed that both editors pummeled him severely. Witnesses to Anderson's condition after the incident, including the doctor who treated him, suggested that Anderson's story was more likely.

After the beating and as he was leaving the office, Anderson pulled a revolver from his pocket and shot Bonfils twice and Tammen once. Neither man was seriously injured. Pry, a witness to the crime, said she used her body to shield Tammen from Anderson, who was attempting to shoot Tammen a second time. According to Anderson, he had gone to the *Denver Post* offices where he was first insulted and then attacked by both Bonfils and Tammen. During the melee and, allegedly to defend himself, he pulled out his gun and shot both men.

DA Malone charged Anderson with two counts of assault to commit murder. Anderson was tried in the West Side Courtroom to a standing-room-only crowd and, naturally, to front page newspaper headlines. The importance of the case was underscored by the fact that Malone himself (with one assistant) tried the first case, involving the attack against both Tammen and Bonfils. After several days of deliberation, the first trial ended in a 6-6 deadlock. A second trial for the assault against Tammen alone ended with the same result, a 6-6 hung jury. A third trial resulted in Anderson's acquittal. Rumors that the jury in the second trial had been bribed for a conviction resulted in the appointment of a grand jury to investigate. The grand jury indicted Tammen and three other officials on bribery charges. Tammen pleaded guilty to attempted bribery, was fined, and given a short jail sentence. Ironically, this was the only criminal conviction resulting from the double shooting.[113]

DA Malone's tenure also included more drama involving Bat Masterson. In the summer of 1900, James L. Smith, aka "Whispering" Smith, was allegedly hired to come to Denver either to kill Masterson or to run him out of town, depending on which character is believed. Smith's previous jobs throughout the West ranged from railroad detective for the Union Pacific, to chief of police on Native American reservations, to stock detective for cattle concerns. During Smith's numerous careers, the gunslinger was involved in several shootings, some of which resulted in deaths, as well as lynchings. He came to Denver at the request of newspaper editor Patrick Gallagher, who had clashed with Masterson over some illegal boxing clubs. When Masterson heard about Smith's arrival at Gallagher's request, he sent a note to Gallagher with a hundred

[113] Dick Kreck. 2016. *Rich People Behaving Badly*, Fulcrum Publishing, Golden, CO; Daniel Diehl and Mark Donnelly. 2006. *Eat Thy Neighbor: A History of Cannibalism,* Sutton Publishing.

dollars inviting Smith and Gallagher to meet him on the street in front of a saloon to settle the matter. Gallagher refused the hundred dollars and denied Smith was in Denver to make trouble with Masterson. Nothing further occurred; presumably, Smith left town and no charges were ever filed.[114]

Later that summer, Bat Masterson again came to the attention of the district attorney when he and Otto Floto, the sports editor for the *Denver Post,* got into a fistfight. Masterson was operating his new "Olympic Athletic Club," and writing a sports column for the Denver newspaper *George's Weekly*. Masterson and Floto were partners promoting boxing matches. After the partnership soured, the two became competitors and enemies. Less a boxing match than a street brawl, the fight was witnessed by many. Malone never charged either man. Floto and Masterson remained enemies, but violence never erupted again between the two, and Masterson eventually left Denver two years later—with an assist from the next Denver district attorney.[115]

Otto Floto, photo from jeffarnoldblog.blogspot.com/2013/07/bat-masterson.html

Police work has always been dangerous, sometimes fatally so. On the night of August 13, 1899, a drunken U.S. Army soldier named Wellington C. Llewellyn shot and killed Denver police officers Thomas C. Clifford and William Griffiths.[116] Llewellyn and two companions

[114] *Rocky Mountain News*, September 22, 1886.
[115] *Svensk-Amerikanska Western*, August 2, 1900, p 8.
[116] Denver Police Department: Officer Down Memorial Page https://www.odmp.org/officer/5764-officer-william-e-griffiths.

from the 34th Infantry Division at Fort Logan had been thrown out of a Denver saloon. When Officer Clifford attempted to disarm the men near 20th and Blake Streets, Llewellyn drew his weapon and shot Clifford, killing him. During the ensuing manhunt, Llewellyn also shot and killed Officer Griffiths under the 16th Street bridge. Llewellyn fled Denver but was identified by his two companions. Malone charged Llewellyn with the murders and a warrant was posted nationally for his arrest. Llewellyn was never caught, and unconfirmed rumors in 1912 had him leading a group of bandits in the Philippines. For months after the murders, Denver police were stopping and questioning every soldier in uniform they encountered on the street. This policy led to poor relationships between the police and the Army, and the searches were eventually abandoned. In 1905, Denver DA George Stidger put Charles S. Wynne on trial for the murders, believing Wynne was Llewellyn. During the trial, prosecution witnesses failed to identify Wynne as Llewellyn and at the conclusion of testimony, the DA ordered the charges be withdrawn. Wynne was turned over to Indiana authorities where he was charged with parole violation and returned to prison.[117]

Thomas C. Clifford and William Griffiths, photos courtesy of the Denver Police Department

On October 31, 1900, Denver police officer Charles S. Secrest was off duty and drinking at Dan Hickey's saloon at 19th and Larimer streets in Denver. Secrest was not in uniform when he got into an altercation over drinks with Henry Reed. During the altercation, Secrest took out his pistol and shot Reed three times through the abdomen. Reed died from the gunshot wounds the next day at the county hospital. When fellow officers arrested the intoxicated Secrest, he said he was "trying out his new gun." In a formal statement, Secrest indicated that he shot Reed in

[117] *Aspen Democrat*, March 28, 1905, p 1.

self-defense after Reed threatened to kill him. Malone refused to charge Secrest because he could not disprove his claim of self-defense beyond a reasonable doubt. A few years later, however, Secrest killed another man under remarkably similar circumstances.

Secrest's second killing occurred on February 9, 1906, when he shot Thomas Johnson in the Cottage Saloon on Curtis Street in Denver. Secrest was again off duty and again intoxicated when he shot Johnson over a dice game. Patrolman Durkin, who earlier had been trying to persuade Secrest to go home, rushed into the saloon while smoke was still coming from the barrel of Secrest's revolver. By this time, George Stidger was district attorney, and he charged Secrest with first-degree murder. On March 27, 1906, a Denver jury, after deliberating over a verdict all night, found the policeman guilty of murder in the second degree. Secrest was sentenced to serve 14 to 20 years in the state penitentiary.

On Election Day, November 6, 1900, ongoing trouble between the Denver Police Department and the Arapahoe County Sheriff's Department turned into a shooting melee, resulting in the deaths of four law enforcement officers—two Denver police officers[118] and two Arapahoe County Sheriff's deputies. Denver was still part of Arapahoe County at the time, which caused jurisdictional disputes. In this incident, Policeman Samuel Charles Carpenter and Officer Charles Green went to 21st and Larimer streets in Denver to supervise the opening of the polls. Denver Police were instructed to enforce the election laws, because there had been reports that the Sheriff's office might attempt to interfere. Several sheriff deputies were present at the polling place. When Carpenter ordered the deputies to back up one hundred feet from the entrance to the polls in accordance with election law, Deputy Hampton Jackson drew a revolver and began shooting.

One bullet struck Carpenter's arm and a second his foot. Green struck Jackson with his club, fracturing his skull and breaking his arm. Other deputies opened fire. Detective Ed Carberry killed Deputy Sheriff Charles Allen and hit Jackson in the head. The deputies and Carberry continued to exchange gunfire. Police Officer Stuart Harvey was shot and died from the wound hours later.[119] Officer Green was shot in the back. Deputy Richard Hardeman was shot twice in the left arm. Both Green and Hardeman survived. Jackson, who had started the shooting,

[118] Denver Police Department: Officer Down Memorial Page, https://www.odmp.org/officer/3162-officer-thomas-c-clifford.

[119] Denver Police Department: Officer Down Memorial Page, https://www.odmp.org/officer/21185-special-officer-stuart-k-harvey.

died a couple of weeks after the incident. Officer Carpenter died 10 years later from medical complications due to the wounds he received in the shooting.[120] DA Malone, after extensive review, refused to charge anyone; he determined that the survivors were either acting in self-defense or were defending others.[121]

Left: Special Officer Stuart Harvey killed in the line of duty. Photo from Denver Police Department "Officer Down Memorial Page"

Right: Patrolman Samuel Charles Carpenter died from the gunshot wound 10 years after the 1900 shooting. Photo from Denver Police Department "Officer Down Memorial Page."

After his single term as district attorney, Malone spent six years on the Denver District Court bench, 1901 to 1907. After leaving the bench and returning to private practice, he was employed to go to Goldfield, Nevada, and take charge of the prosecution of the high-profile case of the People vs. Smith and Preston. Joseph William Smith and Morrie Rockwood Preston were members of the International Workers of the World (IWW) charged with murder during a labor dispute. IWW union members were known as "Wobblies," and the union had a reputation for using violence. Malone obtained convictions of both men and followed the case successfully through the Nevada Supreme Court.[122]

---

[120] Denver Police Department: Officer Down Memorial Page, https://www.odmp.org/officer/21125-patrolman-samuel-charles-carpenter.

[121] Silver Standard, Volume XV, N1, November 10, 1900, p 1.

[122] Sally Zanjani and Guy Louis Rocha. 1986. *The Ignoble Conspiracy—Radicalism on Trial in Nevada*. Reno, University of Nevada Press.

Joseph William Smith and Morrie Rockwood Preston, photos from Nevada State Prison[123]

As a private criminal defense attorney, Malone represented Mrs. Stella Moore-Smith, charged with killing her second husband in Denver.[124] Mrs. Moore-Smith was the daughter of a wealthy California oil businessman. The defendant's first husband, William Moore, was a successful Denver attorney. The case attracted nationwide attention and lasted several weeks. Mrs. Moore-Smith had left William Moore to marry her father-in-law's chauffeur, John Lawrence Smith. Smith had become emotionally and physically abusive to Mrs. Smith, however, even while she financially supported him. After she left Smith and returned to the home of her first husband, Smith, drunk and armed, forced his way into the home and attacked his estranged wife. She was able to get free and shot Smith twice. The second shot was the reason the then district attorney William Foley gave for pursuing murder charges against Mrs. Moore-Smith. Malone used psychiatric testimony, unusual at that time, to argue temporary insanity on the defendant's behavior. The jury acquitted Moore-Smith within 11 minutes of getting the case. Local papers called Malone's closing speech, "one of the greatest forensic efforts ever delivered."[125]

---

[123] *Montana News*, May 30, 1907, p 2; *Salt Lake City Herald*, May 10, 1907, p 9.
[124] *Middle Park Times*, January 26, 1917, p 6.
[125] *History of Colorado*, ed by Wilbur Fisk Stone, S.J. Clarke Publishing Company, 1918 Vol II, p 185.

Mrs. Stella Moore-Smith, along with her murdered second husband (left), and William Moore, her first husband (right), *The Day Book*, Volume 6, Number 96, January 20, 1917

Malone died after being struck and killed by a car on Valentine's Day 1932. The papers recorded his death as the 31st vehicle fatality in and around Denver in that year.[126]

[126] *Rocky Mountain News*, April 11, 1932.

12. Henry A. Lindsley (1901–1904)

HENRY A. LINDSLEY
1901 –1904

Henry A. Lindsley, born in Lebanon, Tennessee on March 30, 1871, was part of an accomplished family. His great-grandfather, Dr. Philip Lindsley, was president of the College of New Jersey (predecessor of Princeton University), as well as president of the University of Nashville. Lindsley's son, Henry Sherman Lindsley, worked as a deputy district attorney in the Denver office in the 1920s before going on to become a District Court judge, Supreme Court judge, and eventually Chief Justice of the Colorado Supreme Court.

Lindsley received his education at Cumberland University in Tennessee, where he graduated with a Bachelor of Law degree at age 19. He came to Denver in 1891 and started the law firm of Whitford & Lindsley in 1893, partnering with another barrister who would soon become district attorney. When Henry Lindsley took office in January 1901, the district attorney's office consisted of the DA and five assistants. Lindsley was the youngest person to serve as Denver district attorney. He was only 28 years old when elected. In 1902, Lindsley served as district attorney, Denver county attorney, and Denver city attorney simultaneously.

In 1904, Robert W. Speer became Denver mayor in what came to be known as the most fraudulent election in the history of the city.[127] Denver newspapers reported that thousands of names of Speer's voters came from local obituaries. Despite this, Speer became mayor, and Lindsley was appointed Denver city attorney soon after. Lindsley continued to serve in the municipal post under Mayor Speer and is credited with advising the mayor on many of the complex negotiations required to develop Denver's City Beautiful public improvement projects during Speer's several terms. In 1908, Lindsley, as city attorney, was able to get the Colorado Supreme Court's decision reversed by the U.S. Supreme Court in the case of Londoner v. City and County of Denver. The ruling allowed the city to tax property owners for the cost of paving the streets of Denver.[128]

---

[127] *Aspen Daily Times*, May 19, 1904; *Denver's Mayor Speer,* Denver: Green Mountain Press 1969; *Robert W. Speer: A City Builder:* Denver Smith-Brooks Printing, 1919.
[128] Londoner V Denver, 210 U.S., 373. 1908.

Denver Mayor Robert Speer photo circa 1905, photo from Colorado Virtual Library

"City Beautiful" Inspired Landscaping in Denver under the Speer/Lindsley tenure, photos from Colorado Virtual Library, credit Denver Public Library and History Colorado

The district attorney had his detractors; one such person was Juvenile Court Judge Ben Lindsey. Early in his judicial career, the judge determined that the county was being overcharged for office supplies as well as being charged for nonexistent supplies. His investigation pointed to the county commissioners. He requested an investigation but with little effect. Lindsley eventually did indict two county commissioners but only after the judge gave his incriminating information to the *Rocky Mountain News* for publication. The commissioners were charged with one misdemeanor, and the criminal case took more than a year to come to trial. They were both found guilty and fined $10 each by a judge brought in from outside the district to ensure an "impartial" trial.[129] Lindsley's office also came under fire when allegations of bribery in the Westside Courthouse were made. Lindsley denied the charges, but District Court Judge F.T. Johnson appointed a special prosecutor to the grand jury to replace the district attorney's office to investigate the allegations.[130]

Another critic was visiting Judge Frank P. Owers from Leadville, Colorado, who severely criticized the authorities, including the Denver police and the district attorney, for permitting Denver to be a wide-open town where immunity was extended to all classes of villains.[131] Owers said the murder of Harold Fridborn and the rape of his sister, Florence Fridborn, were directly traceable to the fact that Denver was a place of safety for robbers, thieves, thugs, and murderers because of law enforcement authorities. The Fridborn teenagers were skating on a frozen lake at Lake Avenue and Alcott Street in Denver when they were attacked by a man with an axe. He killed Harold with two blows from the axe and then choked and raped Florence. Two years later, in 1904, after an exhaustive investigation, Lindsley charged Russell Boles for the attack on the Fridborn children. He was convicted and sentenced to life in prison.[132] In 1916 the State Board of Pardons decided Boles was innocent and Governor George Alfred Carlson (1915–1917), pardoned and released Boles.[133] Years later he returned to prison for a rape in Boulder.

---

[129] Charles Larsen. 1972. *The Good Fight: The Life and Times of Ben B. Lindsey*, Chicago, Quadrangle Books, p 56.
[130] *Elk Mountain Pilot*, Vol 24, No. 10, August 4, 1903, p 2.
[131] *Weekly Courier*, January 16, 1902, p 4.
[132] *Durango Wage Earner*, November 19, 1903, p 2; San Miguel Examiner, Vol XVIII, No 38, March 5, 1904.
[133] *Telluride Daily Journal*, January 15, 1916, p 1.

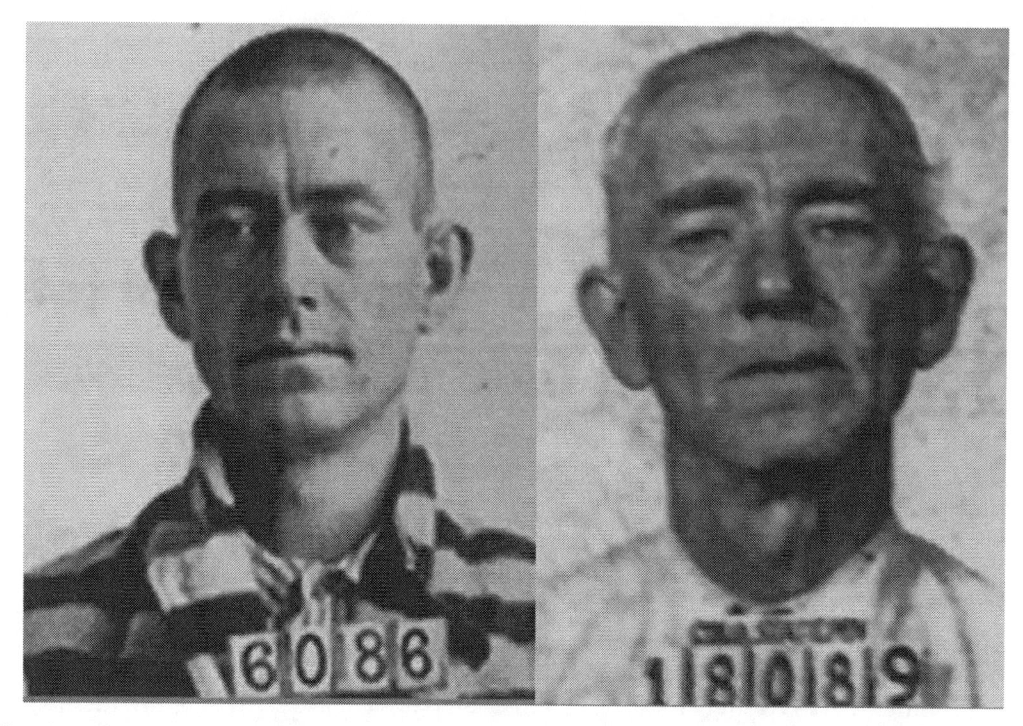

Russell Boles after his conviction in Denver and years later after he was returned to prison for a rape in Boulder, photos from the Colorado State Archives

Lindsley also played a role in the departure from Denver of the famous lawman, gambler, and sometimes gunslinger Bat Masterson. Masterson lived in Denver on and off for more than 20 years and had his share of run-ins with law enforcement in the city. In the 1880s he operated Ed Chase's Palace Saloon and Gambling House. Masterson was alternately a lawman and on the fringes of the law. In addition to his card gambling, Masterson was involved in promoting boxing matches, even though prizefighting was illegal in the city at that time. In 1902, Masterson returned to the city after an extended absence. While attempting to vote in a local election, A female election observer challenged Masterson's vote. Two female candidates were standing for election and Masterson had been vocal about his opposition to women's suffrage. The altercation at the polling place put Masterson in a foul mood, and his subsequent behavior was the result. He went on a drinking bender while conspicuously showing off the fact that he was armed. It was at this time that DA Lindsley stopped in to visit with the long time Denver Sheriff and later Police Chief Hamilton Armstrong. The following story, taken from Lindsley's unpublished manuscript, is relayed in *Guns of the Frontier* by William MacLeod Raine.

Denver Sherriff and later Police Chief Hamilton Armstrong
Photo in the public domain

Armstrong was visibly upset when he stopped in to visit. "What's up?" Lindsley asked.

"It's Bat Masterson. He's on a rampage and I ought to have him arrested, but he is sore as a boil and won't stand for it without a fight. I hate to give the job to any of my boys because two or three of them are likely to get killed."

Just then the telephone bell rang. The call was a long distance one from Cripple Creek.

"Jim Marshall on the line, inquiring about some guy who has skipped out from the Creek," Armstrong mentioned as an aside to Lindsley.

Marshall was a Cripple Creek officer, a man known to be resolute and fearless. He had a large experience in dealing with tough characters.

"Have Jim hold the line a minute, Chief," Lindsley said, and then suggested that Armstrong ask Marshall to come down and make the arrest of Masterson.

Marshall was reluctant to do this. In the first place, it was not his business. Also, he and Bat had been in tight places together during the old Kansas days. In one of the county-seat fights—that between the towns of Cimarron and Ingalls—they had been employed by the Ingalls faction to help get the county records from Cimarron and bring them to Ingalls. In the resulting fight, a Cimarron citizen was killed. Masterson and Marshall were tried for the killing but acquitted.

But Marshall was under obligations to Armstrong, and since somebody had to arrest Bat he thought he had better do the job. He promised to reach Denver early the next day.

By an underworld grapevine route, Bat learned what was afoot. He wired to Marshall that he would be waiting for him in front of the barbershop back of the Scholtz drugstore at ten o'clock. Bat kept his word. He had his morning shave in the shop, and then planted himself in a chair on the sidewalk beside the striped pole. His fingers hovered near the butt of a revolver. From ten o'clock until eleven he sat there, his keen eyes taking in each passer. After an hour of waiting Bat left his post and crossed the street to the saloon in the Tabor Opera House block where he usually had his morning nip. To the barber he mentioned that he would be back presently, to meet the late Mr. Marshall in case he finally arrived. Bat walked up to the bar and gave his order. He lifted his glass to drink.

A familiar voice startled him. "Sorry I was a little late, Bat."

The glass of whiskey stayed poised in the air. Bat realized instantly that he was trapped. Jim Marshall had slipped in a side door and was standing at his right side. He was ready for business, whereas Bat's gun hand was temporarily engaged hoisting one.

Bat showed no disturbance, though he recognized defeat. He looked at the man beside him—a ruddy, hard-eyed man, not quite six feet in height, well dressed, entirely sure of himself.

Quietly Bat put the question that was engaging his attention. "Does this mean a killing, Jim?"

"Depends on whether you are reasonable, Bat."

"Meaning just what?"

"Meaning that it is for you to say."

"What do you mean, reasonable?"

"Denver is too big a town for you to hurrah, Bat. Time for you to move on."

Swiftly Masterson reviewed the situation. Most men of his reputation would have stalled as long as he could, hoping for a break. But Bat knew from long experience that the cards were stacked against him. If he reached for his pistol, he was a dead man. Moreover, he had asked for this. What Marshall said was true. Denver was no longer a frontier town. He had no right to defy the law. Just now Jim Marshall was the law, and it had served notice on him...

Bo Stockton, the saloonkeeper, drew a long breath of relief after Masterson's next words.

"If I leave, how soon do I have to go?" he asked.

"Could you make the four o'clock Burlington, Bat?"

"I reckon so."[134]

Masterson left town that afternoon, never to return to Denver. He moved to New York City and became a literary figure living off his frontier reputation. He wrote disparagingly of the city of Denver for years afterward. Lindsley may have embellished the episode since the incident is not recounted in other histories of Masterson.

Lindsley dealt with other interesting criminal cases during his tenure as district attorney. For example, he prosecuted 14-year-old Albert Thorman for first-degree murder. On October 21, 1901, Gustavus "Gus" Roeghan was passing Thorman on horseback on a road in Akron, Colorado, when words were exchanged and Thorman shot and killed Roeghan. Akron was in far eastern Arapahoe County at that time and therefore under the jurisdiction of the Second Judicial District and the Denver district attorney's office. Thorman had shot Roeghan with his rifle, first in the heart and then in the head. Thorman was charged as a juvenile and at trial claimed self-defense, saying the cowboy raised a whip to strike him. The jury found Thorman guilty of voluntary manslaughter and he was sentenced, as a juvenile, to 14 months at the State Industrial School in Golden, Colorado.[135]

In another notable case, Father Felix Mariano Lepore—pastor of Mount Carmel Catholic Church in north Denver—and Joseph Sorice of Pittsburg, Pennsylvania, shot each other while in the priest's apartment at the rear of the church on February 18, 1903.[136] The men were playing cards when the drunken Sorice stood up and shot Lepore three times. The priest wrestled the gun away from his assailant and shot him once. Both men were fatally wounded and died the next day. In an ante-mortem statement to a member of Lindsley's office, Lepore said he believed Sorice had been sent to Denver to kill him. Sorice refused to say a word either to the district attorney representatives or to the detectives who interviewed him. It was believed that behind the tragedy lay a deep mystery extending back to old times in Italy. In 1907 the Denver Probate Court determined that Father Lepore had a wife and child. The court upheld the claim of Evelyn Benns that she had been the wife of the priest since July 1, 1896, and that a son was born as the result of that marriage.[137] The marital scandal and shooting are still remembered in North Denver's Italian community.

---

[134] William MacLeod Raine. 1940. *Guns of the Frontier*. Boston, Houghton Mifflin Co. the Riverside Press Cambridge, pp 253–257.
[135] *Yuma Pioneer*, November 29, 1901, p 1.
[136] *Telluride Daily Journal* , November 19, 1903, p 1.
[137] *The Colorado Transcript*, September 26, 1907, p 2.

After serving as district attorney, Lindsley continued to serve as city attorney until 1912, for as long as Robert Speer was mayor. Later that year, in December 1912, Lindsley was representing the Denver Civil Service Commission when he got into an altercation with the new Denver Mayor, Henry Arnold. Lindsley was trying to get the mayor to obey the commission's order to reinstate members of the Denver Fire and Police Board,[138] when he was kicked out of the mayor's office for what Mayor Arnold said was "slobbering" over him. Arnold also called Lindsley a "public nuisance." Lindsley responded by saying Arnold should be spending Christmas in jail. Lindsley asked the court to hold the mayor in contempt for ignoring the commission's order. Judge and former Denver DA Greeley Whitford dismissed the contempt charge but criticized Arnold for calling Lindsley names.

Henry Lindsley died May 18, 1934, at the age of sixty-three.

13. George Stidger (1905–1908)

GEORGE STIDGER
1905-1908

George Stidger was born in Keosuaqua, Iowa in January 1860. He graduated from Simpson College, Iowa in 1880, studied law in Red Oak, Iowa, and was admitted to the Iowa and Colorado bars in 1882. That same year he joined two brothers who had moved to Colorado to practice law and began his Colorado practice in Boulder. He moved to Denver in 1888, was appointed justice of the peace in 1890, and elected to that same office in 1892. He was elected district attorney in 1904 as a Republican. During his tenure, unlike his predecessor, Stidger was known for prosecuting election crooks for violating Denver election laws. One reason George Stidger defeated Lindsley in the 1904 election for district attorney was that Lindsley was vigorously opposed by the "Honest Elections League" for not prosecuting any election fraud cases.[139]

In attempting to clean up Denver's elections, Stidger charged election officials Peter Miller and Michael Dowd with election fraud after the 1904 municipal election. The two men stole 318 ballots in the election and substituted them with illegitimate votes. The lights were extinguished for a few minutes after the polls had closed at the polling place where these men

[138] *Fire and Water Engineering*, Vol 52, p 57; *Herald Democrat*, December 23, 1912, p 3.
[139] *Grand Junction Daily Sentinel*, Vol 11, November 9, 1904, p 1.

were officers, allowing the ballots to be switched. After Miller and Dowd were found guilty, former Denver district attorney and then-District Court judge Booth Malone sentenced the men to three to five years in the state penitentiary. Malone, recognizing that the crime was part of a conspiracy involving many others, characterized the crime as treason and said the people who paid for such work were worse than those who performed the act.[140]

In another election fraud case, Stidger charged Denver police officers J.J. Keane, Charles Barberri, and William Sick with bribing voters in the November 4, 1905, municipal election.[141] The trial was again in front of Denver District Court judge Booth Malone. None of the witnesses Stidger needed for the case could be located. Without witnesses the prosecution could not go forward, and Stidger reluctantly withdrew the charges.

When Stidger was DA, two Denver officers were killed in one incident on March 14, 1905.[142] For many years, the police department had a police surgeon on staff who responded to incidents where injuries had occurred or were likely to occur. On this date, Police Surgeon Frank Dulin and Captain William Bohanna were responding to a reported shooting at a residence. George Shissler had used a shotgun to kill his neighbors, and then then barricaded himself in his home and shot and killed both Captain Bohanna and Police Surgeon Dulin when they came on the scene. A gun battle with other responding Denver officers ensued, and when the shooting was over, Shissler was dead. At the coroner's inquest it was determined that Shissler shot himself.

[140] *Lamar Register*, Vol 19, No. 37, February 22, 1905, p 3.
[141] *Herald Democrat*, March 4, 1905, p 1.
[142] Denver Police Department: Officer Down Memorial Page https://www.odmp.org/officer/4347-police-surgeon-frank-dulin; https://www.odmp.org/officer/1991-captain-william-bohanna.

Police Surgeon Frank Dulin (left) and Captain William Bohanna (right), photos courtesy of the Denver Police Museum

From 1904 to 1909, Vaso L. Chucovich ran a gambling operation in Denver in association with Edwin Gaylord and "Big Ed" Chase. Chucovich was a close friend of Mayor Robert Speer and would underwrite Speer's city improvement projects in exchange for police protection and the ability to operate his gambling house openly. As much as he may have wished to prosecute Chucovich, Stidger was unable to do so without police enforcing the gambling laws. When the public demanded action, Speer would often have the police focus on small-time operations or those run by Black or Chinese gamblers, ignoring the Chucovich operations.

Left: Vaso L. Chucovich, photo from Denver Public Library Special Collections, Z-2889.
Right: "Big Ed" Chase, photo published in *From the Grave: A Roadside Guide to Colorado's Pioneer Cemeteries*

The early 20th century was a period of active labor organizing as well as ownership pushback against unions, often expressed through violence. Colorado was no exception. On May 15, 1904, ex-policeman Lyte Gregory was killed in the early morning when returning to his home from a night of drinking at a saloon in west Denver. Gregory was shot down at the entrance of an alleyway, his body riddled with buckshot. Gregory had recently worked for the Reno Detective Agency and was one of the men accused by William Wardjon— the national committeeman of the United Mine Workers of America—with assaulting him on a Rio Grande train near Salida, Colorado. Wardjon was badly beaten and claimed that four Reno Detective Agency men were his assailants. On January 6, 1906, Albert Edward Horsely, aka Harry

Orchard, confessed that he and Steve Adams had murdered Gregory. Adams later confessed to his involvement in the murder as well.[143] Orchard and Adams were paid union terrorists who, among other crimes, blew up the Vindicator mine in Colorado in 1903, killing two men. The next year they planted a bomb at an Independence, Colorado train depot, killing 13 non-union miners and crippling many more.

Albert Edward Horsely, aka Harry Orchard (left) and Steve Adams (right), photos from *The Confessions and Autobiography of Harry Orchard*

[143] Albert Edward Horsely. 1907. *The Confessions and Autobiography of Harry Orchard*, The S.S. McClure Company, pp 125–127; "The Confessions and Autobiography of Harry Orchard," Victor Heritage Society, http://www.rebelgraphics.org/wfmhall/harry_orchard_confession01.html; *Routt County Sentinel*, May 20, 1904, p 2.

Independence, Colorado train depot after explosion on June 6, 1904, in which 13 people were killed. Photo from Cripple Creek Museum captioned "Waiting for the dogs," shared by Jean Greeson.

Orchard was also tried and convicted in March 1908 for setting a bomb that killed former Idaho Governor Frank Steunenberg. He was sentenced to death for this crime, but had his sentence commuted to life in prison. He died in the Idaho State Penitentiary in 1954. Adams, again Orchard's accomplice, repudiated his confession and was acquitted at trial of the murder of Steunenberg. Stidger did not extradite either man to Colorado for Gregory's murder nor for the murder of Denver resident Merritt Walley that had occurred when Orchard and Adams were attempting to assassinate Colorado Supreme Court Justice William Gabbert, to which Orchard also confessed.

Former Idaho Governor Frank Steunenberg, photo from *The Confessions and Autobiography of Harry Orchard*

On May 24, 1905, at 10 a.m., Merritt Walley was walking across a vacant lot on Emerson Street near Colfax Avenue in Denver's Capitol Hill neighborhood. He kicked a strange object and was killed instantly by a dynamite bomb.[144] The police and the coroner were puzzled by the explosion and why Walley would be targeted. They examined various scenarios, including whether it was an accident, a suicide, or a planned killing of Walley, but were unable to uncover any reason this man might have been deliberately killed. It was not until the arrest of union terrorist Alfred (Horsely) Orchard on December 30, 1905, for the bombing murder of ex-Governor Steunenberg, that the mystery was solved. Orchard confessed to setting the bomb that killed Walley—the intended target of the bomb had been Colorado Supreme Court Chief Justice William Gabbert. Orchard, by his own admission, had committed 16 murders in addition to a lifetime of burglaries, insurance fraud, and even bigamy. His published autobiography outlined how he planned the Gabbert assassination.

"I went to Pettibone's store, and in the basement he had some old eight-day clocks. I took the spring of one of these, and practiced with it to see if I could get it so it would break those little vials that I had with sulphuric acid in for the bombs. I had tried a few vials with it, and it broke them every time. Then I made this new bomb in a wooden box and fixed it with this spring. I fastened the spring along the underside of the cover, and bent the spring back, and held it there

[144] Stewart Hall Holbrook. 1956. *Rocky Mountain Revolution*. Holt, p 177; *Colorado Transcript*, June 1, 1905, p 2.

with a piece of stiff wire that went down through the box. I had a little eye in the top of the wire to hook the pocket-book on, and left this so I could see it. When this wire was pulled out, it let the spring hit a couple of half-dram vials that were filled with acid, and broke them, and the giant-caps were right under these. This wire pulled out very easily, and I knew the spring was sure to break the bottles.

I buried this second bomb as close to the first as I dared, and not touch it. The next morning I found the sidewalk clear when the judge was coming, and had Pettibone's bicycle, and rode along, and stopped at the bomb and hooked on the pocket-book, and rode away. I listened, and knew that something had happened to it, or else he did not see it, for I did not hear it go, and I did not have time to get more than a block away by the time he would be there. However, I was afraid to go back there for fear someone had been watching me, or for fear something might have happened that it did not go, and they had discovered the bomb. Anyway, I was too big a coward to go back, and made up my mind I would let it go. I did not think the judge would walk over it and not notice the pocket-book.

I went on downtown, and about an hour afterward I heard the bomb go off; but it was not the judge that got it, but another poor unfortunate man by the name of Merritt W. Walley. There were about ten pounds of dynamite in each of these bombs, and they both went off. It blew this poor fellow to pieces and broke the glass in the windows for many blocks around. There were many theories advanced in regard to the cause of this explosion, but not any of them came anywhere near the truth. Some thought that a yeggman had buried nitroglycerin there and Walley stubbed against it. I have been told since that Judge Gabbert saw a friend on the corner and followed the walk around instead of going across the vacant lot that morning. I thought when this failed I was out of luck sure, and that there would not be any chance to work there any more, as I did not suppose Judge Gabbert would go across there for the present. So I gave up trying to do him any harm for the present at least, but I thought I would make one more attempt, nearly on the same line, with Judge Goddard."[145]

Although attempts were made on both justices Gabbert and Goddard, the only Denver citizen killed by Orchard or his accomplices was the innocent bystander Merritt Walley.

[145] *Confessions and Autobiography of Harry Orchard.* Victor Heritage Society, http://www.rebelgraphics.org/wfmhall/harry_orchard_confession01.html.

Chief Justice William Gabbert, Justice Luther Goddard, and Merritt Walley, photos in public domain

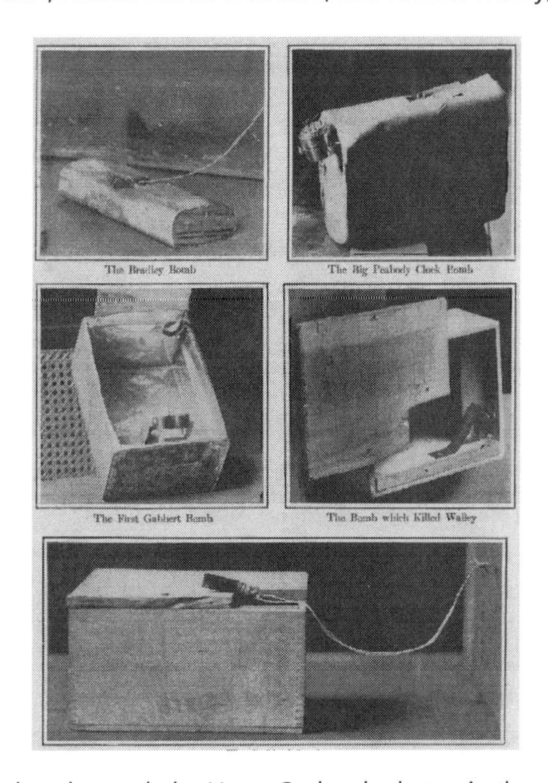

Models of the bombs made by Harry Orchard, photos in the public domain

Also during Stidger's term, a Catholic priest was murdered in Denver; this was the second such killing in five years. On Sunday morning, February 23, 1908, Father Joseph "Leo" Heinrichs was shot and killed while giving communion at mass at Saint Elizabeth's Church in Denver.[146] Father Heinrichs, a German-born priest, had been assigned to the parish church for

[146] *Brush Tribune*, No 19, February 28, 1908, p 7.

only five months. Denver Police Patrolman Daniel Cronin was off duty and attending the Sunday service when Italian anarchist Giuseppe Alia pulled out a revolver as he knelt to receive communion and shot the priest. When Alia attempted to flee, Cronin leaped over three church pews to apprehend the shooter on the front steps of the church after Alia was tripped by another parishioner. Cronin immediately commandeered a buggy and transported Alia to police headquarters, keeping the angry church crowd from attacking the anarchist. At the jail, Alia boasted of his anarchist beliefs, saying he had a grudge against all priests and that he had gone to the church's communion rail to get a better shot at the priest. He said his only regret was that he could not shoot the whole bunch of priests in the church. Based upon Cronin's testimony, the testimony of other eyewitnesses, and Alia's confession, DA Stidger convicted Alia of first-degree murder.[147] He was sentenced to death by hanging within weeks of the shooting. Alia never expressed any remorse and made two escape attempts from death row. He went to the gallows, fighting, biting, and snarling.[148]

[147] *Fort Collins Courier*, March 11, 1908, p 1.
[148] *Weekly Courier*, July 15, 1908, p 9.

Catholic Priest Father Joseph "Leo" Heinrichs was killed at mass in 1908. Photo from "Priests of the Eucharist," http://catholictradition.org/Priests/fr-heinrichs.htm

Italian anarchist Giuseppe Alia, photo in the public domain

1908 file photo from the Denver Catholic Register archives shows a full St. Elizabeth of Hungary Parish for

the funeral Mass of Father Leo. Thousands attended, with the majority of attendees likely outside of the church. His body, lying in the open casket, can be seen near the center of the photo. St. Elizabeth's Church is now located on the Auraria campus in Downtown Denver.

Officer Cronin saw many changes in the police department in his 28 years as a Denver police officer. Later in his career he promoted to Captain, overseeing the Traffic Unit in the 1920s. The Traffic Unit at this time included the "Bandit Chaser" armored car, the Denver Police Department's first aircraft, and the "Flying Squad" riot response teams.

Officer Daniel Cronin around the time of the arrest of Alia, photo courtesy of Denver Public Library, Special Collections

Captain Daniel Cronin and Denver police "Bandit Chaser" 1921, photos courtesy of Denver Public Library Special Collections #Rh-2143 and X-29731

"Machine Gun Squad at Civic Center" Photo of the Denver Police Department's "Flying Squad," March 1921. The unit was created to respond to well-organized and well-armed criminal gangs. Photo Courtesy of Denver Public Library Special Collections X-29671

In 1905, a woman named Helen Schmidlap—whom Colorado newspapers called "the most beautiful woman ever lodged in the Denver County Jail"—killed her ex-husband. In July, Schmidlap arrived in Denver from California armed with a pistol, and immediately went to the boarding house where her ex-husband William Schmidlap was living. She was resolved to kill him for failing to support their children. A witness overheard Helen tell William that she had come all the way from California to kill him, and then three shots rang. DA Stidger tried Schmidlap for first-degree murder twice. The first jury could not reach a verdict. The victim had a history of alcohol abuse and assaulting his wife, and it was alleged that he tried to convince her to engage in prostitution to support the family. The trial received so much press that there was speculation whether it would be possible to secure twelve men in Denver to try her again. The second jury found Schmidlap not guilty. At the conclusion of the trial, the judge took the extraordinary step of telling the jury that their verdict was not in accord with his idea of justice.[149]

Helen Schmidlap, photo from *Wicked Denver: Mile-High Misdeeds and Malfeasance* by Sheila O'Hare and Alphild Dick

Ambiguous justice was not confined to attractive female defendants. On Christmas Day 1905, Phillip Lynd and Philip Keiser verbally harassed Jewish workers Jacob Weisskind and Mendel Slotkin for working on "Christ's birthday." Weisskind and Slotkin were loading scrap iron on a flatcar of the Colorado and Southern Railroad at the Larimer Street crossing a few blocks from downtown. Lynd and Keiser went to the nearby saloons of Larimer Street where they were able to gather a mob of outraged men from among those drinking at the bars on Christmas Day—being drunk on Christmas apparently was more acceptable than working on that day. The mob of 15 to 20 men returned to the tracks and attacked Weisskind and Slotkin. They beat the two men with stones, bricks, and iron, slashing their faces and breaking bones. They crushed Weisskind's skull. During the attack, Lynd and Keiser yelled that they were avenging the blood of Christ by shedding the blood of Christ killers.

---

[149] *Aspen Daily Times*, January 30, 1906, p 1; *Grand Junction Daily Sentinel*, Vol 12, February 5, 1906.

The attacks made national news, and Denver was described as rife with anti-Semitism. The *Los Angeles Times* stated that the situation in Denver "seemed just like Russia" where pogroms were occurring. Stidger charged three men, Lynd, Keiser and James Bohanna with first-degree murder and assigned former DA Greeley Whitford as special prosecutor to pursue the case. When the case went to trial, many of the defendants' supporters were in the room to intimidate Whitford and the witnesses. Despite the intimidation, those who witnessed the crime took the stand and testified. The prosecution called a total of eighteen witnesses. The *Jewish Outlook* newspaper in Denver reported that Whitford tore the defense argument to "shreds." Unfortunately, the jury was less was impressed with Whitford; only Lynd and Keiser were convicted. Lynd was sentenced to four to six years in the state penitentiary, and Keiser was sent to the county jail for seven months and fourteen days. Bohanna was acquitted.[150]

Less than two years later, two other Jewish residents of west Denver—Michael Weisblye and Tevyah Bokser—were also attacked and brutally murdered.[151] The perpetrators, Harold McKnaw and Wilbur F. Gilmer, belonged to a street gang that had a reputation for targeting Jews. Stidger charged both men with first-degree murder and again convictions were obtained, albeit to lesser offenses, and again, lenient sentences by the court. The results suggested that even when the prosecutor pursued the cases strenuously, they could not overcome community-wide anti-Semitic views.[152]

Other murderers were held to stricter penalties. For example, police officer John Spellman was shot and killed while attempting to arrest three drunken men.[153] The suspect was arrested the next day, tried, convicted, and sentenced to 10–15 years in prison. Another police officer killed during Stidger's term was William Beck.[154] Beck was on routine patrol on 16th Street when he noticed the rear door of a business open. He went into the business to leave a note for the owner when he was shot and killed. The suspect was never apprehended. A fourth officer was killed on August 25, 1908.[155] Policeman William Stephens was questioning a person

---

[150] Michael Adam Lee. 2017. "The Politics of Antisemitism in Denver, Colorado, 1898–1984." PhD Thesis, University of Colorado at Boulder.
[151] *Jewish Outlook*, Vol 3, No. 16, February 15, 1907, p 1.
[152] Michael Adam Lee. 2017. "The Politics of Antisemitism in Denver, Colorado, 1898–1984." PhD Thesis, University of Colorado at Boulder; Jewish Outlook, Vol 3, No. 16, February 15, 1907, p 1.
[153] Denver Police Department: Officer Down Memorial Page, https://www.odmp.org/officer/12604-policeman-john-spellman.
[154] Denver Police Department: Officer Down Memorial Page https://www.odmp.org/officer/1660-policeman-william-h-beck.
[155] Denver Police Department: Officer Down Memorial Page

suspected of stealing a horse. The individual was riding one horse while leading a second one. While being questioned, the suspect pulled out a gun and shot officer Stephens. The murderer then sold the horse but was captured when his customer noticed a bullet wound in the horse and contacted police. The suspect was sentenced to prison, where he died 22 years later.

Denver police officers John Spellman, William Beck, and William Stephens, photos courtesy of the Denver Police Museum

The district attorney's office also investigated white-collar crime cases. On October 17, 1905, Stidger signed an indictment from the Denver grand jury charging Leonard Imboden and James A. Hill with conspiracy to embezzle funds and property of the closed Denver Savings Bank. Indictments were also returned against eight other people connected with the Denver Savings Bank.[156] Imboden was a promoter connected with several banks. Hill was the president of the Denver Savings Bank when it closed its doors. At trial, the evidence showed that both Imboden and Hill had conspired to defraud the depositors of the bank of thousands of dollars. Both men were convicted and sentenced to nine to ten years; they were paroled in 1911. Stidger dismissed the charges against the others.

The district attorney's office continued to deal with violent crime. On October 7, 1907, Denver police found a package containing 51 sticks of dynamite on a vacant lot in the rear of Edward "Big Ed" Chase's residence at 1402 Race Street in Denver. The search was made after Kemp Bigelow reported that he had overheard two men near the city park plotting to blow up Chase as well as Governor Henry Buchtel and several other prominent citizens of Denver. Chase

---

https://www.odmp.org/officer/12769-policeman-william-p-stephens.

[156] *The Enid Events* (Enid, OK), Vol 14, No. 16, Ed. 1, January 11, 1906, p 1.

was the wealthy head of the gambling syndicate in the city and an associate of Mayor Speer's friend Vaso Chucovich. The next day, Governor Buchtel, bankers David H. Moffat and Charles Brewer Kountze, and steel magnate Lawrence Phipps received in the mail packages containing "infernal machines," i.e., homemade bombs. The packages contained enough dynamite to cause extensive destruction if they had been opened. Bigelow later confessed to police that he had planted and mailed the dynamite. Stidger charged Bigelow with assault to kill all the victims.[157] He pleaded guilty and was sentenced to prison.

Left to right: Henry Buchtel, Edward Chase, David H. Moffat, Charles Brewer Kountze, and Lawrence Phipps. All photos in the public domain; photo of Phipps courtesy of the Senate Historical Office

Stidger's office also dealt with domestic violence murder/suicides; in fact, two occurred within two weeks of each other. On February 6, 1908, carpenter Jacob Koretsky fatally shot his wife Rebecca on Grove Street between 16th and 17th Avenues in Denver. One report indicated that Koretsky suspected his wife of infidelity and believed she planned to take their two children away. Another report said that Koretsky was extremely ill, thought that he was about to die, and did not want to leave his wife free to receive the attentions of other men. Regardless, Stidger never charged Koretsky with the crime because after killing his wife he placed the weapon against his own head and pulled the trigger. The murder/suicide orphaned the two Koretsky children.[158]

Just over a week later, on February 15, boilermaker Clyde B. Jolly shot and killed his wife in the couple's home at 2304 Curtis Street in Denver. According to detectives, the Jollys had been quarreling all day over Clyde's jealousy. Stidger never had the opportunity to prosecute

[157] *Telluride Daily Journal*, October 9, 1907; *Grand Junction Daily Sentinel*, Vol 15, No. 21, December 14, 1907, p 1; *Telluride Daily Journal*, December 16, 1907, p 2.
[158] *Telluride Daily Journal*, October 9, 1907; *Grand Junction Daily Sentinel*, Vol 15, No. 21, December 14, 1907, p 1; *Telluride Daily Journal*, December 16, 1907, p 2.

Jolly for the murder because after he murdered his wife, Jolly shot himself. The sole witness to the murder/suicide was the couple's six-year-old child.

A few months later on May 1, 1908, Denver Police Chief Michael Delaney and his driver, Captain William H. Gray assaulted T.S. Matthews as Matthews was coming out of Delaney's girlfriend's house. Delaney, who was married started slugging him in a jealous rage. Matthews was merely a plumber who was leaving the address after repairing a leaking pipe. Delaney, the former Police Captain of Detectives, was known as "Third-Degree Delaney" because he would at times personally assault suspects to get them to talk. Stidger lost many cases because of Delaney's brutal tactics. In the Matthews case, Stidger charged Delaney and Gray with assault and battery.[159] Delaney became the third Denver police chief in 15 years to be criminally charged. Delaney resigned from the force, furnished bond, and skipped town.

Denver Police Chief Michael "Third-Degree" Delaney, photo courtesy of the Denver Police

Captain Gray pleaded guilty to accessory to a crime and was sentenced to six months in jail. Delaney returned to Denver and met with Mayor Robert Speer and Democratic leaders. They advised him to leave the city and stay away. Delaney took the next train for the East but a failure-to-appear warrant forced him to return to Denver. On October 8, 1908, Stidger announced that the victim, Matthews, could not be located. Without the victim, the DA could not proceed with the prosecution of the former police chief, so the case was dismissed. Delaney went on to work as a bodyguard for *Denver Post* newspaper owner Frederick Bonfils.

[159] *Fort Collins Courier*, May 20, 1908, p 7.

Stidger served as district attorney until 1908 and he died in Denver in 1918 at the age of 58.[160]

14. Willis V. Elliott (1909–1912)

Willis V. Elliott was born in Mansfield, Pennsylvania on June 13, 1871. Elliott's father was a Denver District Court judge and then a justice of the Colorado Supreme Court. Elliott graduated from East High School in Denver when the school was known as East Side High School and was located at 19th Street between Stout and California Streets. After graduation, he attended the State Normal School in Mansfield, Pennsylvania. He then went to law school at the University of Michigan at Ann Arbor and graduated in 1894. DA Booth Malone appointed Elliott as a deputy district attorney in 1897, and Elliott ran for and won the district attorney election in 1908 as a Republican. He served one term and did not seek reelection.[161]

Portrait of Willis Victor Elliott, a senior at Denver High School in 1890, photo courtesy of Denver Public Library Special Collections #Z-8364

Elliott was a staunch Republican with a strong opposition to unions. Before he was elected Denver DA, Elliott represented companies, utilities, and individuals with strong anti-union positions. When he took office as district attorney in 1909, he, like others before him,

---

160 *Bench and Bar of Colorado*, Bench and Bar Publishing Co, 1917, p 174.

161 *The Bench and Bar of Colorado*, p 93.

retained his private practice and continued to represent anti-union clients. At times Elliott's interests in his civil practice and his elite clients led local newspapers to question his independence as the lead prosecutor in Denver. In one instance, he represented the Gas and Electric Company in its effort to defeat a labor-sponsored referendum.

Another example of Elliott's anti-union proclivities was his involvement with John Chase. During the Colorado Labor Wars of 1903 and 1904—a series of large-scale strikes of miners and mill workers across Colorado that was met with violence—General John Chase was the commander of the Colorado National Guard in three areas of the state that dealt with significant mine labor strikes: Lake City, Cripple Creek, and Trinidad. While commanding National Guard troops during this time, Chase aggressively harassed and incarcerated striking workers and their allies. Chase ordered a raid on the offices of the *Victor Daily Record* newspaper in Victor, Colorado in September 1903 and took the entire staff as "prisoners of war" because the newspaper supported striking miners in the Cripple Creek area. When a Colorado judge issued writs of habeas corpus to release some of the newspaper prisoners, Chase ordered three hundred troops to bring all the prisoners to the courthouse, where he posted a Gatling gun as well as sharpshooters on nearby buildings. To say this was an attempt at intimidation would be an understatement. When the judge ordered the prisoners released, Chase refused to comply unless Colorado Governor James H. Peabody so ordered. Chase was court-martialed for perjury and disobedience of orders.[162] Elliott, who was not yet the Denver district attorney at this time, represented Chase at the court martial. Chase was acquitted of perjury and convicted of disobedience of orders. Colorado Governor Peabody set aside the guilty verdict and returned Chase to the command of the National Guard.

[162] *Castle Rock Journal*, October 23, 1903, p 3.

General John Chase of the Colorado National Guard, and Frank E. Gove stand outdoors in Trinidad, Las Animas County, Colorado. Both men are present to quell the demonstration to free Mother Jones and support the UMW Ludlow strike against CF&I. Photo courtesy of Denver Public Library Special Collections X-60525

One police officer was killed in the line of duty during Elliott's four years in office. On March 9, 1912, Policeman William McPherson was shot and killed while talking to a barkeeper in a saloon.[163] The patrolman was ambushed when two masked men entered the bar, announced a robbery, and opened fire. McPherson returned fire and wounded Oscar Cook, one of the suspects. The barkeeper died at the scene and McPherson died three days later from his injuries. Both suspects, Cook and Edward Seiwald, were captured and convicted. Cook, the identified shooter of the officer and the barkeep, was convicted by Elliott and sentenced to hang; Seiwald was given a 20-year prison sentence. Cook was hanged on February 29, 1916.[164]

[163] Denver Police Department: Officer Down Memorial Page https://www.odmp.org/officer/9137-policeman-william-mcpherson.
[164] *Raymer Enterprise*, Volume 5, Number 24, October 29, 1914, p 8.

Officer William McPherson, photo courtesy of the Denver Police Museum

Elliott also prosecuted the case against Frank Harold Henwood, the perpetrator of the "Brown Palace Murders." The presiding judge was former DA Greeley Whitford. Henwood was charged with murdering two men, Sylvester "Tony" Von Phul and George E. Copeland; a third man was injured in the melee. Copeland was an innocent bystander, but Von Phul was Henwood's rival for the affections of Isabelle Springer. Mrs. Springer was the wife of a prominent Denver banker, John Springer. She was very generous with her attentions and had been dating both Henwood and Von Phul.

Brown Palace Hotel, circa 1900, in the public domain

Frank Henwood (left), photo from the Denver Public Library Special Collections # Rh-1446, Isabelle Springer (center), Sylvester "Tony" Von Phul (right), photos courtesy of Colorado Historical Society

On May 24, 1911, the day of the shooting, Von Phul and Henwood were in the Brown Palace bar. Von Phul was an aerialist who was in Denver for a balloon ascent of Pikes Peak. When Isabel Springer's husband became suspicious of her affair with Von Phul, she tried to end it, but Von Phul extorted her into continuing with him by threatening to make her incriminating love letters public. Springer asked Henwood to retrieve the letters and he agreed. After an altercation with Von Phul over the letters, Henwood showed up at the bar and shot him, Copeland, and another bystander. Elliott charged Henwood with two counts of first-degree murder of Von Phul and Copeland.

John Springer divorced Isabel five days after the shooting. All the scandalous gossip and romantic affairs of Mrs. Springer were brought out in the trial. Henwood was found guilty, but the Colorado Supreme Court reversed the conviction because the judge had not allowed the jury to consider manslaughter. On May 28, 1913 (after Elliott's term concluded), DA John Rush tried Henwood in a second trial for Copeland's murder. Henwood was again found guilty and was sentenced to death by hanging. Just before his scheduled execution, however, the governor commuted Henwood's sentence to life imprisonment. He served 10 years before being paroled. Less than three months later, Henwood was returned to prison for a parole violation. He died in prison in 1929. Isabel Springer, meanwhile, moved to New York and her life spiraled downward. She died of a morphine addiction in 1917. The entire sordid affair is chronicled in Dick Kreck's book, *Murder at the Brown Palace*.[165]

In another high-profile case, on May 15, 1912, Elliott charged Frederick Bonfils and Harry Tammen (the owners of the *Denver Post)* with criminal libel after the paper ran a series of articles about William G. Evans and his deals and efforts to buy judges and politicians. Evans was the oldest son of Colorado's second territorial governor John Evans and president of the Denver Tramway Company.[166] Ten days later, on May 25, 1912, Elliott followed up, charging Evans and former Denver mayor Robert Speer (the owners of the *Denver Times)* with criminal libel for articles they ran in their paper attacking Bonfils. While the case was pending, Judge Hubert Shattuck held Speer, Bonfils, and Tammen in contempt for articles they published in their respective newspapers questioning the impartiality of the court. On September 23, 1912, Elliot dismissed the libel cases against all defendants, concluding that these were civil matters.

[165] Dick Kreck. 2003. *Murder at the Brown Palace: A True Story of Seduction and Betrayal*, Fulcrum Publishing. Golden, Colorado.
[166] *Montrose Daily Press*, Number 224, May 18, 1912, p 1; *Daily Journal* (Telluride), May 25, 1912, p 1.

Meanwhile, former Denver Police Chief Michael Delaney was running three brothels on 21st Street in Denver. In July of 1912, Elliott hauled Delaney before the grand jury. Delaney, the former chief of detectives as well as police chief ("Third-Degree Delaney"), described to the panel how he would lose ballot boxes during elections and manufacture evidence in cases when he was in office from 1904 to 1908.[167] The statute of limitations had passed, and Delaney was never indicted for any of these crimes. At the end of the investigation the grand jury issued a report criticizing former mayor Robert Speer and his political machine, but no one was ever indicted.

Governor John Shafroth, on the other hand, earned the nickname "Honest John" after he resigned a congressional seat when it was shown that illegal ballots were cast in his favor. His actions were not always without question, however—like when he pardoned a drunk driver in the following high-profile case. In 1910, wealthy young businessman Morris Mayer was driving his car drunk and at a high speed when it collided with two street cars. Three people were killed, and one seriously injured. Mayer was thrown clear and was found hours "afterwards wandering the streets, only slightly injured but half demented." DA Elliott charged Mayer with manslaughter. He was convicted and sentenced to a year jail. Mayer served about three months before being granted a "Christmas pardon" by Governor Shafroth. Many people, including newspaper editors, were outraged. The governor said that "prominent citizens" urged the pardon.[168]

Elliott's prosecutions also included police violence. On the evening of May 27, 1910, Denver police officer Frank Campbell was on duty on Market Street in Denver. He approached 17-year-old William Bell, who was sitting on the doorstep in front of a market and talking with brothers Roy and Harry Blackford. Harry said something to Bell and started to sit down next to his brother when Officer Campbell grabbed Harry and threw him on the steps in front of the market. Campbell then punched Harry, chased him down the street a short distance, and brought him back to where the others were. Roy Blackford told Campbell, "That is my brother; you hadn't ought to do anything like that." Campbell then hit Roy three times with his club, fracturing his skull. Neither Bell nor the Blackfords had insulted or threatened Campbell. The three were arrested, and although Roy Blackford sustained his injuries at 8:30 p.m., he received no medical attention until after 6 a.m. the next morning. He lay bleeding

[167] Herald Democrat, August 31, 1912, p 4.

[168] *Daily Sentinel Golden Transcript*, Volume 105, Number 135, June 23, 1972, p 4; *Montrose Daily Press*, Volume III, Number 114, December 27, 1910, p 2.

and unconscious for 10 hours on the floor of the "bull pen" in the Denver jail, while prisoners tried to get the jailer to call a doctor. Roy Blackford died of his injuries, and Elliott charged Campbell with murder.[169] At trial, witnesses testified that Campbell hit Blackford three times "with his billy club with all his force." Campbell testified that he had the two others in custody and was holding them with one hand while he struck Blackford. He said the reason he struck him was because Roy had "his fist drawn back" and Campbell was protecting his prisoners and himself. A jury returned a verdict of voluntary manslaughter, and Campbell was sentenced to the penitentiary for two to three years. This was one of the incidences that Police Commissioner George Creel used in 1912 to justify his order to remove nightsticks from all Denver police officers.

Another interesting case was a sensational murder that happened at Denver's Richthofen Castle on May 5, 1911. A witness walking on the grounds heard a gunshot and saw Gertrude Gibson Patterson standing over her husband and firing a second shot into his back, killing him. She fired a total of four shots, two hitting their mark. It appeared an open and shut case of premeditated and unprovoked murder for DA Elliott. The case drew national attention and the Denver newspapers, again referring to a female defendant's appearance, called Patterson, "The most beautiful woman in America."[170] At trial, only moments before closing arguments, the defense introduced a last-minute surprise witness who said he saw Patterson act in self-defense. Patterson had reported repeated physical and emotional abuse throughout her marriage to her former football-playing husband. The all-male jury found Patterson not guilty. Following her acquittal, at least four of the male jurors visited Patterson in her hotel room, one bringing flowers. Patterson fled the attention of the press for Europe. For her voyage back she booked her passage on the Titanic, where her luck ended. She never made it home, going down with the great ship along with more than 1,500 others. Of the 705 survivors, one from Denver would become famous: Margaret "The Unsinkable Molly" Brown.

---

[169] *Herald Democrat*, June 22, 1910, p 1; *Herald Democrat*, June 23, 1910, p 1.
[170] *Aspen Democrat-Times*, September 28, 1911; *Chronicle-News*, October 11, 1911, p 1; *Crime History*, Sept. 25, 1911: "'Most Beautiful Woman in America' shoots husband to death," https://dccrimeandpunishment.wordpress.com/2013/09/25/crime-history-sept-25-1911-most-beautiful-woman-in-america-shoots-husband-to-death/.

Gertrude Gibson Patterson and the grounds of the Richthofen Castle, photo from *Front Porch Northeast Denver News*, August 1, 2017

Meanwhile, corruption continued to be a problem in Denver. On August 20, 1912, Denver District Court judge Hubert Shattuck ordered a grand jury to investigate city officials receiving bribes and using extortion, blackmail, and graft to protect the gambling houses and sex parlors in the Tenderloin, a lower downtown district of Denver. Because it was alleged Elliott was "whitewashing" these crimes, Judge Shattuck prohibited him from overseeing the presentation of the investigations.[171] Elliott responded by refusing to prosecute any of the grand jury's complaints, claiming their work was illegal. Shattuck appointed a special prosecutor to run the grand jury, which issued sixty-four indictments, ranging from former Denver Mayor Robert Speer and former Denver Police Chief Hamilton Armstrong to 24 property owners who allowed their buildings to be used for "immoral purposes." All those indicted went before a different District Court judge, who tossed out the indictments, ruling that the special prosecutor who signed the indictments lacked the legal authority to do so based on an illegal appointment.

In a final note about Elliott, he gained renown for ordering the closing of saloons at midnight during the week and entirely on Sundays. Elliott was only 42 years old and out of the office of district attorney for 5 months when he suffered a fatal asthma attack in May 1912 while on a business trip in Wiggins, Colorado.

15. John A. Rush (1913–1916)

[171] *Las Animas Leader*, Volume XXXVIII, Number 26, November 25, 1910, p 3; *Herald Democrat*, August 27, 1912, p 1; *Chronicle-News*, November 23, 1912, p 1.

John A. Rush was born in Richland County, Illinois on March 9, 1865. His family moved to a farm in Kansas when Rush was in high school. After graduating from Topeka high school, Rush taught in the Topeka school system for a year, saving money so he could attend the University of Kansas at Lawrence. After graduation in 1890, he was briefly city editor of the *Lawrence Daily Journal* and a reporter for the *Kansas City Journal*. Rush entered law school at the State University of Kansas in 1891, continuing to work as a journalist to help pay the cost of his schooling. He moved to Denver in 1893 and opened his law practice. He was elected Denver district attorney in 1913 and served one term.[172]

Rush's time in office saw yet another violent incident involving *Denver Post* owner Frederick Bonfils. On February 9, 1914, a fight broke out in the Denver courthouse corridor between Bonfils and attorney Thomas O'Donnell. The two men had a history of bitterness between them, which increased during a campaign by the Denver Union Water Company to secure a new franchise. Bonfils and O'Donnell were in the courthouse because Bonfils had a lawsuit pending against the water company. Bonfils claimed that O'Donnell insulted him, so he struck O'Donnell in the face with his right hand, on which he wore a heavy ring that cut a deep gash in the attorney's face. O'Donnell then drew a revolver and attempted to shoot Bonfils. When O'Donnell pulled the trigger, the gun did not fire because Bonfils had jammed his thumb under the pistol's hammer. When O'Donnell tried to shoot a second time, Bonfils's bodyguard, ex-Denver police chief Michael Delaney, disarmed O'Donnell. Rush initially issued a warrant for O'Donnell's arrest, but he subsequently refused to file charges based on self-defense.[173]

[172] *Bench and Bar of Colorado*, 1917, p 164; *New York Times*, November 2, 1943.

[173] *Herald Democrat*, February 10, 1914, p 1; *Routt County Sentinel*, February 13, 1914, p 1.

Denver Post owner Frederick Bonfils (left) and attorney Thomas O'Donnell (right), Bonfils photo from Britannica, The Editors of Encyclopedia. "Frederick Gilmer Bonfils". *Encyclopedia Britannica*, 17 Dec. 2021, https://www.britannica.com/biography/Frederick-Gilmer-Bonfils. Accessed 29 December 2021; O'Donnel photo in the public domain

DA Rush was himself the victim of a crime about a year after he took office. On February 18, 1914, Rush and his wife were ambushed outside their home at home at 1250 Emerson Street in Denver. They were held prisoner at gunpoint for more than half an hour by attorney Don Blackwood and his wife, Bernice. Blackwood attempted to force the district attorney to sign papers that showed Rush had plotted to incarcerate Blackwood in an insane asylum. Rush convinced the Blackwoods to go into the house, where his life was saved by the heroism of his wife, who distracted the Blackwoods so Rush could call the police. When the officers arrived, the Blackwoods were arrested. Mr. Blackwood was incarcerated at the county hospital, and the wife was taken to jail. She was later released on the condition that she leave Denver. Blackwood was charged with lunacy and was adjudged insane by a commission appointed by the Denver County Court. He was sent to the State Insane Asylum in Pueblo. In 1920, however, Blackwood escaped from the state asylum. His wife was with him when he was arrested a week later in Lincoln, Nebraska. He was returned to Colorado and again sent back to the asylum.[174]

[174] *Herald Democrat*, February 20, 1914, p 1; *Cheyenne Record*, Volume 8, Number 46, February 5, 1920, p 7.

District Attorney Rush and His Staff. Seated, Left to Right—H. N. Sales. Chief Deputy; John A. Rush, District Attorney; Wayne C. Williams, First Assistant; Hazel Kelly, Stenographer; Robert H. Kane, Deputy. Standing, Left to Right—Nathaniel Halpern, Foster Cline, B. L. Pollock, R. E. Young, Charles T. Mahoney, Paul McGovern, Lewis C. Rush, Deputies.

Rush (seated, second from left) and DA office staff. Photo from the City of Denver municipal magazine, Vol. 11, No. 4, Nov. 22, 1913

On March 25, 1915, Rush announced a grand jury investigation into "the maze of charges and countercharges" that for years had centered on the Denver Juvenile Court and Judge Benjamin Lindsey. The investigation was an attempt to get at the real facts of a situation that had been the source of endless bickering and political scandals. On April 12, the grand jury issued a report exonerating Lindsey of any charges of misconduct. Frank Rose was instead indicted on the charge of criminal libel in connection with affidavits reflecting on Judge Lindsey's character. During Rose's trial Lindsey was ejected from the courtroom after he called Rose's lawyer a liar for accusing the judge of "maligning" Denver and its people. The jury in Rose's trial resulted in a hung jury, and Rush dismissed the case.[175]

[175] *Weekly Courier*, April 16, 1915, p 5; *Middle Park Times*, October 22, 1915, p 6.

Judge Ben Lindsey with his wife, December 4, 1915. Judge Lindsey was known as the father of juvenile law. Photo courtesy of the Library of Congress.

One crime spree case prosecuted by Rush's office was the "Candy Kid Bandit." In May of 1915, the armed robber known as the "Candy Kid Bandit" shot Denver police officer Thomas J. Lahey during a running gun battle. The youthful robber was running from the stickup of a Denver drug store when he shot Lahey, dangerously wounding the officer. The bullet struck Lahey in the mouth, took a downward course and lodged in his throat. Even after Lahey was shot, he chased the criminal to 16th Avenue and Clarkson Street, but he was weakened, and the robber escaped.[176] The next night the "Candy Kid" entered the store of V.D. Bond at 201

Broadway in Denver and collected $40 and, as always, some candy at the point of a gun. It was his eighth successful armed robbery and he had evaded a police dragnet. It took several months for 17-year-old David Franklin Tyler to finally be arrested by the Littleton sheriff after he and another man stole two horses. Tyler confessed to being the "Candy Kid Bandit."[177] Rush charged Tyler with robbery with intent to kill and the assault on Lahey. He was convicted of all charges and sentenced to prison for 13 to 15 years. On September 27, 1919, Tyler's sentence was commuted to 6 to 15 years because of his good behavior in prison and efforts to get an education while incarcerated.

Police during Rush's tenure relied heavily on horses (mostly to pull patrol wagons), which were stabled at fire stations. Mounted patrols also covered large areas like the Denver Stockyards and open spaces in the city. On one such patrol, mounted patrol officer William H. Cabler, was shot to death on April 21, 1916, while attempting to apprehend Ralph Bertram and Fred Jones after they held up the crew of a Burlington Northern freight train in the Denver Stockyards, the current site of the National Western Stock Show.[178] Cabler was chasing the robbers on his horse "Goldie" when Jones shot Cabler. A squad of mounted Denver police, cowboys, and other citizens—numbering around 2,000 people—searched for the criminals for hours before apprehending them. DA Rush charged the two men. Jones was convicted of first-degree murder and sentenced to life; Bertram was convicted of robbery and sentenced to 11 to 13 years in prison. Cabler's wife brought an action for compensation, which was denied because her husband's killing was intentional and not an accident.[179]

By 1932, motorcycles and automobiles put Denver's mounted patrol out of business. Most of the horses were sold at auction, with some kept for use by the Parks Police; all were gone by 1935. In the early 1980s, a volunteer Mounted Patrol for special events was put together by officers who owned horses. The Mounted Patrol was officially brought back in 1985 and still works in Denver today.

---

[176] *The Elbert County Tribune,* Volume 31, Number 33, May 28, 1915, p 5.
[177] *The Colorado Statesman*, Volume 21, Number 41, May 29, 1915, p 2.
[178] Denver Police Department: Officer Down Memorial Page
https://www.odmp.org/officer/21121-patrolman-william-h-cabler.
[179] *Alamosa Courier*, Volume XXVII, Number 9, April 29, 1916, p 7; *Bayfield Blade*, April 28, 1916, p 2; "First Report of the Colorado Industrial Commission," August 1, 1915 to December 1, 1917 p 31.

The early days of the Denver Mounted Patrol, posing in front of Colorado State Capitol building, circa 1921–1928 (Denver Police Department Facebook photo)

Robert Speer had been elected mayor of Denver back in 1904. Boss Speer and his political machine, known as the "Big Mitt," allowed gambling, prostitution, and other forms of vice so long as the administration got its cut. The Big Mitt often resorted to election fraud to remain in control. In 1912, Speer left office and the Denver citizens voted in a measure that changed city governance from a strong mayor to a commission. When the commission government experiment failed, Speer was poised to return. No one was more vocal in opposition to Speer's return to power than DA Rush, who had investigated Speer's corruption. Nevertheless, in March of 1916, the voters returned Speer to office.[180] Rush finished his term as Denver DA and did not seek reelection. He returned to private practice and in 1920 moved to Los Angeles to practice law with his son. In 1936, Rush served on the Citizen Committee on Governmental Reorganization in Los Angeles. He published a series of papers on making Los Angeles a City and County, much like Denver.[181] Rush died on November 1, 1943, in Los Angeles.

---

[180] "Robert Speer's Denver 1904–1920," Volume 2 of *Denver From the Bottom Up*, by Phil Goodstein, Denver, New Social Publications, 2004.

[181] John Rush. 1936. "Legal questions involved in the creation of a city and county of Los Angeles: An opinion."

An interesting final note on Rush's tenure relates to prohibition. The 18th Constitutional Amendment outlawing the sale of alcohol took effect nationally in January 1920, but Colorado voters had decided to prohibit the sale and consumption of booze six years earlier in a November 1914 vote, to take effect January 1, 1916. Prohibition saw the rise of a variety of illegal activities as well as the expansion of organized crime. During Prohibition, a series of Denver district attorneys—from John A. Rush (1913–1916) to Earl Wettengel (1929–1936)—had to overcome police corruption to enforce anti-bootlegging laws and the violence that went with the illegal sale of alcohol. An interview with retired Denver officer Samuel Finnie on September 10, 1963, vividly described the situation in law enforcement during Prohibition. Finnie worked in the Denver Police Department as a patrolman in 1925, became a detective in 1929, and served as head of the vice squad from 1932 until 1947. As a rookie officer in 1925, Finnie was ordered to report any actions he was going to take regarding bootleggers. When Finnie would report on bootlegging operations to his superiors, nothing happened. The stills and speakeasies he discovered and reported were never raided or shut down by the police. It became clear to Finnie that his superiors were on the take and he became aware of other police officers who received protection money from the bootleggers. Finnie turned down many bribe offers. This situation did not stop Finnie from enforcing the liquor laws, but it did lead to his reassignment to a different beat.[182] Without support of the police, there was little the prosecutors of the era could do to enforce the state Prohibition laws.

[182] *Colorado Magazine*, L/1, 1973, p 17.

16. William E. Foley (1917–1920)

William E. Foley was born in Terre Haute, Indiana July 10, 1879. Foley's father was a miner who moved the family to Colorado in 1895. Foley senior became wealthy in gold mining in Cripple Creek but through poor investments, lost everything he had made. William Foley graduated from La Salle Institute in Chicago in 1897. He obtained his law degree from the University of Denver in 1905. Foley was a successful athlete and captain of the university football team. He opened a private practice after graduation, was elected to the Colorado general assembly in 1908, and then was elected to the position of district attorney in 1917.[183]

In 1916, as a Democratic primary candidate, Foley ran advertisements in Denver newspapers that read: "A Public Defender and not a Persecutor 'A Big Man with a Smile WILLIAM E. FOLEY FOR DISTRICT ATTORNEY.'"[184] After he won the primary, Foley's advertisements for the general election made no mention of his size nor his smile, nevertheless he was still elected Denver district attorney.

Foley 1916 political advertisement, photo in the public domain

[183] *Bench and Bar of Colorado*. 1917, p 113; *The Ordway new era*, January 05, 1917, p 2.
[184] *Denver Star*, Volume 27, Number 152, September 9, 1916, p 7.

On September 14, 1918, Denver police officers John Ryan and Harry Wilson approached a home at 815 East 17th Avenue in Denver that was being used as a hideout by the Lewis-Jones gang—a notorious group of robbers known for quick getaways and violent methods.[185] Denver police had surrounded the house earlier in the evening because they were looking for gang members who had shot and killed a Colorado Springs police officer that day. In the Colorado Springs incident, Chief of Detectives John Rowan was killed in a shootout while chasing the gang members after a bank robbery.

Chief of Detectives John Rowan, photo in the public domain

Several of the gang members escaped the police-surrounded hideout and fled in a car, firing on two detectives in the alley. The police cleared the house and arrested everyone remaining. Hours later, however, gang members quietly returned and were again inside the hideout. When officers Ryan and Wilson came to the door, Dale Jones, Marjie Dean, and Roscoe "Kansas City Blackie" Lancaster were waiting for them. Jones asked, "Who are you?" When Ryan told Jones they were police officers, Jones stuck a gun in Ryan's stomach and took both officers inside and tied them up. Ryan and Wilson were eventually freed when other officers came to the house after Jones, Dean, and Lancaster left.

On the same day, police officer Luther McMahill finished his shift and was headed home on his bicycle when he saw a suspicious high-powered touring car with its lights out on Colorado

[185] *Montrose Press*, Volume XXXVII, Number 38, September 20, 1918; *Cañon City Record*, Volume 40, Number 2, January 9, 1919, p 7; Jeffrey S. King. 2013. *Kill Crazy Gang: The Crimes of the Lewis-Jones Gang*, The Frank Manley Publishing Company, Washington D.C.

Boulevard near 16th Street. Inside the car were Marjie Dean and Dale Jones, who was second in command of the Lewis-Jones gang. When McMahill pointed his flashlight at Jones, he shot the officer directly above the heart, killing him instantly.[186] The car then moved toward 17th Street, picking up fellow gang member Lancaster. Jones, Dean, and Lancaster fled Colorado. Foley never charged anyone in either incident because the three gang members were soon dead—Lancaster was killed in a shootout with Kansas City police officers in 1918,[187] and Jones and Dean were killed in a shootout with Los Angeles sheriffs.[188]

Officer Luther McMahill, photo courtesy of the Denver Police Museum

Dale Jones and Marjie Dean, photos in the public domain

[186] Denver Police Department: Officer Down Memorial Page, https://www.odmp.org/officer/9079-policeman-luther-mcmahill.
[187] The Weekly Courier, September 27, 1918, p 1.
[188] *Douglas County News Press*, February 1, 2012. https://douglascountynewspress.net/stories/notorious-gang-rides-through-local-history,66540.

Car used in a shootout on February 16, 1918, by Jones and Dean. Inscription reads: "Car used by Dale Jones, Kansas City Blackie, and Margie Dean in their fight with officers in Colorado Springs on Sept. 13, 1918." Photo courtesy of Palmer Lake Historical Society

In 1920, Denver experienced a labor crisis that resulted in several deaths. The Denver Tramway Company threatened to cut wages for its employees unless the city allowed it to increase fares. Tramway workers wanted a raise after taking other recent wage cuts, but the city would not allow the fare increases. The workers, who were members of Local 746 of the Amalgamated Association, voted to strike on August 1, 1920. More than nine hundred workers walked out.[189] The company brought in strike-breakers and used them to operate the streetcars. Union supporters responded by heaving bricks at the streetcars, tipping them over, and burning them. Four days after the strike began, on August 5, strike-breakers fired on a labor crowd, killing two teenagers. On the same day, a crowd of union supporters attacked the *Denver Post* headquarters at 15th and Curtis Streets in downtown Denver.[190] *The Post* had been extremely critical of the strikers and was well known for its anti-union positions. In fact, *Post* owner Frederick Bonfils was closely aligned with the Boettcher family, who were the majority owners of the Tramway Company. That night, about 4,000 people assembled in front of the *Post* building. Some protesters entered the offices, damaging equipment, breaking out windows, and

---

[189] *Morgan County Republican*, Volume 20, Number 32, August 6, 1920, p 1; *Loveland Reporter*, Number 18, September 4, 1920, p 1.
[190] *Herald Democrat*, August 7, 1920, p 1–2.

attempting to set the building on fire. Bonfils stayed in his home at 10th Avenue and Humboldt Street after hiring security guards who placed machine guns on his balconies to ward off the mob.[191] The members of the mob who damaged the *Post* headquarters were not identified and, as with the rioting strikers, Foley never charged anyone for the damage to the *Post* building.

The next night, strike-breakers again fired on protesters, this time killing five people and wounding thirteen others. None of the victims were strikers or brick-throwers. Federal troops were called in to restore peace the next day. The troops disarmed the strike-breakers, protected the streetcars, and the strike was broken. Denver police never arrested any of the shooters, and Foley never prosecuted anyone for the killings.

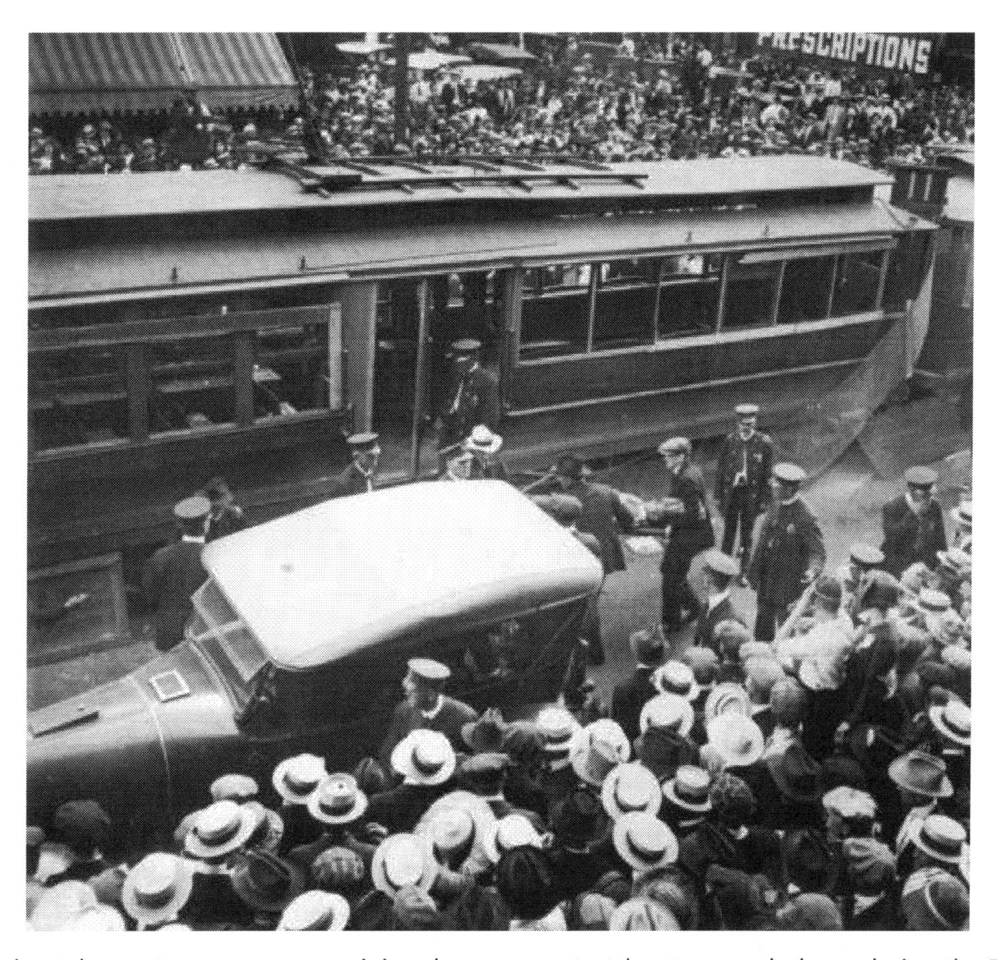

A crowd watches as two men carry an injured man on a stretcher to an ambulance during the Denver Tramway Company strike in 1920. Denver Police officers stand in front of the crowd. Photo by Harry Rhoads Collection. Denver Public Library Special Collection Rh-5948

[191] Stephen J. Leonard and Thomas J. Noel. 2016. *A Short History of Denver*, University of Nevada Press.

On June 9, 1919, World War I veteran Jerry Corbetta was shot in the back by Denver Police Detective George Klein during a raid on a north Denver bootlegging operation at West 14th Avenue and Pecos Street.[192] Klein was the chief of Denver's liquor squad, and when he and other officers told the occupants of the "soft drink parlor" to submit to a search, Corbetta ran and Klein shot him. Foley charged Klein with first-degree murder.[193] More than 2,000 Italians, angered by the bond set for Klein, marched to city hall and demanded that Klein be placed back in jail and discharged from the police force. Chief of Police Hamilton Armstrong worked with a Roman Catholic priest to calm down the crowd. At the coroner's inquest, Klein claimed the shooting was accidental and he was cleared by the jury. On August 29, 1919, Klein received three blasts from a shotgun, killing him outside his home at 1438 Newton Street in west Denver. Homicide detectives and DA investigators were never able to solve Klein's murder or determine if the motive was the Corbetta shooting or his anti-bootlegging assignment.[194]

About six months later, in early January 1920, Denver Patrolmen James E. Boggio was killed in a shootout. Boggio, along with several other officers, fought a pistol battle with wanted thief Adrian Pearl Thompson in Thompson's mother's Denver home. While searching the home for Thompson, one officer was attacked by Thompson's mother as he entered the kitchen—the woman started beating him with a fireplace poker. As Patrolman Boggio entered the kitchen to assist the officer, he was shot by Thompson, who was hiding in a stairwell.[195] The other officers returned fire and killed Thompson. Boggio was transported to a local hospital where he died two days later.[196] Thompson, a deserter from the Marine Corps who held a sharpshooter's medal, also shot two of the other officers in the gun battle. Both officers survived their wounds. Foley found that the officers were justified in killing Thompson.

---

[192] *Herald Democrat*, June 11, 1919, p 1; *Herald Democrat*, June 12, 1919, p 1; *Herald Democrat*, June 10, 1919, p 8; Dick Kreck. 2009. *Smaldone: The Untold Story of an American Crime Family*, Fulcrum Publishing.
[193] *Fort Collins Courier*, August 29, 1919, p 1; *Cañon City Record*, Volume 40, Number 36, September 4, 1919, p 1; Dick Krek. 2009. *Smaldone: The Untold Story of an American Crime Family*, Fulcrum Publishing.
[194] Denver Police Department: Officer Down Memorial Page. https://www.odmp.org/officer/7605-detective-george-c-klein.
[195] *Summit County Journal*, January 10, 1920, p 2.
[196] Denver Police Department: Officer Down Memorial Page https://www.odmp.org/officer/1987-patrolman-james-e-boggio.

Denver Detective George Klein (left) and Patrolmen James E. Boggio (right), photos courtesy of the Denver Police Museum

Two more Denver police officers died during Foley's time in office. On December 1, 1920, Officer Roy Downing was shot and killed while responding to a residential burglary.[197] The subject fled the scene and was never caught. Downing had been with the Police Department for just one year. The next officer, Policeman Emerson McKinnon, died an on-duty death while assisting Denver firefighters. He fell through an opening in an elevator shaft while battling a fire.

Turning again to corruption, Foley faced the new decade of 1920 under investigation. The headline in the January 31, 1920, issue of the *Denver Post* reported, "Grand Jury Probe Demanded for W.E. Foley Administration and Airing of Recent Scandals."[198] The *Post* noted that 18 Denver citizens had petitioned Judge Henry Hershey to appoint a special prosecutor to probe the "connections" Foley had with some criminal matters he had prosecuted during the prior two years. Signers of the petition included several notable Denver citizens of the time: Rev. Charles Mead, pastor of Trinity Methodist Episcopal Church, Dr. May Bigelow, a member of the state legislature, and Mrs. Mabel Stearns Noble, secretary of the Denver social health committee.

The petition requested investigation by a special prosecutor, providing five specific reasons: "First – For the connection of the district attorney with the notorious Nolan case.[199] Second – For his failure to prosecute gamblers in West Side court, thus enabling them to get off

[197] Denver Police Department: Officer Down Memorial Page https://www.odmp.org/officer/21967-policeman-roy-o-downing.

[198] *Herald Democrat*, February 1, 1920, p 1; *Herald Democrat*, February 3, 1920, p 2; *Herald Democrat*, February 15, 1920, p 3.

[199] The Nolan diamond case referred to the robbery of Irene Nolan, wife of a wealthy motion picture executive.

with a minimum fine of $10 and costs in police court, where the fine is usually suspended. Third – Because of the suspicion and censure brought on his office in connection with the Bush case. Fourth – For his failure, despite his statements to the contrary, to close houses of prostitution by means of the injunction and abatement law. Fifth – Because of the numerous reports current that the office of the district attorney, or employees of said office are offering continued protection to the underworld."[200]

Two special prosecutors, a private attorney, and the Colorado Attorney General Victor E. Keyes were appointed by Judge Hershey. The final report of the investigation issued on March 18, 1920, fully exonerated the DA and his staff, although it did indict one deputy sheriff and recommended the appointment of a special committee to fight vice in the city, which was described as operating on "a scale to create the worst condition in many years." After Judge Hersey thanked the jury and congratulated the DA on the outcome of the investigation, a heated exchange occurred between the DA and the judge. Foley told Judge Hershey that he did not "share in the appreciation and gratification felt by the court for the jury's returns."[201]

Colorado Attorney General Victor E. Keyes (1919–1922), photo in the public domain

If Foley hoped that the report clearing him of corruption was the end of his political troubles, he soon found out otherwise. Just weeks before the November 1920 election, one of

[200] *Herald Democrat*, March 19, 1920, p 1.
[201] *Herald Democrat*, March 19, 1920, p 1.

Foley's deputies, Paul McGovern, resigned and went public with complaints against Foley, accusing him of leniency, negligence in prosecuting bootleggers, and favoritism in handling criminal complaints. McGovern accused Foley of being "in a political alliance with the bootleggers of this city." He also accused Foley of filing criminal charges as political favors to businessmen without regard to the facts of the allegations. The most serious criticism he leveled was that the district attorney, by his inaction, had allowed evidence to be lost and multiple murderers to leave the state. Foley's behavior resulted in no charges being brought against these men according to the eight-year former deputy district attorney. McGovern felt there was probable cause to file criminal charges and, in his statements to the media, he reported that he had argued forcefully with Foley to charge the suspects.[202]

Deputy DA Paul McGovern, photo from *The Bench and Bar of Colorado,* 1917

Foley's political troubles began much earlier in his administration. On January 13, 1917, Denver's African American newspaper, the *Denver Star*, published an editorial about the newly elected district attorney after he was sworn in and had become active in the management of his office. They noted that Foley was elected by a majority of 2,220 votes. *The Star* claimed that without the Black vote, Foley could never have been elected, yet he had not considered any Black people in any capacity as appointees. Foley had assured many people before the election that he would appoint a Black man to work in his office. *The Star* had urged Foley's election and

[202] Svensk-Amerikanska Western, October 28, 1920, p 3; Denver Star, Volume 27, Number 161, November 11, 1916; Denver Star, Volume 27, Number 170, January 13, 1917, p 4.

[203] *Denver Star*, Volume 27, Number 161, November 11, 1916; *Denver Star*, Volume 27, Number 170, January 13, 1917, p 4.

trusted that Foley would make good on his promise.[203] During his tenure, however, Foley never appointed a Black person to work as a deputy district attorney. It was not until the administration of DA Burt M. Keating (1948–1967) that the first Black man, James Flanigan, was appointed to serve as a deputy district attorney in Denver.

James Flanigan, the first Black deputy district attorney in Denver. Photo in the public domain

Foley ran for reelection in 1920 but even in a heavily Democratic city, Democratic candidate Foley lost to his reform-minded Republican challenger Philip Van Cise.

17. Philip S. Van Cise (1921–1924)

Philip S. Van Cise was born in Deadwood, Dakota Territory (now South Dakota) in 1884. His father was Edwin Van Cise, a well-known lawyer who moved the family to Denver in 1900. Philip graduated from East High School in 1903, obtained a B.A. from the University of Colorado in 1907, and received his law degree in 1909. While in college he worked as a cub reporter at the *Rocky Mountain News*. Upon graduation from law school, he went into private practice in his father's law firm. From 1910 to 1914 Van Cise served as a captain in the Colorado Army National Guard. His company was called out to prevent violence at the southern Colorado coal strike near Ludlow, Colorado. On November 30, 1913, Van Cise risked his life to prevent violence when a train carrying strikebreakers arrived at Ludlow. Hundreds of strikers and their wives rushed to the train station intending to murder the strikebreakers, but Van Cise kept the two sides apart. In the end, he was able to convince the strikers to return to their tents, and he ordered the strikebreakers to continue to Trinidad in accordance with the governor's orders. Before returning to Denver after being relieved of duty, Van Cise warned his superiors that Karl E. Linderfelt's Company B was a serious threat to peace at Ludlow months before Company B committed the Ludlow Massacre—an attack on striking miners and their families that left two dozen dead. After the labor violence, Van Cise served on a three-member National Guard board that investigated the Ludlow Massacre. The board recommended a general court-martial for all National Guard members that participated in the massacre.[204]

At the start of the First World War, Van Cise joined the army as an active-duty officer. After the war, he returned to Denver and went into private practice. In 1920 he campaigned and was elected Denver district attorney. When he took office in 1921, Denver was a "wide-open town" for gambling, prostitution, and confidence games. Van Cise was committed to enforcing the law and changing Denver. During his tenure as district attorney, Van Cise is credited with dismantling the "Million Dollar Bunco Ring" run by con man Lou Blonger and for his bitter fight against the Ku Klux Klan's efforts to control the city and state both politically and economically. These efforts resulted in threats against the life of Van Cise and his family.

---

[204] *Denver Post*, December 10, 1969, p 2; *Rocky Mountain News*, Dec. 9, 1969; *Westword*, February 7, 2008; *The Colorado Lawyer, Philip S. Van Cise* by Edwin P. Van Cise, Vol. 15, No. 7, 1986, July, p 1,165.

1920 Van Cise campaign leaflet, photo in the public domain

As district attorney, Republican Van Cise was described as crusading, crime fighting, and graft busting. He was often blunt and a bit rough and said, "the bulk of practicing criminal attorneys in Denver are as crooked as their clients." At one point he engaged in a courtroom fistfight with the defense counsel for a group of Bunco criminals. He gave opposing counsel William Bryans a black eye in a pretrial hearing and subsequently obtained convictions on his clients. Van Cise also once referred to Denver jurors as, "A bunch of bums hanging around the courthouse … usually picked up" to serve on juries.[205] His colorful quotes and brawling style may be one of the reasons he served only one term as prosecutor. Notwithstanding his abrupt style, Van Cise was able to amass an incredible 44 criminal convictions out of the 45 felony trials conducted by his office during his single term.

Overall, Van Cise believed that laws were made to be enforced regardless of the identity of the offender—and his enforcement efforts were aggressive. With the help of some law

[205] *Denver Post*, December 10, 1969, p 2.

enforcement officers and many public-spirited private citizens, most of the gambling establishments in Denver were raided and closed. The gambling fixtures and furniture were seized, and Van Cise donated billiard tables, chairs, card tables, and cards to every firehouse in Denver, enough to last them for years. He sent letters of warning to Denver property owners who rented or leased their buildings to persons conducting gambling activities. The letters stated that charges would be filed against the owners unless they made their tenants stop the gaming operations in their buildings. Sixty years later, Denver DA Norman S. Early (1983–1993) used the same technique to get crack cocaine dealers out of Capital Hill apartments. Van Cise also launched raids against most of the brothels and temporarily cleared the streets of prostitutes.[206] The raids, however, had an unforeseen result. The prostitutes, who had been primarily concentrated in a 12-block downtown area, left the district and spread to all parts of the city.

In the early 1920s the Denver police force was riddled with corruption. Charges such as accepting bribes, selling bootleg whiskey, associating with prostitutes, and drinking on duty were regularly lodged against Denver police officers. The corruption was not confined to the poorly paid patrolman but spread to the upper echelons of the department. Van Cise convened two grand juries during his term to look at corruption in Mayor Dewey Bailey's administration. The 1923 grand jury censured eight law enforcement officials, including the manager of safety and the city constable as "totally unfit to hold any office in this city and should be discharged forthwith."[207] Van Cise declared, "The present city administration is a disgrace to American government." Shortly after being elected district attorney, Van Cise was escorted on a tour of the gambling houses, bootleg joints, and places of prostitution in town by Police Captain August Hanebuth. Afterward, Police Chief Hamilton Armstrong explained which individuals controlled what crime and warned Van Cise whom to watch out for in the court system and in the police department. Armstrong warned Van Cise that Lou Blonger "owned the town" with tight control of crime and had men installed throughout the police department and in political jobs to maintain control. Armstrong offered to help the new DA "smash the whole damn bunch of them," but two months later the longtime police chief died of heart disease. However, the inside information helped Van Cise clean up the city.

---

206 *The Colorado Lawyer, Philip S. Van Cise* by Edwin P. Van Cise, Vol. 15, No. 7, 1986, July, p 1,165.
207 *Westword*, Alan Prendergast, February 7, 2008.

Dewey Bailey, Denver mayor 1919–1923, photo courtesy of Denver Public Library Special Collections H-6

In 1920, before Van Cise was elected, Leonard DeLue of the DeLue Detective Agency arranged for a meeting between Lou Blonger and Van Cise. Lou Blonger's criminal syndicate had operated openly in Denver for more than 20 years. At the meeting, Blonger offered to take care of the election campaign expenses of the candidate in return for Van Cise capping the bonds of the charged Bunco ring members at $1,000. Incensed, Van Cise rejected the offer.

Leonard DeLue and Lou Blonger; DeLue photo in the public domain, Blonger photo his official mug shot[208]

Van Cise declared war on Blonger and his associates.[209] Using law enforcement techniques that the Denver weekly newspaper *Westword* described as decades ahead of their time, including planting a Dictaphone inside Blonger's office, going through Blonger's trash, and using a crooked detective to feed Blonger false information, Van Cise destroyed Blonger and his gang, changed the city's political establishment, and made headlines across the country. *Fighting the Underworld*, Van Cise's book about the case, became a source for the classic Paul Newman-Robert Redford movie, *The Sting.*

Until Van Cise, Blonger had operated with impunity in Denver since the late 1890s. An 1899 *Denver Times* article described Blonger's card swindling of "suckers" in great detail, even to the extent of running a photo of one victim with one of Blonger's "chief crooks" on his way to being robbed. The article bluntly reported, "Seventeenth street is infested by a gang of bunco steerers, headed by Lou Blonger." By the 1920s, Blonger was credited with international criminal operations, all of which were headquartered in Denver. Blonger's gang was netting between $1 million and $5 million annually by selling worthless stock. The arrests in 1922 and prosecutions of these men in 1923 made local and national headlines for weeks. The defendants were tied to criminal activity in multiple states.

---

208 The Mark Inside: A Perfect Swindle, a Cunning Revenge, and a Small History of the Big Con, Amy Reading, Knopf Doubleday Publishing, 2012, p 163.
209 *Westword*, February 7, 2008. "Phil Van Cise: Scourge of Denver's Underworld."
https://www.westword.com/news/phil-van-cise-scourge-of-denvers-underworld-5097432.

When Van Cise went after Blonger, he knew he could not trust the Denver Police Department because many officers were on the take. During the roundup of the con men and the raid on their businesses, Van Cise's men recovered a bankbook for a joint account in the name of ringleaders Lou Blonger and Adolph W. Duff.[210] The bankbook showed payments were made from the bosses to Washington A. Rinker, captain of the Detective Bureau of the Denver Police Department. Blonger's memorandum book also showed a payment of $600 to another Denver police officer. The evidence of payoffs to Rinker did not impact his career; in fact, he became Chief of Police in 1925.

Denver Police Chief Washington A. Rinker, photo courtesy of the City and County of Denver

[210] *The Mark Inside: A Perfect Swindle, a Cunning Revenge, and a Small History*, by Amy Reading, Vintage Books, 2013, p 218.

Mug shot of Adolph W. Duff, alias "Kid Duffy," photo in the public domain

To work around the corrupt officers in the Denver Police Department and the Dewey administration, Van Cise used Adjutant General P.J. Hamrock of the Colorado State Rangers and 18 of Hamrock's rangers to arrest 34 members of the "Million Dollar Bunco Ring" in Denver.[211] The roundup took place over two days starting on August 24, 1922. Many of those arrested had train tickets in their possession so they could make a quick getaway. Van Cise arranged for gang members to be held in the basement of the Universalist church on the corner of Colfax Avenue and Lafayette Street instead of the Denver County Jail, in case Denver jailers decided to tip off the con men.

[211] *Denver Post*, August 25, 1922, p 1.

The Colorado Rangers, photo courtesy of Colorado Mounted Rangers

The Universalist church on the corner of Colfax Avenue and Lafayette Street, photo in the public domain

Although Lou Blonger was one of the first arrested in the day-long raids, his name did not appear in the *Denver Post's* story the next day.[212] Van Cise found out later that Blonger's name had been suppressed because Blonger was one of co-publisher Harry Tammen's best friends. Tammen told his reporter Forbes Parkhill, "Lou taught me the most valuable thing I ever knew.

[212] *Fighting the Underworld*, by Philip S. Van Cise, Van Cise, Houghton Mifflin Co., 1936, p 213.

He taught me how to catch a sucker. Tammen continued, "I caught one," jerking his thumb toward co-publisher Frederick Bonfils' office, adding, "I've still got him."[213]

Harry Tammen, photo in the public domain

After his arrest, Lou Blonger sued Van Cise, members of the district attorney's staff, and the citizens that Van Cise deputized to drive the arrested gang members to their temporary custody in the Universalist church. Blonger claimed unlawful arrest and that he had suffered $200,000 in damages. The civil lawsuit, a tactic to divert the prosecution team's time and resources prior to the ring's criminal trial, was eventually dismissed.

Blonger bonded his top con men out of jail but made the mistake of failing to post bail for Len Reamey, alias J.K. Ross. Reamey had worked his way up from a "steerer" to top bookmaker in the organization. Feeling slighted by having to remain in jail and suffering the pangs of opium withdrawal, Reamey cut a deal with the DA for complete immunity in exchange for sharing his knowledge of the inner workings of the gang.[214] Reamey knew who had played what part in dozens of scores and how the money was divided up among the "steerer," the "spieler," the bookmaker, and Blonger and Duff for "overhead," including cop payoffs. He knew that no con

---

[213] *Fighting the Underworld*, by Philip S. Van Cise, Houghton Mifflin Co., 1936, p 213.
[214] *Fighting the Underworld*, by Philip S. Van Cise, Houghton Mifflin Co., 1936, p 256–267.

man could operate in Denver without Adolph W. Duff's okay. At trial, the defense attorneys attacked Reamey mercilessly, calling him a liar and his wife a whore. They professed shock at his arrest record and his dope use. Reamey faced real danger by testifying; in fact, one of Blonger's associates tried to bring a gun into the courtroom while Reamey was on the stand, but he was frisked and arrested. Reamey's testimony dovetailed well with the many victims who testified, leading to the convictions of those members of the ring who were on trial.

Blonger's men also attempted to escape justice by paying a woman to come to Denver to lure DA Van Cise into a compromising situation. This con was known as "the old badger game," an extortion scheme often perpetrated on married men, in which the "mark" was tricked into an embarrassing position to make him vulnerable to blackmail.[215] The plan to compromise Van Cise failed when the woman double-crossed the gang and left town with the con men's money and without ever seeing the district attorney.

Los Angeles DA Thomas Lee Woolwine told Denver's Assistant DA Kenneth Robinson that if one of Blonger's men, J. Roy Farrell, were arrested in the take-down, he would be interested in prosecuting Farrell in California. Farrell was one of the slickest con men in the United States, and Woolwine had many cases against him in Los Angeles. Although Denver had a good case against Farrell, Robinson turned him over to California. As Farrell was being escorted out of the Denver jail, however, he told Van Cise how much he appreciated being sent to California. Once Farrell was jailed in Los Angeles, he posted a phony $20,000 bond through a "straw bondsman" and was released.[216] Woolwine was completely embarrassed and told Van Cise that a clerk in the Criminal Court had authorized Farrell's release on the bond without consulting his office. Farrell was never again arrested in Los Angeles or Denver.

---

[215] *Fighting the Underworld*, by Philip S. Van Cise, Houghton Mifflin Co., 1936, p 309–311.
[216] *Fighting the Underworld*, by Philip S. Van Cise, Houghton Mifflin Co., 1936, p 229.

Los Angeles DA Thomas Lee Woolwine and con man J. Roy Farrell, photos in the public domain. Woolwine photo courtesy Bain News Service publisher

The trial of the Million Dollar Bunco Gang began on February 5, 1923, and almost immediately there were rumors that members of the gang had fixed the jury. Blonger's men approached at least four of the jurors with bribes, including juror Herman M. Okuly who played along with the offer of $500, but immediately reported the deal to his boss at work, who informed Van Cise.[217] Day after day the prosecution called victims, bilked out of their life savings, to the stand. Reamey was the star witness because he was one of the gang's bookmakers and was fourth in the hierarchy of the organization behind Blonger, Adolph W. "Kid" Duff, and bookmaker Jackie French. Reamey provided the inside story of how the gang defrauded hundreds of victims and divided the spoils among themselves. When the prosecution rested after seven weeks of testimony, the defense attorneys felt so secure in the fix they surprised everyone by resting their case without presenting a witness, and further by offering to forgo their closing arguments if the prosecution did the same. Van Cise directed the special prosecutors to call their bluff, so the case went immediately to the jury without any closing arguments.[218] After four days of deliberations, with three jurors still favoring acquittal, Okuly told the holdouts "the difference between me and you is that I got my five hundred dollars, but turned it over to the Judge, and you've still got yours."[219] The three hold-out jurors relented, and the jury returned a verdict of

[217] *Fighting the Underworld*, by Philip S. Van Cise, Houghton Mifflin Co., 1936, p 323–326.
[218] *Fighting the Underworld*, by Philip S. Van Cise, Houghton Mifflin Co., 1936, p 337–338.

guilty for all 20 defendants on trial. After the trial Reamey left Denver and never again got in trouble with the law.

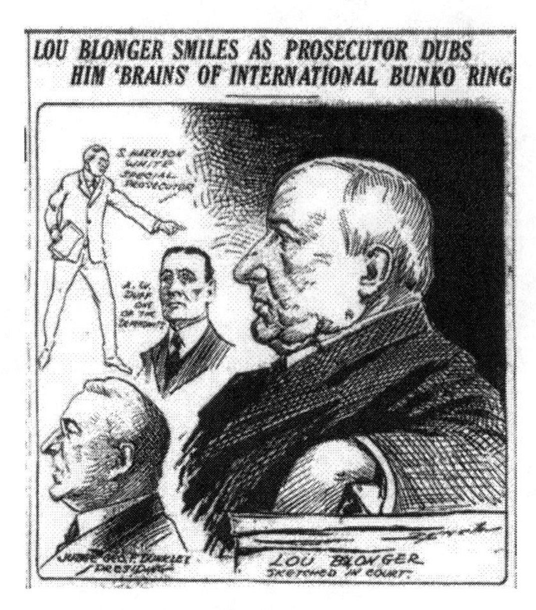

Newspaper sketch of the Blonger trial from the *Denver Times*

June 1, 1923, was sentencing day. Blonger, Duff, French, and eight associates were sentenced to serve from seven to ten years in prison on the two counts of conspiracy to commit grand larceny, and from seven to ten years on the single charge of conspiracy, the sentences to run concurrently. The additional eight Blonger con men were sentenced from three to ten years upon the same counts. Grove Sullivan, alone of the 20 men convicted, escaped sentence. He was declared insane and eventually sent to the state insane asylum. All the convictions were upheld on appeal, and Blonger died in prison in April of 1924.[220]

Not all the members of the Million Dollar Bunco Ring were charged, however. There were three lucky con men: "The Blind Man" Roy Yeaman, "Fat" Jack Ryan, and Puss McCaskey, alias "J. R. Barry" escaped prosecution. According to Van Cise, the "three lucky ones were released too soon." Van Cise clarified, "We found out later that we had enough evidence to send that trio to the pen with the rest, but they were gone... someday they'll slip up and be caught." He believed "once a con man—always a con man. They never change."[221] Yeaman, Ryan, and McCaskey were never tried for their crimes in Denver.

[220] *Denver Post*, Monday, April 21, 1924.
[221] *Fighting the Underworld*, by Philip S. Van Cise, Houghton Mifflin Co., 1936.

Three lucky con men, Roy Yeaman "The Blind Man," Jack Ryan "Fat," and Puss McCaskey, alias "J. R. Barry"
Photos are mug shots in the public domain

Even after arrests of the Bunco group, not all of Denver's government officials were pleased. Mayor Dewey Bailey accused the DA of being a dupe of jealous stockbrokers.[222] And the Colorado Law Enforcement League, with support and encouragement from the Denver Police Department, led an unsuccessful recall effort against the prosecutor. Van Cise's actions were vindicated. In addition to convicting Blonger and 19 of his confederates, a special grand jury investigation only weeks after the Blonger gang convictions declared that the city administration was "rotten," including eight officials who were "totally unfit to hold any offices in this city."[223]

In addition to organized crime, Colorado was rife with organized discrimination. The Ku Klux Klan was an exceptionally powerful political force in Colorado and Denver during this time; in the 1920s, the Klan had control of Republican governor Clarence Morley, reputedly U.S. Senator Lawrence Phipps, and Denver Mayor Benjamin Stapleton, as well as a number of Colorado house representatives.[224]

---

[222] Record Journal of Douglas County, September 8, 1922, p 2.
[223] *Westword*, February 7, 2008. "Phil Van Cise: Scourge of Denver's Underworld." https://www.westword.com/news/phil-van-cise-scourge-of-denvers-underworld-5097432.
[224] https://www.colorado.gov/pacific/sites/default/files/Morley.pdf.

Members of the Ku Klux Klan march in a parade, May 31, 1926, on Larimer Street in Denver, Colorado.
Photo from Denver Public Library Special Collections X-21543

Before becoming governor, Clarence Morley was a Denver District Court judge while also being Colorado's Grand Cyclops of the Ku Klux Klan. Virulently anti-Catholic, Morley was elected judge with the backing of Colorado Klan leader Dr. John Galen Locke. At one point, Morley locked Van Cise out of grand jury proceedings. Grand juries are normally run by the district attorney but Van Cise had to go to the Colorado Supreme Court to gain entrance to his own grand jury room. Morley was elected the 24th governor of Colorado, serving one two-year term from 1925 to 1927. After leaving office, he was convicted of mail fraud and imprisoned.

Prominent Klansmen: Colorado Governor Clarence Joseph Morley (left) and Dr. John Galen Locke (right), photos in the public domain

In the 1920s, Colorado's 126,000 Catholics became "public enemy number one" for the Ku Klux Klan. The Klan spied on Catholic priests, leaders, organizations, and businessmen to gather damaging information with the intention of ruining reputations. The Knights of Columbus, a Catholic organization that advocated serving one's church, community, and family, took the Klan very seriously. On October 27, 1923, five Klansmen kidnapped Knights of Columbus member Patrick Walker, took him to a spot near Riverside Cemetery, and pistol-whipped him. Walker could not identify the attackers and Van Cise could do nothing about the kidnapping and assault.[225]

O. Otto Moore, who eventually rose to Chief Justice of the Colorado Supreme Court, was an early hire by Van Cise who helped investigate Klan members. An obvious problem with identifying the hooded "knights" was their anonymity. To identify members, Van Cise assigned Moore, another deputy, and two secretaries to park on West Colfax near Table Rock, the site of Klan meetings. One group was to write down the license plate numbers of passing cars prior to a Klan meeting. The other group beyond Table Rock wrote down the numbers of the cars continuing to Golden. All those on the first but not on the second list were assumed to be attending the Klan meeting.

[225] *Herald Democrat*, October 29, 1923, p 1; *Hooded Empire The Ku Klux Klan in Colorado*, by Robert Alan Goldberg, University of Illinois Press, 1981, p 31.

As Moore and his companions were doing their assigned duty, they were accosted by two Klansmen with Jefferson County deputy sheriff badges. "You're obstructing traffic," they told Moore, "Move on!" Moore replied, "We're not obstructing anything. If you want to arrest us, you name the charge and take us to jail, but otherwise let us alone." He flashed his own district attorney's badge. Shortly thereafter, a car full of hooded Klansmen, with several other cars surrounded Moore's vehicle. The men encircled the car and lifted it bodily onto the highway. "Then they gave us a shove with a big Stutz roadster," he recalled. "Of course, they also grabbed all our papers and records."[226]

The Ku Klux Klan burning a cross in Denver, circa 1921–1930
Photo courtesy of Denver Public Library Special Collections Collection, X-21542

A recall drive was started by the righteous sounding Colorado Law Enforcement League, a Ku Klux Klan front group. The recall attempt ended abruptly when the signed petitions were stolen from the Law Enforcement League offices.[227] A grand jury investigation intimated that the

[226] "O. Otto Moore Papers," The Denver Public Library Western History/Genealogy Department.
[227] *Surface Creek Champion*, Volume 19, Number 20, November 16, 1922, p 2.

purported theft could have been an attempt at framing the district attorney and covering up the apparently unsuccessful petition drive. Van Cise's problems with the Klan continued even after he left office, and in June 1926, the Klan burned a cross on the front lawn of his home. The Klan was also responsible for a threat against Van Cise's life as well as a kidnapping attempt.

A disturbing example of Klan control of Denver justice was the 1920 trial of Denver resident William W. Clawson for the murder of Joseph Zuckerman, a local Jewish resident.[228] Van Cise charged Clawson with murder, but even with overwhelming evidence of his guilt, the jury acquitted him. The not guilty verdict was attributable to the KKK influence on the judge and jury. Reporting on the verdict, the *Denver Jewish News* declared that it was a "miscarriage of justice." In the same article, attorney Joseph F. Jaffa remarked: "The season for the ruthless mauling and slaying of Jewish horse and cattle traders and peddlers seems to be an open one in Denver."

The primary target of the Klan, of course, had always been African Americans. In the 1920s, Dr. Clarence Holmes, president of the Denver NAACP, launched a drive to integrate the downtown Denver movie theaters. In response, the Ku Klux Klan sent Holmes a threatening letter and burned a cross in front of his dental office.[229] As African Americans began buying homes in white neighborhoods, they received a hostile reception. In 1920, a threatening white mob forced Mrs. Emma Davis to leave her home at 2540 Gaylord Street. On July 7, 1921, a bomb ripped apart the newly acquired home of a Black family at 2112 Gilpin Street, and four months later the house was bombed again.[230] In December 1926, bombs were hurled at E.E. Carrington's home at 22nd Avenue and Vine Street; a second attempt a month later drove the family from the neighborhood. None of the bombers were apprehended, so there were never any prosecutions by Van Cise or his successor Foster W. Cline.

---

[228] *Denver Jewish News*, Volume 6, Number 18, May 5, 1920, p 1.
[229] *Hooded Empire: The Ku Klux Klan in Colorado*, Robert Alan Goldberg, University of Illinois Press, 1981, p 25.
[230] *Hooded Empire: The Ku Klux Klan in Colorado*, Robert Alan Goldberg, University of Illinois Press, 1981, p 26.

Left: Dr. Clarence Holmes, photo from findagrave.com/memorials
Right: Dr. Holmes's office and burned cross, Denver Public Library Special Collections #X-22320

On January 27, 1922, Ward Gash, a Black janitor, received a letter from the Ku Klux Klan warning him to leave Denver because he was having "intimate relations with white women" and using "abusive language to, and in the presence of white women."[231] Before leaving town, Gash turned the letter over to the district attorney's office. This resulted in a series of grand jury probes into Klan operations in the city. The Denver police chief was a Klansman, and the department was heavily infiltrated by the KKK. The Denver city attorney, manager of safety, manager of revenue, clerk and recorder, manager of parks, city accountant, and others were all Klansmen. Members of the KKK also served as justices of the peace and District Court judges in Denver. The threat to justice also derived from potential jurors who were drawn from Klan membership lists. During this era in Denver, DA Van Cise was one of the few elected officials willing to exert government power against the bigotry and illegal activities of the Klan.

Van Cise also prosecuted Denver city officials for criminal activities not related to official corruption or Klan activities. On October 25, 1922, he indicted warden Frank Kratke of the Denver county jail and guard Edward Allison, charging them with assaulting an invalid prisoner named Alpha E. Ransom. Ransom was sent to jail for being unable to pay a $10 assessment in police court. He died three days later from injuries he received in the jail. During a brawl between prisoners, Kratke and Allison intervened and beat Ransom senseless. At trial, the

[231] *Hooded Empire: The Ku Klux Klan in Colorado*, Robert Alan Goldberg, University of Illinois Press, 1981, p 17.

main witnesses for the prosecution were prisoners. The defense was that the prisoners, not Kratke and Allison, inflicted Ransom's injuries. The verdict of not guilty was returned to a packed courtroom.[232]

Meanwhile, after his election as mayor in 1923, Ben Stapleton named Klansman Rice Means as manager of safety and later city attorney.[233] Klansman Reuben Hershey succeeded Means as manager of safety after first serving as manager of revenue. The police department was heavily infiltrated, with seven sergeants and dozens of patrol officers all card-carrying Klansmen. Mayor Stapleton refused for almost a year to appoint a Klansman as chief of police but facing a recall election led by Ku Klux Klan Denver leader Locke, Stapleton named William Candlish as Denver's new chief of police in return for Klan support.[234] At a Klan rally on July 14, 1924, Stapleton made it clear that if reelected, he would "give the Klan the kind of administration it wants." Stapleton was reelected. In 2020, voters in the Stapleton neighborhood of Denver officially changed the name to Central Park because of the KKK connections of the former mayor.

---

[232] *Fort Collins Courier*. October 26, 1922, p 3; *Herald Democrat*, November 2, 1922, p 1.
[233] Municipal Facts, published by the City and County of Denver, Volume 6, 1923, p 4.
[234] *Hooded Empire The Ku Klux Klan in Colorado*, Robert Alan Goldberg, University of Illinois Press, 1981, p 32.

Denver mayor and KKK supporter Ben Stapleton, photo courtesy of the City and County of Denver

KKK city leaders appointed during Stapleton's tenure: Denver City Attorney Rice Means (left), Manager of Safety Reuben Hershey (middle), and Denver Police Chief William Candlish (right). Photo of Means, National Photo Company Collection – Library of Congress Catalog, photo of Hershey courtesy of City/County of Denver, and Candlish photo from: ourcampaigns.com/candidatedetails.

Chief Candlish was a former newspaper editor, state senator, and radium experimenter with no previous police experience, but he was loyal to the Klan and to Locke. Candlish made the police department an instrument of the Klan's will. He promoted Protestant police officers that became Klansmen and gave them choice assignments. Protestant officers who refused to join the Klan received shorter work hours and were denied promotions. Non-Klan Protestant officers joined the Jewish and Catholic officers who were assigned to night shifts on undesirable beats. Candlish's men began enforcing forgotten city ordinances to make life hard for Black, Jewish, and Catholic shopkeepers in Denver. The Klan also took advantage of the situation to requisition men and vehicles from the department for their own use.

In October 1924, Candlish ordered Denver police officers to oust all white women from establishments of any kind owned and operated by Greeks, Japanese, and Chinese within the city of Denver. The order was based on an old state law.[235] Scores of women were thrown out of employment by this action, more than a dozen being employed in a single Chinese restaurant. Van Cise refused to prosecute anyone under the law, and felt he had little power to stop Candlish's harassment.

Still, Van Cise fought corruption where he could. In 1924, he charged several Denver police officers in the bootleg squad with larceny and embezzlement. Officer James R. Kilpatrick, leader of the squad, and his officers were seizing cases of bootlegged alcohol and instead of putting the cases of booze in the evidence vault, they were selling them for personal profit. Most members of this unit were Klansmen and they were living far beyond their means thanks to the revenue from the bootlegged alcohol they were seizing. After the jury was selected and Deputy DA O. Otto Moore began presenting his case, the defense moved to have Klansman Judge Henry Bray throw out the case, claiming that since bootlegged liquor was illegal it had no value and could not then be the basis of theft and embezzlement charges. Judge Bray agreed and dismissed the case. Moore was convinced that the Colorado head of the Klan, Galen Locke, influenced Bray's absurd ruling. The district attorney's office appealed the ruling and the Colorado Supreme Court ruled that the bootlegged liquor, although it was illegal, had value and could be the basis of theft and embezzlement charges.[236]

---

[235] *Aspen Daily Times*, October 2, 1924, p 1.

[236] *Craig Empire*, Number 19, June 3, 1925, p 8, "O. Otto Moore Papers," The Denver Public Library Western History/Genealogy Department.

O. Otto Moore (left) and Judge Henry Bray (right). Moore's photo from the Colorado State Archives, Bray's photo from *The Bench and the Bar of Colorado* 1917.

In 1924, Van Cise helped create the "Visible Government League" to counter Ku Klux Klan influence in the Denver Republican primary.[237] The League successfully ran a petition drive to put anti-Klan candidates on the Denver Republican primary ballot. As part of the League's effort, Van Cise agreed to deliver an anti-Klan speech on September 4 at the Denver Auditorium. The talk was entitled "Morley and the Courts—The Klan Boycott," and Van Cise intended to expose and condemn Klan attempts to ruin Catholic businesses in Colorado, influence judges and juries, and disrupt the Republican Party. The night of the speech, Klan members filled the hall, outnumbering the rest in the audience and shouted Van Cise down when he attempted to speak. This screaming went on for hours, and even Klan leaders and the Denver police officers could not quiet the crowd. Finally, Van Cise gave up and walked out while the Klan supporters sang "Onward Christian Soldiers." It was after one in the morning when Van Cise and his chief investigator left through a back door. The district attorney's car was chased, and shots fired.[238]

The DA was not the only elected official to speak out against the Ku Klux Klan's domination of Denver's government. During the recall election of Mayor Ben Stapleton in

[237] *The Invisible Empire in the West: Toward a New Historical Appraisal of the Ku Klux Klan in the 1920s*, edited by Shawn Lay, University of Illinois Press, 2004, p 55; *Cañon City Daily Record*, October 7, 1924, p 11; *Hooded Empire The Ku Klux Klan in Colorado*, by Robert Alan Goldberg, University of Illinois Press, 1981, pp 75–76.
[238] *Westward*, Feb. 7, 2008.

March of 1924, Judge Ben Lindsey appealed to Denver voters "to rescue their homes and their fair city from this white hooded menace—the blackest it has ever faced. At this juncture this can be done only by voting against Klansman Benjamin F. Stapleton."[239]

In a significant blow to the Klan, on January 9, 1925, Van Cise indicted Ku Klux Klan Grand Dragon, Dr. John Galen Locke, and six of his men for kidnapping 15-year-old East High student Keith S. Boehm. Locke had fellow Klan members pose as police detectives, abduct Boehm, and deliver him to Locke's downtown Denver office. Professing the need to uphold moral values, Locke threatened Boehm with castration unless he married his pregnant ex-girlfriend, Mae Nash. Colorado Governor-elect Clarence J. Morley posted Locke's $1,000 bond. The kidnapping case was eventually thrown out on a technicality by a Klan judge, but it brought ridicule on the KKK leader.[240]

Turning to police officer deaths, five Denver police officers lost their lives in the line of duty during Van Cise's four-year tenure.[241] Policeman William Steam was killed in February 1921, shot in the back of the head by a gunman angry that the officer had shut down a dance hall. Van Cise successfully prosecuted Keil O'Neill, aka Lee Williams, for the ambush murder. O'Neill was sentenced to life in prison.[242] Policemen Clarence Zietz and Forrest Ross both died in car crashes in April 1921, one crash occurring while responding to the first fatal crash. On May 30, 1921, police officer Arthur Pinkerton was electrocuted by an electric arc light while moving it out of the path of pedestrians. Policeman Richie Rose was ambushed and murdered by several assailants. Rose had just finished eating breakfast with his wife and was walking to a call box when he noticed a suspicious vehicle sitting in the street. As he approached it, suspects in the vehicle opened fire. Rose ran to a nearby pole to take cover and returned fire. However, several more men were waiting behind him and shot him. After he fell to the ground, the men approached him, took his gun and shot him several more times. No suspects were ever identified or prosecuted, although Policeman Rose's last words were reported as, "Mafia, mafia, mafia." Officials at the time surmised bootleggers were responsible for the murder.[243]

---

239 *The Ku Klux Klan in the City, 1915-1930*, by Kenneth T. Jackson, Oxford Press 1967, p 224.
240 *New York Daily News*, January 8, 1925, p 32; *Hooded Empire The Ku Klux Klan in Colorado*, by Robert Alan Goldberg, University of Illinois Press, 1981, pp 98–99.
241 Denver Police Department: Officer Down Memorial Page https://www.odmp.org/officer/21175-policeman-william-o-steam, https://www.odmp.org/officer/14674-policeman-clarence-e-zietz, https://www.odmp.org/officer/11541-policeman-forrest-ross, https://www.odmp.org/officer/10694-policeman-arthur-j-pinkerton, https://www.odmp.org/officer/11523-policeman-richie-rose.
242 *Denver Post*, May 13, 2011.

Denver Police Officers William O. Steam, Clarence Zietz, Forrest Ross, Arthur Pinkerton, and Richie Rose. Sketch and Photos courtesy of the Denver Police Museum

Some of the violence Denver police officers faced may have been aggravated by the attitude and policy of top police officials. On February 16, 1921, for example, Denver's manager of safety and excise Frank M. Downer ordered members of the Denver police department to "shoot to kill" all bandits attempting to escape from police officers.[244] This proclamation followed reports of numerous crimes in Denver alleged to be attributed to an influx of criminals from eastern cities. The crimes were attributed to a gang of yeggmen (slang for burglars and safe crackers), stickup men, and other criminals who had found their way to Denver after being driven from Chicago, St. Louis, Kansas City, and other cities. Eight members of the Denver police department who used their guns in dealing with criminals during the week before Downer's proclamation were commended by Downer and Chief of Police H. Rugg Williams. Patrolman Leslie G. Sayer, who had shot and killed a bandit in Denver three days earlier, received a personal commendation from Downer. "We might as well haul a few bandits to the morgue as the hospital" was the declaration of the safety manager.[245] DA Van Cise had no comment on Downer's proclamation.

In 1923, Van Cise refused to be nominated as a candidate for mayor of Denver,[246] although he did work to defeat Mayor Bailey and called his administration "a disgrace to American government." Van Cise continued his colorful proclamations even after his public service. In 1927, he accused Juvenile Court Judge Lindsey of making it impossible to effectively run the Juvenile Court after the judge convinced many of the court staff to resign. Van Cise accused the judge of removing and destroying public records of the court as well as unethical

[243] Officer Down memorial page. www.odmp.org/officer/11523-policeman-ritchie-rose.
[244] *Colorado Daily Chieftain*, February 17, 1921, p 1.
[245] *Fort Collins Courier,* Feb. 16, 1921, p 8.
[246] *Denver Post*, December 9, 1969, p 2.

behavior for accepting a fee for legal services while he was a judge. This was the incident that eventually led to the judge's disbarment.[247]

In 1936 Van Cise wrote *Fighting the Underworld,* which describes his exploits battling crime. In 1945, Van Cise was shot at twice by the husband of a divorce client Van Cise was representing, but both shots missed their intended target. Two kidnapping attempts were also made against Van Cise, once by the Klan and once by unknown assailants in 1943 when he fought off two would-be abductors in his front yard at 1080 Sherman Street.[248] No arrests were ever made in either incident. In the 1950s, Van Cise served as a special prosecutor and brought charges against the Smaldone family for running crooked gambling operations in Adams County.

Just as Isaac Stevens became the legal representative of the *Denver Post* in another era, Van Cise represented the *Rocky Mountain News* in the 1930s. In August 1932, the *News* printed an article quoting two prominent Democratic politicians lambasting the *Post* and Frederick Bonfils directly. Bonfils filed suit against the *News* for $200,000. Van Cise represented the *News* and based his defense on the fact that what was published about Bonfils was true.[249] Bill Hosakawa, in *Thunder in the Rockies*, reported that Van Cise set about to show that "Bonfils did not have a good name and his reputation was so bad it was impossible to damage it further." Van Cise's aggressive investigation into Bonfils's life and background turned up file cabinets full of unflattering material. Two trial delays extended the case, but Bonfils died in early 1933 before the libel case came to trial. Even though Bonfils was dead, Van Cise's name was banned from being mentioned in the *Post* until Edwin Palmer Hoyt's ascension to publisher in 1946. Ironically, the *Post* hired Van Cise and his son in 1954 to defend against a suit brought by chiropractor Leo Spears. Van Cise represented the *Post* until his death, and his son continued to work with the paper for many years after.

Van Cise also served as president of the Denver Bar Association and as a member of the Colorado and American Bar Associations. In 1926, he was appointed one of three members of the National Crime Commission that worked with the States Association of Attorneys General in an unsuccessful attempt to set up model legislation to control and regulate the use and possession of handguns.[250] He also served as chair of the Judiciary Committee of the Colorado Bar

---

[247] *Daily Times*, Volume XXXIII, Number 198, August 4, 1927, p 6; *Daily Times*, Volume XXXIII, Number 250, October 3, 1927, p 1; *Steamboat Pilot*, December 13, 1929, p 8.

[248] *Denver Post*, December 9, 1969, p 2; *Westword*, February 7, 2008.

[249] *The Colorado Lawyer*, Philip S. Van Cise by Edwin P. Van Cise, Vol. 15, No. 7, 1986, July, p 1,165.

Association, which developed and oversaw the successful implementation of their proposal for the non-partisan selection of state judges, the system that is currently in place.[251] These policies were the first significant change in the selection of judges since Colorado became a state; prior to these changes, judges campaigned for election under a party standard.

After a life as a political reformer, Van Cise died on December 8, 1969, at the age of 85. Van Cise's son wrote of his father's uncompromising stand for what he believed was right, and summarized that although he was disliked by many, he was admired by most. Denver honored his contributions with the opening of the Van Cise-Simonet Detention Center in 2010.

18. Foster W. Cline (1925–1928)

FOSTER W. CLINE
1925 - 1928

Foster W. Cline was born November 2, 1880, in Roanoke, Virginia and attended school in Russell, Kansas. He obtained his bachelor's degree from McPherson Kansas College and worked as a teacher before obtaining his law degree from the University of Kansas at Lawrence. Cline practiced in Walsenberg, Colorado for several years before moving to Denver. While in Walsenberg, he was hired by the Huerfano County Law and Order League to fight the corrupt political machine of Sheriff Jeff Farr. After he became the target of threats for demanding the Sunday closure of saloons and enforcing the anti-gambling ordinances in Walsenburg,[252] Cline moved to Denver, where he had two brothers, attorney Carl Cline and Furman Cline, president of an investment company. In 1913, Cline became a deputy under Denver DA John A. Rush. Cline served in the district attorney's office until 1917 and then formed a law partnership with Rush. In 1918 Cline ran for the state senate and was defeated, but in 1924 successfully ran in a four-way race for district attorney with the campaign slogan: "Get in line and vote for Cline."[253] Although Cline assured the *Jewish News* he was not a member of the Ku Klux Klan, it was rumored that he had promised to hire Klansmen, and he received the

---

[250] *Denver Post*, December 9, 1969, p 2.

[251] Colorado Judicial Merit Selection—A Well-Deserved 40th Anniversary Celebration by Gregory J. Hobbs, Jr. Colorado Bar Association, 35 The Colorado Lawyer 13, (April 2006), p 16.

[252] *Walsenburg World*, Volume XXIII, Number 22, June 1, 1911, p 1.

[253] TARRYALL/CLINE RANCH, Anderson/Cline Ranch South Park, Park County, Colorado, Historic Structure Assessment. October 2011. Prepared by Merrill Ann Wilson, Historical Architect, Inc., p 23. Colorado and its People, a biographical work from 1948.

group's support in the election.[254] Despite the rumors, Cline did take steps to challenge and prosecute various Klansmen after his election. Like those before him, he faced obstacles from the group's corrupt control of Denver city administration, the Denver Police Department, and the Denver jury system. Cline launched an investigation into the jury commissioner's involvement in improperly loading jury panels with Klansmen.[255] He vowed to crack down on bootleggers, and in 1925 he joined with Mayor Stapleton in "the Good Friday Raids,"[256] which were a massive set of raids to round up and prosecute bootleggers, prostitutes, pimps, and gamblers. Nearly 200 criminals were arrested and charged with various state, city, and federal crimes. These raids and follow-up investigations exposed a web of graft that involved the Police Vice Unit, the Klan, and organized crime. A dozen officers lost their jobs, but none were prosecuted.[257]

On June 10, 1925, Klansman Governor Clarence Morley invoked an anti-liquor law to commission men to serve as "Prohibition Enforcement Agents," and then filled those positions with Klansmen and vested them with the same authority to investigate liquor violations as law enforcement personnel. By the end of 1925, Morley had appointed nearly 200 Klansmen to these positions throughout the state; three-quarters of them kept their identities secret.[258] In Denver, Morley's men used unconstitutional raids, claiming searches for liquor, as a cover to harass anti-Klan businesses. Their activities went on throughout Colorado and led to two shootings, one of a suspected bootlegger and the other of a fellow prohibition agent. Cline denounced these activities as "un-American" and called the agents Morley's "secret spy system."[259] Cline made it clear that he would prosecute any agent that violated the law in Denver, and the warden of the Denver County Jail refused to accept prisoners taken by the Prohibition Enforcement Agents.

---

[254] *In the Shadow of the Klan, When the KKK Ruled Denver 1920-1926*, by Phil Goodstein, New Social Publications, Denver 2006, p 295.
[255] *Daily Times*, Volume XXXII, Number 47, February 10, 1926, p 1; *Aspen Daily Times*, February 25, 1926, p 1; *In the Shadow of the Klan, When the KKK Ruled Denver 1920-1926*, by Phil Goodstein, New Social Publications, Denver 2006, p 343.
[256] *Encyclopedia of Politics of the American West,* edited by Steven L. Danver, CQ Press, 2013, comment by Ralph Hardstock; *In the Shadow of the Klan, When the KKK Ruled Denver 1920-1926*, by Phil Goodstein, New Social Publications, Denver 2006, p 300.
[257] *Palisade Tribune*, Volume 22, Number 47, April 24, 1925, p 2.
[258] *Daily Times*, Volume XXXI, Number 152, June 10, 1925, p 1; *Aspen Daily Times*, December 31, 1925, p 1; COLORADO GOVERNORS, Clarence Morley, https://www.colorado.gov/pacific/sites/default/files/Morley.pdf.
[259] *Aspen Times*, November 23, 1925, p 1.

Prohibition agents destroying alcohol c 1921, Public domain

Together with Arapahoe county DA Joel E. Stone, Cline publicly admonished Governor Morley for the deeds of his prohibition or "dry" agents. Stone claimed the governor's agents undermined law enforcement as a whole by creating a perception in the community that the entire justice system was out of control. Cline particularly called out agent Fred W. Kuenzel, threatening to arrest him if he continued his lawless raids on behalf of Governor Morley.[260]

On January 20, 1926, commissioner of Weld County and chair of the Association of County Commissioners legislative committee Dan C. Straight was subpoenaed by Cline to appear as a witness before a Denver grand jury to give evidence as to Straight's claim that Governor Morley had vetoed a bus bill in 1925 after being paid $6,000 out of a slush fund. Cline had the allegation probed thoroughly, but no indictment was ultimately brought against the Klansman governor.[261]

[260] *The Aspen Daily Times*, November 25, 1925, p 1.

While dealing with prohibition-related crimes as well as the Klan, Cline's office continued to handle the types of cases always seen by a prosecutor's office. On June 9, 1927, for example, Joseph Minter, a telephone office manager, shot and killed Colorado state senator and prominent attorney Albert B. Bogdon in Minter's estranged wife's apartment. Minter and his wife had been separated since January after she had filed for divorce. On the day of the shooting, to spy on his wife, Minter rented a hotel room under an assumed name across from the Alrose apartments where she lived. As he watched though a window, Minter saw the married Bogdon calling on his wife. When the couple got into a compromising position, Minter knocked down the door and shot and killed Bogdon. Mrs. Minter said she heard three or four gunshots and found Bogdon's body on the floor, and her husband holding a smoking revolver. "I ought to shoot you, too," Minter told his wife and then ran to a telephone in the hall, notified police, and disappeared.[262] The next morning a bedraggled and mud-spattered Minter surrendered to police and Cline charged him with first-degree murder. At trial, Minter admitted that he broke into the apartment and shot Bogdon but claimed that he had gone into an uncontrollable rage when he saw his wife in Bogdon's arms. The jury found Minter guilty of involuntary manslaughter and he was sentenced to one year in prison.[263]

Also in 1927, Cline indicted three Denver dairy companies and their officers, known as the "Milk Trust," for conspiracy to violate the Colorado Anti-Trust Law by fixing the price of milk in Denver. The dairy companies took their case to the U.S. Supreme Court and in "Cline, District Attorney v. Frink Dairy Company (1927)," Chief Justice William Taft delivered the opinion of the Court, ruling the Colorado Anti-Trust Law to be unconstitutional.

Three Denver policemen lost their lives in the line of duty during Cline's term. James Shannon was killed April 4, 1925, while attempting to arrest a man near 34th and Williams streets[264] The suspect, Albert Dorchak, was apprehended, prosecuted by Cline, convicted, and sentenced to life. On March 23, 1927, patrol officer Elmer Rich entered a home on a domestic disturbance call when a gunman opened fire, killing Rich and then taking his own life. Rich had been on the force for only six months at the time of his death. Denver Patrolman Harry Ohle was killed the following November while searching a home for suspected illegal alcohol. Ohle and

---

[261] *Aspen Daily Times*, January 20, 1926, p 1.
[262] *Xenia Evening Gazette*, June 10, 1927, p 1.
[263] *Daily Times*, Volume XXXIII, Number 152, June 10, 1927, p 1.
[264] *Daily Times*, Volume XXXI, Number 117, April 29, 1925, p 1.

two other officers entered a darkened room when a man inside shot all three police officers and a citizen named Louvenia Reese. Patrolman Ohle was hit in the heart and died instantly; Reese died as well.[265] The suspect, Eddie Ives, a six-time convicted felon, was convicted by Cline of the double homicide and sentenced to death by hanging. He was executed in 1930. Ives, who weighed only 80 pounds, was escorted to the gallows but the first attempt to hang him failed because he was too light. The rope jumped off the pulley and Ives fell to the floor, gasping for breath. "You can't hang a man twice," he said. But they did.[266]

Denver policemen James Shannon (left), Elmer Rich (middle), and Harry Ohle (right), photos courtesy of the Denver Police Museum

One of the more novel cases handled by Cline's office occurred at the end of his tenure. In the first two weeks of April 1928, there was a series of armed robberies in Denver where the bandit committed the crimes in blackface. It did not take long before the local Denver newspapers referred to the robber as "the blackface bandit." In mid-April, after he blackened his face to pull additional robberies, bandit Pete Moran entered an alley and was confronted by Denver patrol officer Clarence Alston. There was an exchange of gunfire, in which Alston fired five rounds at Moran, striking him once in the foot. Moran ran with Alston chasing after him. The foot chase lasted a few blocks and ended with Moran's apprehension and arrest. Moran survived his wound and told police he committed the robberies to get the money to pay for the divorce for a woman named Mrs. Bobby Laestcher, who Moran claimed wanted to divorce her husband to marry him. When Laestcher was questioned about Moran's claim, she said that she

[265] *Eagle Valley Enterprise*, January 4, 1929, p 6.
[266] *Westword*, April 8, 2013.

knew nothing about the robberies and would get the money for her divorce herself. She also told police that due to her abusive estranged husband and now this, she was probably through with men.[267] Cline charged Moran with robbery with intent to kill. He was convicted and sentenced to 10 to 15 years in prison.[268]

In the last year of his term as district attorney, Cline established the Tarryall-Cline Ranch house, which is just off Highway 285 in Park County, Colorado. Cline himself never intended to live there full time, but his family used it in the summer months and he rented it out to a steady succession of ranch managers who operated hay and livestock businesses on-site. The 1,635 acres on the west side of the highway (which includes the main ranch headquarters complex) was purchased in 2011 by Park County and is now part of a unique public program that allows access for fly-fishing on private ranches for a daily rod fee.

Cline did not run for reelection in 1928, but two years later he ran unsuccessfully for state senate. He went on to serve as the regional administrator of the Securities and Exchange Commission. Cline continued to practice law and remained active in the Democratic Party. He died in Denver on November 30, 1969.[269]

[267] *Steamboat Pilot*, April 20, 1928, p 7.
[268] *Steamboat Pilot*, May 4, 1928, p 7.
[269] *Denver Post*, December 6, 1969.

Main ranch house at the Tarryall-Cline Ranch, Park County, Colorado, photo from the Twila Hamilton Brompton collection

Foster and Mildred Cline and their sons, Foster Jr. and Stephen, and Bertha Furman (background) outside the main ranch house at the Tarryall-Cline Ranch. Family friend Bertha Furman seated in rear. Photo from the Twila Hamilton Brompton collection

Foster Cline Jr. gained notoriety as a prominent child psychiatrist who, in the 1970s, developed "attachment therapy," a treatment method for children suffering severe mental and behavioral disorders.[270] Part of the treatment involved immobilizing an out-of-control child through physical restraint. Children might be tightly held or wrapped in a blanket until they stopped their behavior. The therapy resulted in more than one child's death while being restrained. Cline Jr. found himself testifying across the country as a defense witness for parents and treatment providers who had used his methods to disastrous results. In at least a few instances, he testified for the defense in courtrooms where his father had worked for the prosecution.[271]

[270] *Adoption Resources for Mental Health Professionals*, edited by Pamela V. Grabe, Transaction Publishers, 1986, p 137.
[271] https://www.chicagotribune.com/news/ct-xpm-2000-06-08-0006080068-story.html; *Westword,* July 27, 2000.

19. Earl Wettengel (1929–1936)

Earl Wettengel was born in Denver on October 2, 1888. He was the son of Denver mining pioneer John W. Wettengel and was the first elected Denver DA to be born in the city of Denver. When reelected in 1932, he also became the first person to be reelected as Denver DA since David Graham 52 years earlier in 1879. Wettengel graduated from the University of Denver, where he was a football star. He served honorably in the Army in the Philippines during World War I. He was city commander of the American Legion, president of the United Veteran's Council, and president of the Colorado District Attorney's Association.[272]

Wettengel was a deputy under both Philip Van Cise and Foster Cline and had a reputation as an aggressive crime fighter and expert litigator. He was first elected DA in 1928 after serving as a deputy district attorney for six years. He easily won reelection in 1932. Wettengel was a respected Republican leader in Denver and was considered a skilled orator and trial attorney. The local papers praised his prosecutorial record. One *Denver Post* article noted that Wettengel's staff convicted five murderers in his first six months as DA. He was also renowned during his first term for his speakeasy raids during Prohibition. At the start of his second term, he continued to increase his crime-fighting reputation through his raids on fortune-tellers and "bucket shops"—early white-collar criminals who engaged in high-pressure selling of fraudulent stocks over the telephone. Wettengel's promising career came to an abrupt and humiliating end in his second term, however.

---

[272] *Denver Post*, January 3, 1965, p 25.

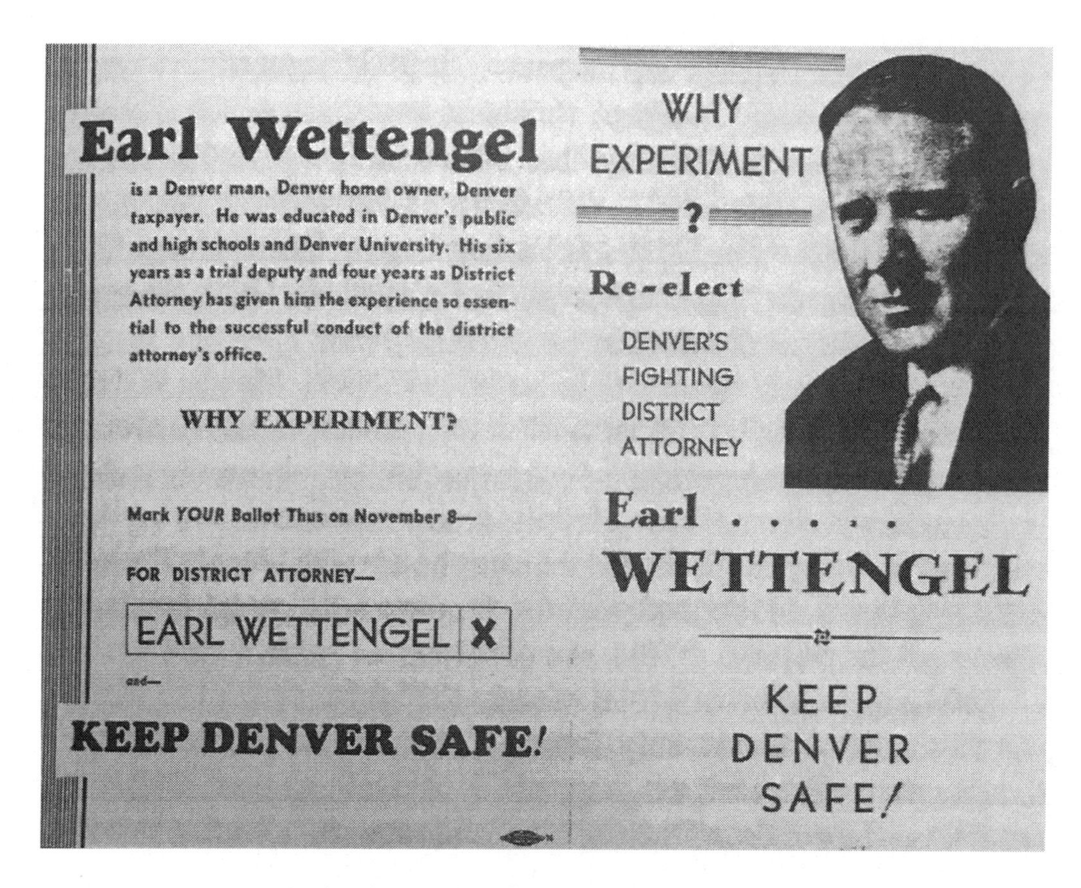

Wettengel reelection handbill, photo in the public domain

In December 1934, Wettengel was indicted on perjury charges by a special grand jury.[273] He was accused of meeting with the slot machine king of Colorado in Kansas City and Saint Joseph, Missouri, and subsequently lying about those meetings to hide his connections to organized crime. Max Melville, a prominent private attorney, was named special prosecutor and he stubbornly pursued the case against Wettengel.[274] During the case, Melville and his family faced threats against Melville's four-year-old daughter, threatening phone calls, and an armed break-in at his home. In response, the Denver police put a guard around Melville's home. Melville would later serve as assistant district attorney for Denver DA Bert M. Keating.

Although criminal charges against Wettengel were dropped in 1935 when witnesses from Kansas City refused to come to Denver to testify, Melville followed through, requesting administrative sanctions.[275] He successfully pursued his case to the State Supreme Court, seeking Wettengel's disbarment. On April 21, 1936, the Supreme Court did exactly that; suspending the

[273] *Aspen Daily Times*, April 23, 1936, p 8.
[274] *Greeley Daily Tribune*, April 10, 1936, p 9; *Greeley Daily Tribune* March 12, 1938, p 3.
[275] *Greeley Daily Tribune*, April 8, 1936, p 2.

DA indefinitely from the practice of law for fabricating evidence. The court found that a hotel registration card presented by Wettengel as evidence that he was at a Kansas City hotel "was clearly and convincingly shown to be a forgery, fabricated by and for the respondent with intent on his part to mislead and deceive." The high court disbarred the DA.[276] Incredibly, the court still allowed Wettengel to continue to serve as Denver's DA through the end of his second term. In issuing its ruling, the Court stated, "The respondent is district attorney of the second judicial district. The question is not before us as to whether our order works a forfeiture of the office. Doubt nevertheless may arise concerning the effect of our judgment upon the right of the respondent to continue in the office and the validity of his act as such official, with resultant uncertainty and litigation. Let it be further ordered, therefore, that the suspension of the respondent shall not forbid his performance of the duties of his present term." The Colorado Supreme Court eventually reinstated Wettengel's law license in 1938, but his political and prosecutorial careers were over. Wettengel was the only Denver DA, and possibly the only elected DA in the country, to lose his law license and continue to serve as a chief prosecutor.

At the height of his popularity in 1934, Wettengel was a strong candidate for Denver mayor.[277] Wettengel was even knighted by the fascist Italian king Victor Emmanuel in 1933. Wettengel withdrew from the mayoral race when he was indicted, calling his indictment a political campaign organized by the city's loan sharks out to stop him from prosecuting them.

Even without Wettengel's personal legal problems, the Denver district attorney's office would have been busy. During Prohibition, mob bootleggers were responsible for at least 14 murders in the Denver area. The victims were police officers, rival mobsters, and mobsters' relatives; most went unsolved. The first Prohibition-era murder in Denver was of police detective George Klein in 1919, and the last was mobster Augie Marino in 1933. The bloodiest years were during Wettengel's tenure, with nine bootlegging-related killings. After alcohol again became legal, the mob moved into illegal gambling.[278]

Famous bootleggers Pete and Sam Carlino set up a "Bootleggers Convention" scheduled for January 25, 1931, at the La Plamarte Roadhouse in Wheat Ridge, Colorado, to avert an all-out war between the Carlino brothers and other Colorado bootleggers.[279] The Carlino brothers

---

[276] *Greeley Daily Tribune*, March 16, 1936, p 1; *Greeley Daily Tribune*, April 9, 1936, p 7.

[277] *Steamboat Pilot*, March 13, 1931, p 5.

[278] *Smaldone The Untold Story of An American Crime Family*, by Dick Kreck Fulcrum Publishing, Golden, Colorado, 2009, pp 68–69.

[279] *Denver Post*, January 25, 1931, p 1; *Colorado's Carlino Brothers: A Bootlegging Empire* by Sam Carlino,

were from Pueblo and were looking to take over the illegal liquor business in Denver and the rest of Colorado. Denver Police got wind of the plan and arrested 29 gangsters at the meeting. Pete Carlino and the others were charged by Wettengel but released. Guiseppe "Joe" Roma and the Smaldone brothers were not at the meeting. Some observers believe that had the police not broken up the meeting, the all-out war that followed for the next few years might have been prevented.

Pete Carlino and Guiseppe "Joe" Roma, photo courtesy of Denver Public Library Special Collections

On March 16, 1931, Sam and Pete Carlino and four others blew up Pete's home at 3357 Federal Boulevard as part of an insurance scam.[280] The Carlinos were being squeezed by other bootleggers and needed cash to import booze. Wettengel charged Pete and several others with arson (the Carlino henchmen were convicted, but Pete went into hiding).[281] Three days before the arson trial, Sam Carlino was murdered in his Denver home by Bruno Mauro, an 18-year-old gangster apprentice.[282] Mauro was part of Carlino's gang but was upset that Carlino did not keep his promise to take care of Mauro's family after Mauro's father was arrested for running a

---

History Press, Charleston, SC, 2019, p 86.

[280] *Craig Empire Courier*, Volume 40, Number 43, March 25, 1931, p 4.

[281] *The Clovis New Journal*, May 13, 1931, p 1.

[282] *Denver Post*, May 8, 1931, p 1; *Craig Empire Courier*, Volume 40, Number 50, May 13, 1931, p 3; *Lafayette Leader*, Volume 28, Number 9, March 4, 1932, p 6.

whiskey still. Mauro also shot two eyewitnesses, Jim Colletti and Carlino's wife, but they survived. Wettengel charged Mauro with the murder but by the time of the trial Mrs. Carlino had left Denver out of fear for herself and her family. Eyewitness Colletti could not be found. The jury found Mauro not guilty of the murder.[283]

In early 1931, Ignacio Vaccaro—a nephew of the Carlino brothers and bodyguard for Pete—was believed to have been murdered.[284] Local law enforcement theorized that Vaccaro had been killed by rival Denver bootleggers headed by Joe Roma. Vaccaro's car was found outside of Colorado Springs, but his body was never recovered. On February 18, 1931, Pete was shot at from a moving car in front of the Johnson Brothers Garage in Denver, but all four bullets missed. Three days earlier, prominent Denver bootlegger Joe Barry had been shot by unknown assailants, and the public was abuzz about a Denver gang war. These attacks spurred Denver police chief of detectives Albert T. Clark into action. Clark ordered the arrest of all known bootleggers on vagrancy charges and the closing of pool halls and soft drink parlors in North Denver. During this time, Mayor Ben Stapleton and Police Chief Dick Reed were assuring constituents that there was no gang situation in the city, but Wettengel understood the city was in the middle of a bloody battle for control over illegal alcohol distribution.[285]

On March 3, 1931, Denver DA investigators Ray Humphreys and Stanley Maus were chasing a car of suspected bootleggers through downtown Denver. As the two cars went over the 20th Street viaduct headed toward north Denver, another car, driven by Eugene "Checkers" Smaldone, pulled in front of the DA investigators and pinned their car against the curb. Maus responded by firing three shots into Smaldone's car, one missing Smaldone's head by mere inches. As potentially deadly as the incident was, Smaldone received a ticket and was fined $60. The bootleggers got away.[286]

---

[283] *Denver Post*, April 27, 1932, p 12; *The Pueblo Chieftain*, April 27, 1932, p 1.
[284] *Smaldone: The Untold Story of An American Crime Family*, by Dick Kreck Fulcrum Publishing, Golden, Colorado, 2009, p 69.
[285] *Denver Post*, May 9, 1931.
[286] *Denver Post*, March 3, 1931, p 1; *Smaldone: The Untold Story of An American Crime Family*, by Dick Kreck Fulcrum Publishing, Golden, Colorado, 2009, p 98.

A young Eugene "Checkers" Smaldone, mug shot from the Denver Police Museum

Denver attorney investigators Stanley Maus (left) and Ray Humphreys (right), photo courtesy of the Denver district attorney's office

Later that same month, Wettengel questioned and then arrested two men regarding a plot to kill chief investigator Ray Humphreys. The arrest of John Debalme and James Percelle followed a tip that a mysterious invitation would be transmitted to Humphreys to investigate a liquor shipment, supposedly coming into Denver. When Humphreys followed up on the tip, he would be killed. Police said that Debalme and Percelle had been under surveillance, but that their arrest was ordered in the hope that if there were such a plot planned, it would be thwarted. Wettengel took the threat seriously, knowing that bootlegger gang members had been suspected of killing law enforcement officers in the past. As mentioned previously, detective George Klein and patrol officer Richie Rose had been gunned down a few years earlier. Even more recently, federal agent Dale F. Kearney had been killed in Aguilar, Colorado. Federal agent Ray Sutton also disappeared and was presumed murdered by bootleggers. The case, according to the district attorney's office, presented a new angle on the recent outbreak of gang warfare in Denver. Debalme and Percelle were never charged, however, and the plot to kill Humphreys was assumed abandoned. Humphreys continued to serve as chief investigator at the Denver district attorney's office for another 28 years, until 1959. Humphreys died in 1973.

Clarence "Chauncey" Smaldone, left, and Eugene "Checkers" Smaldone leave U.S. District Court in Denver in 1982 after each was sentenced to 10 years in jail and fined $20,000 for loan sharking and income tax evasion. Behind them is attorney Peter Ney. Photo from Denver Public Library Special Collections, Photo donated to the Denver Public Library by the Rocky Mountain News / David L. Cornwell RMN-030-0053

On Saint Patrick's Day 1932, a gangland "execution car" forced the car driven by whiskey runner and gangster Vincent Mortellaro into the curb. Mortellaro's car was then riddled with shotgun slugs. Mortellaro died, but three other occupants survived. A few days later the small sedan used in the assassination was seized by district attorney investigators. At the time it was seized, the brother-in-law of Joe Roma drove it. The Smaldone brothers, Clyde and Eugene, were arrested and jailed during the investigation, but never charged. The seven guns that the Denver Police seized from Eugene at his arrest were returned. The car turned out to be the sole clue to the identity of the execution squad, and Mortellaro's murder was never solved.[287]

On April 12, 1931, undercover federal agent Lawrence L. "Baldy" Baldesareli was leaving the Mayflower Hotel at 17th and Grant in Denver when he was shot in the arm by both a

[287] *The Times,* Shreveport, Louisiana, March 18, 1932, p 16; *Mountain Mafia: Organized Crime in the Rockies* by Betty L. Alt, Sandra K. Wells, Cold Tree Press Nashville Tennessee, 2008, p 81.

revolver and shotgun. His injury resulted in a long stay in a Denver hospital because the slugs had been soaked in garlic water (a technique used by gangsters to make the bullets poisonous and prevent wounds from healing). Baldesareli had come to Denver under the supervision of U.S. Attorney Ralph Carr. The undercover agent had worked his way into the confidence of the well-organized gang of bootlegger-killers headed by Pete and Sam Carlino. Posing as a fight promoter, and later as a Chicago gunman, Baldesareli finally was accepted by the big shots of the mob and eventually was made the personal bodyguard of Sam Carlino. The agent was a constant companion of the Carlinos and gained detailed information on the gang's activities. After Baldesareli healed from the gunshot wounds, he supplied evidence that resulted in federal indictments against the gang for conspiracy to commit arson and several murders. Sam and Pete Carlino were never brought to justice due to their untimely and violent deaths, and others in the gang were either slain or sentenced to long prison terms. No one was ever charged in the shooting of Baldesareli.[288]

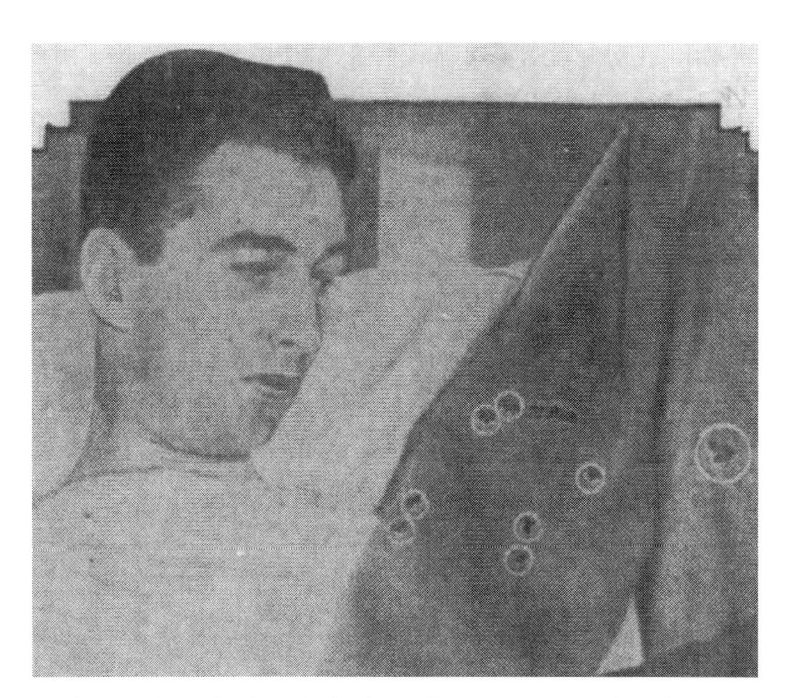

Lawrence L. "Baldy" Baldesareli in the hospital, photo from *The Journal and Courier*, Lafayette, Indiana, April 18, 1931

On June 19, 1931, Pete Carlino was captured near Pueblo and taken to jail in Denver for the arson of his own home. He was bailed out by gang boss Joe Roma. Pete's body was found

[288] *Trail of Shadows: The Unsolved Murders of Prohibition Agents Dale Kearney and Ray Sutton*, by Chuck Hornung and B. Lee Charlton, McFarland and Company, Jefferson, North Carolina, 2019, pp 158–160.

September 14, 1931, on a road near Pueblo. The top of his head was almost torn off by bullets. His murder was never solved.[289]

The murders of Pete and Sam Carlino left Joseph Roma as the organized crime leader in Denver and all of Colorado. Nicknamed "Little Caesar" or "Little Joe" due to his five-foot-one stature, Roma continued as crime boss until his murder on February 18, 1933. Roma referred to himself as a grocer because he ran a grocery store at 3420 Quivas street. Having acquired his position as "mob boss" through violence and murder, he was gunned down in his North Denver home after talking with some unidentified acquaintances. As they rose to leave, they riddled Roma with seven bullets, six of the shots to his head. His wife, Nettie, found him slumped in his favorite chair. Although there were good suspects, the Denver Police and DA Wettengel were never able to charge anyone with Roma's murder. His right-hand men, Clyde and Eugene Smaldone, succeeded him as crime leaders in Denver.[290]

Not all the violent crime in Denver during this period was due to organized crime. On May 24, 1932, Joseph A. Hayes shot and killed his 17-year-old girlfriend, Alta Lee Armstrong, of Rocky Ford, Colorado. Hayes, a former U.S. Marine, killed Armstrong after she refused to marry him. She had left Rocky Ford and gone to Denver to attend nursing school. Two days later Hayes followed Armstrong and shot her to death. After killing Armstrong, Hayes turned the weapon on himself. He shot himself in the jaw, but the wound was not fatal. While at the hospital Hayes confessed to homicide detectives, believing he was on his deathbed. Wettengel charged Hayes with first-degree murder. Future Denver DA Bert M. Keating was one of Hayes' defense attorneys. The jury found Hayes guilty of first-degree murder and he was sentenced to life in prison.[291]

Eleven Denver police officers were killed in the line of duty during the seven years Wettengel was district attorney; six in vehicle accidents and five by gunfire. Patrolman Thomas Durkin had served as a Denver police officer for more than 27 years and, at age 65, was preparing for retirement when he was struck by a vehicle and killed while on duty in January 1929.[292] In March of that same year, Patrolman Clarence Alston was shot and killed by two

[289] *Record Journal of Douglas County*, April 17, 1931.
[290] *Wray Gazette*, Volume 31, Number 9, February 23, 1933, p 2; *Smaldone The Untold Story of An American Crime Family*, by Dick Kreck Fulcrum Publishing, Golden, Colorado, 2009, pp 1–2.
[291] *Miami Daily News-Record* from Miami, Oklahoma, October 13, 1932, p 6; Record Journal of Douglas County, November 11, 1932, p 2.
[292] Officer Down Memorial Page, https://www.odmp.org/officer/4402-patrolman-thomas-j-durkin.

suspects when he was investigating suspicious activity in a vehicle at Colfax and Broadway.[293] One of the two suspects subsequently committed suicide. Two suspects shot Officer William Keating he had apprehended while they were attempting to burglarize a store. Both suspects were apprehended after the shooting and, upon their convictions by Wettengel, each was sentenced to 65 years in prison.[294] Detectives George Schneider and John Dea were both killed February 11, 1933.[295] The detectives were called to an auction house by the owner who suspected a person was trying to sell stolen tools. When the detectives were escorting the suspect to a back room to question him, he pulled out a gun and shot both Dea and Schneider, then went on a shooting rampage in the auction house, killing one patron and wounding two others. When the shooter got close to the wounded Dea, the detective shot and killed the suspect. Schneider died almost instantly from his wounds. Dea died after being transported to the hospital.

From left to right: Patrolmen Thomas Durkin, Clarence Alston, William Keating and Detectives George Schneider and John Dea, photos courtesy of the Denver Police Museum

Patrolman Thomas O'Connor died in March 1934 after being struck by a vehicle.[296] Patrolman John O'Donnell and Patrolman Clarence Fraker both died in an automobile accident in March 1934 while responding to a call,[297] and Patrolman Alson McCasland died in a motorcycle collision with a car at East 19th Avenue and Clarkson Streets.[298] Sixty-eight-year-old Robert Campbell was the second Denver police surgeon to die while on the job.[299] He too was killed in an on-duty vehicle accident. Detective Pasquale Marinaro was shot and killed trying to

---

[293] Officer Down Memorial Page, https://www.odmp.org/officer/1169-patrolman-clarence-w-alston.
[294] Officer Down Memorial Page, https://www.odmp.org/officer/7362-police-officer-william-c-keating.
[295] https://www.denverpolicemuseum.org/2018/08/22/detectives-george-schneider-and-john-dea/.
[296] Officer Down Memorial Page, https://www.odmp.org/officer/10106-patrolman-thomas-j-oconnor.
[297] Officer Down Memorial Page, https://www.odmp.org/officer/5063-patrolman-clarence-e-fraker.
[298] Officer Down Memorial Page, https://www.odmp.org/officer/8819-patrolman-alson-e-mccasland.
[299] Officer Down Memorial Page,https://www.odmp.org/officer/2727-police-surgeon-robert-m-campbell.

apprehend a murder suspect.[300] Before dying, Marinaro was able to return fire and wound the suspect who then killed himself as other officers were closing in.

From left to right: Patrolmen Thomas O'Connor, John O'Donnell, Clarence Fraker, Alson McCasland, Dr. Robert Campbell, and Detective Pasquale Marinaro, photos courtesy of the Denver Police Museum

After his public humiliation, Wettengel's private life also suffered. During the prosecution of his perjury case, Wettengel was stopped in Wakeeney, Kansas and arrested on a charge of driving while under the influence of liquor. His 24-year marriage to Lillie Holbrook also ended in 1939. Over the next decade, Wettengel dropped out of public life. He returned to the Denver courts in the 1950s, where his reputation as an expert litigator was resurrected.

When Wettengel died in 1965, the headline in the *Denver Post* was, "DA of Denver's 'Rough and Tumble' Days Dies at 76." Upon his death, Denver DA Bert Keating said, "Wettengel was one of the best trial attorneys I ever faced. He was DA when I started out as a lawyer. He was very able, very fair, and very helpful to young trial lawyers like myself."[301] Ray Humphries, Wettengel's chief investigator for eight years, was quoted in the same article as saying the former DA was a fair and decent man who would never ask his staff to do anything, he wouldn't do himself, and that Wettengel was often the first man in during DA-conducted criminal raids.[302]

---

300 Officer Down Memorial Page, https://www.odmp.org/officer/8550-detective-pasquale-c-marinaro.

301 *Denver Post*, January, 3, 1965, p 25.

302 *Denver Post*, January, 3, 1965, p 25.

20. John Albert Carroll (1937–1940)

JOHN A. CARROLL 1937–1940

John Albert Carroll was born in Denver on July 30, 1901. Carroll joined the Army at age 16 and served in both World Wars and, like his predecessor in the district attorney's office, served in the Philippines. Unlike Wettengel, however, Carroll had a long and distinguished political career. After the first military stint, his professional experience began as a Denver police officer walking a beat in the 1920s. While serving as a street officer, he attended Westminster Law School at night. In the 1930s he began his political career working on Senator Edward Costigan's successful reform campaign for U.S. Senate. Carroll also managed the 1932 gubernatorial campaign of Josephine Roche, the labor leader and businesswoman. Carroll headed the Denver Democratic Party in the early 1930s and was named an assistant U.S. attorney in 1932. In 1936 he was elected Denver DA.[303]

One of Carroll's most notable cases while district attorney was the indictment of members of the General Assembly for bribery after they accepted free liquor from the liquor lobby. In the 1937 session of the Colorado Legislature, liquor industry lobbyist Donald F. Clifford gave many of the legislators bottles of liquor to influence their votes on questions affecting liquor legislation. He had a delivery boy take receipts for the packages delivered. These receipts were discovered during another investigation, and they showed that more than half of the members of the two houses had accepted the liquor. Carroll not only indicted Clifford for bribing and attempting to bribe legislators, but he also indicted Senator Homer Preston, and Representatives Marion Strain, William Jennings, and Truman Hall for receiving liquor bribes from Clifford. The lobbyists' attorneys applied for and secured from the District Court a demurrer that quashed the indictments on the grounds that Clifford had been compelled to testify against himself while in the grand jury room. Carroll appealed the demurrer, and the Colorado Supreme Court reversed the District Court and sent the case back for trial. On March 7, 1940, Deputy DA Anthony Zarlengo notified District Judge Floyd Miles that some State witnesses were no longer available, and Judge Miles authorized dismissal of the cases.[304]

---

[303] *Rocky Mountain News*, September 1, 1983, p 10; https://bioguideretro.congress.gov/Home/MemberDetails?memIndex=C000189.
[304] *Steamboat Pilot*, June 9, 1938, p 2; *Steamboat Pilot*, November 23, 1939, p 2.

In another high-profile case, Anna Marie Hahn—aka the "Arsenic Anna or the Blonde Borgia"—came to Denver from Cincinnati via Chicago in July 1937 with her 11-year-old son Oscar and her traveling companion Johan Georg Obendoerfer.[305] Obendoerfer was the latest in a string of older gentlemen the young Hahn had befriended and romanced—and each had contracted a mysterious illness before dying. Hahn had lured numerous suitors to their deaths, profiting financially from her scheme. While the trio stayed at the Oxford Hotel on 17th Street, a hotel porter noticed Obendoerfer writhing on his bed and inquired about him. To avoid further scrutiny, Hahn moved them all to the Midland Hotel, at Arapahoe and 17th streets in Denver. She wrote a letter on Oxford Hotel letterhead to Obendoerfer's bank requesting that they send all his money to Colorado. The day the money showed up in Denver, Hahn fled to Colorado Springs, despite the staff at the Midland Hotel demanding that she take Obendoerfer to the hospital. Hahn had been feeding Obendoerfer watermelon to ease his dry throat and sprinkling what appeared to be salt on it from a shaker. It turned out the saltshaker was filled with arsenic—watermelon was a well-known method for feeding arsenic to rats. All her victims were given arsenic with a chaser of croton oil because the croton oil would scrub the arsenic from the stomach (and the oil was not tested for in a standard autopsy of the time). On August 1, 1937, Obendoerfer died in Colorado Springs and the next day Hahn and Oscar returned to Denver where she pawned two diamond rings she had stolen from a room in the hotel. Before Hahn left Colorado Springs, she checked Obendoerfer's wicker satchel in at the train depot. Inside were his clothes, a pipe, and a saltshaker containing 82% arsenic trioxide. Hahn and Oscar left Denver and caught a train back to Cincinnati arriving on August 9. The next day police were knocking at her door. Colorado Springs Detective Inspector Irvin B. Bruce sent a telegram to Cincinnati police, asking that Hahn be questioned for grand larceny. She was arrested for taking the two diamond rings, but Colorado Springs police also were curious about the body she had left in their city.

[305] *The Cincinnati Enquirer*, December 8, 1938, p 2.

Mug shot of Anna Marie Hahn, photo from Wikipedia

Under police questioning, Hahn's stories began to unravel, and Cincinnati police found connections between her and several bodies. Hahn was charged for these murders and at trial, the prosecution put a staggering ninety-five witnesses on the stand, while the only people who would vouch for Hahn were herself and Oscar. Even her husband, Philip, did not testify on her behalf. DA Carroll and his staff helped ensure the witnesses from Denver got to Cincinnati for the trial. The prosecutor, Dudley Miller Outcalt, in his closing argument said that Hahn was "the only one in God's world that had the heart for such murders." He argued to the jury that "she sits there with her Madonna face and her soft voice, but they hide a ruthless, passionless purpose the likes of which this state has never known." Hahn was convicted and sentenced to death. She was executed in Ohio's electric chair on December 7, 1938. All told, Hahn killed eight people and attempted to poison five more.[306]

[306] Diana Britt Franklin. 2006. *The Goodbye Door: The Incredible True Story of America's First Female Serial Killer to Die in the Chair Kent,* State University Press.

Cincinnati Prosecutor Dudley Miller Outcalt holding one of Hahn's saltshakers[307]

Four Denver police officers died in duty-related incidences during Carroll's four years in office. On March 8, 1937, Patrolman Forrest Sawyer was shot and killed by a man who called the police station and said he wanted to be arrested because he was a madman.[308] When Sawyer arrived at the suspect's home, the man opened fire and killed him. The suspect then killed himself. The following February, Patrolman Jacob Benner died from blood poisoning he had contracted after injuring his leg in a November 1937 raid on an illegal gambling den.[309] Denver Detective Fred Renovato was shot four times when he attempted to stop a man from assaulting his girlfriend.[310] The suspect was dragging his girlfriend by her hair when the detective intervened. After the shooting, the suspect was apprehended, convicted by Carroll's office and executed for his crime. Finally, Patrolman Earl Burns died on duty after falling down a flight of stairs in February 1939.[311]

---

[307] Photo from https://www.findagrave.com/memorial/150524628/dudley-miller-outcalt.
[308] Officer Down Memorial Page, https://www.odmp.org/officer/11797-patrolman-forrest-e-sawyer.
[309] Officer Down Memorial Page, https://www.odmp.org/officer/20383-patrolman-jacob-benner.
[310] Officer Down Memorial Page, https://www.odmp.org/officer/11181-detective-fred-renovato.
[311] Officer Down Memorial Page, https://www.odmp.org/officer/2554-patrolman-earl-f-burns.

Left to right: Patrolmen Forrest Sawyer, Jacob Benner, Earl Burns, and Detective Fred Renovato
Photos courtesy of the Denver Police Museum

After serving as DA, Carroll ran unsuccessfully for Colorado Governor in 1940 and then World War II interrupted his political career.[312] During the war, Carroll worked in military administration, serving as a major in Italy. He returned to politics after the war and successfully ran for a seat in the U.S. House of Representatives in 1946. After serving two terms in the House, he ran for U.S. Senate and lost. This was at the height of the McCarthy era and, as a progressive Democrat, Carroll was accused of being a communist by his opponent.

On April 11, 1951, President Harry Truman relieved General Douglas MacArthur of his command of the U.S. Armed Forces. MacArthur was extremely popular and the decision to relieve him was not. Former DA Carroll contacted the White House and offered to come to Washington to help Truman with members of Congress concerning the MacArthur issue. Truman knew he could face a storm of opposition for firing the popular general and needed to get the facts to his supporters in Congress and the nation. Carroll was a former congressman, well known, and came highly recommended. Truman accepted Carroll's offer and things went so well that after a month, Truman made him a permanent member of the White House staff. Carroll served as Truman's administrative assistant and as a foreign policy adviser until the end of 1952.[313]

---

[312] *Rocky Mountain News*, September 1, 1983, p 10;
https://bioguideretro.congress.gov/Home/MemberDetails?memIndex=C000189.
[313] John A. Carroll Papers 1915–1982 Special Collections & Archives, University Libraries - Norlin Library,

Carroll again ran for Senate in 1954 and was again smeared as a communist and a Catholic. The oil and gas industry also opposed his candidacy based on Carroll's opposition to the oil depletion allowance and his support of government control of offshore oil drilling. He lost his second Senate bid to Gordon Allott. One Allott tactic was to "waive the red banner" and frighten voters regarding the communist takeover of the country. His newspaper ads asked voters to send a "real American" to the Senate to join the crusade to drive out communism and corruption.[314] The third time was a charm for Carroll, and he won the Senate race in 1956 by beating former Governor Dan Thornton. True to his liberal reputation, one of the first bills the freshman senator introduced was a call for federal voting rights for Blacks.

Carroll served only one Senate term. He was defeated in 1962 by Peter Dominick. After his Senate career, Carroll returned to private law practice in Denver. He died at the age of 81 in 1982.[315]

University of Colorado. Extensions of Remarks in the U.S. House of Representatives, Remarks of Patricia Schroder, September 12, 1983, p 23763.

[314] Extensions of Remarks in the U.S. House of Representatives, Remarks of Patricia Schroder, September 12, 1983, p 23762.

[315] *Rocky Mountain News*, September 1, 1983, p 10, https://bioguideretro.congress.gov/Home/MemberDetails?memIndex=C000189.

21. James T. Burke (1941–1948)

JAMES T. BURKE
1941–1948

In 1940, James Burke defeated O. Otto Moore (a fellow Denver deputy district attorney) for district attorney, an office he would hold for eight years.[316] Born in Minneapolis in 1898, Burke served in WWI as an infantry sergeant and was wounded in France. He earned his law degree at Westminster Law School in 1926 and ran a private practice prior to joining the district attorney's office in 1929.

Burke was district attorney when a Denver grand jury indicted 10 Denver police officers on criminal charges. These indictments were the tip of a much larger culture of crime rampant within the department. It would be up to the next district attorney to expose the full extent of the corruption, however.

An interesting case during Burke's tenure was that of Theodore Coneys. In 1941, Coneys, a middle-aged drifter, broke into the westside Denver home of an acquaintance named Philip Peters. In the ceiling of a closet, Coneys found a small trapdoor that led to an attic where he decided to stay after stealing food. He remained in the home undetected for weeks until October 17, when Peters discovered him at the refrigerator. Panicking, Coneys bludgeoned the 73-year-old Peters to death and returned to the attic. Peters' body was discovered later that day, but police found no signs of forced entry. They noted the trapdoor in their search of the home but thought that it was too small for any adult to crawl through. Coneys remained in the house undetected, even after Peters' wife returned to the house from a hospital convalescence. A few months later, after complaining the house was haunted because of the noises she heard, she moved to live with an adult son on the Western Slope. Coneys stayed in the vacant home until being discovered on July 30, 1942, while police were making a routine check on the house. Running upstairs, police caught sight of Coneys' legs as he was going into the attic. Once in custody, he confessed to the crime. Newspapers dubbed him the "Denver Spider Man." Burke charged Coneys with Peters' murder; he was convicted and sentenced to life imprisonment

[316] State of Colorado, Abstract of Votes Cast in 1940, compiled by Walter Morrison, Secretary of State 1940, p 22.

where he died.[317] An episode of CSI: Las Vegas ("Stalker") as well as a Simpsons' episode ("The Ziff Who Came to Dinner") appear to have been inspired by the "Spider Man" case.

Left: Coneys' mug shot; right: the attic where Coneys resided for months[318]

In February of 1943, Theodore Meyers, his brother Emmett, and M. E. Dunston went on a weeks-long robbery spree in both Denver and Adams County. The trio was responsible for 28 robberies, during which they used a fake patrol car to pull over motorists to beat and rob them. They became known as Denver's elusive "squad car thugs" or the "road terrors," and the Denver Police along with Adams County Sheriffs conducted a massive manhunt to catch the bandits. The robbers were always armed with guns, wore masks, swore profusely, and threatened or beat the victims out of their money. Then they made the mistake of attempting to rob a car full of detectives north of the Denver airfield. The police exchanged gunfire with the robbers and Emmett Meyers was killed. Burke charged Dunston and Theodore Meyers with multiple counts of aggravated robbery. They pleaded guilty and were sentenced to fifteen to 20 years each at hard labor in the state penitentiary.[319]

On July 3, 1943, *The Denver Star*—the newspaper that served the African American community in Colorado, Wyoming, Montana, Utah, and New Mexico—criticized Burke's refusal to file charges against a Denver restaurant owner for violating Colorado's public accommodations law. Black World War I veteran John Oliver was told by the restaurant owner that he would not be served in the dining room and would have to go to the restaurant's kitchen to be served. When the situation was brought to Burke's attention, he advised Oliver's attorney

---

[317] *Rocky Mountain News*, September 20, 1992, p 4M; *Rocky Mountain News*, September 12, 1999, p 19D; https://en.wikipedia.org/wiki/Theodore_Edward_Coneys.

[318] Photo from Metaweb/GNU Free Documentation License

[319] *The Gaffney Ledger*, March 30, 1943, p 5.

that because the statute afforded his client a choice of civil or criminal remedies, Burke felt no obligation to bring criminal charges against the restaurant owner. *The Star* condemned Burke for condoning a "Jim Crow policy."[320]

In 1944 Burke ran for reelection against Ralph J. Cummings, who was Earl Wettengel's assistant. Burke focused the voters on his experience, his scandal-free administration, and his experience as a World War I veteran. When he won reelection, Burke became only the third district attorney in Denver's history to secure a second term.

Burke reelection flyer, photo in the public domain

On April 25, 1944, investigators for the district attorney's office followed up on an anonymous telephone call at Denver's Cosmopolitan Hotel. In one of the hotel rooms, they found Gertrude Martin suffering from the effects of an illegal abortion. Dr. Julius A. Wolf,

---

[320] *The Denver Star*, July 20, 1940, p 3; *The Denver Star*, July 3, 1943, p 1.

whose office was in the Republic Plaza building in Denver, was arrested and charged by Burke in two different cases with conspiracy to commit illegal abortions. In both trials, the principal evidence against Wolf were his daybooks, which were seized without a search warrant. Based on those daybooks, prosecutors found other patients whom Wolf had aided in securing abortions. The juries in both cases found Wolf guilty and he was sentenced to prison. Wolf appealed his conviction all the way to the U.S. Supreme Court, arguing that the daybooks should have been suppressed. The Supreme Court refused to expand the "exclusionary rule," requiring the suppression of unconstitutionally obtained evidence, to the states.[321]

Meanwhile, author Jack Kerouac's friend Neal Cassady's "on the road" experiences began in Denver behind the wheel of stolen cars. Between the ages of 14 and 21, Cassady stole some five hundred cars, was arrested 10 times, and convicted six times. As a result of the convictions, Cassady spent 15 months in reform schools. When he was not in custody, he was "joy-riding" in stolen cars through the streets of Denver. In June of 1944, DA Burke charged Cassady with receiving stolen property when he was arrested in possession of a stolen car. He was convicted and served 11 months of a one-year prison sentence. After Cassady's release, he became friends with Jack Kerouac, and their series of cross-country adventures became the subject of Kerouac's book, *On the Road*, published in 1957. Cassady later met author Ken Kesey and embarked upon a new series of road adventures, joining Kesey's psychedelic troupe "The Merry Pranksters."[322]

---

[321] Wolf v. Colorado, 338 U.S. 25 (1949)

[322] "Wild in Denver: Neal Cassady's Teen Years." http://teenagefilm.com/archives/freak-party/wild-in-denver-neal-cassadys-teen-years/%20.

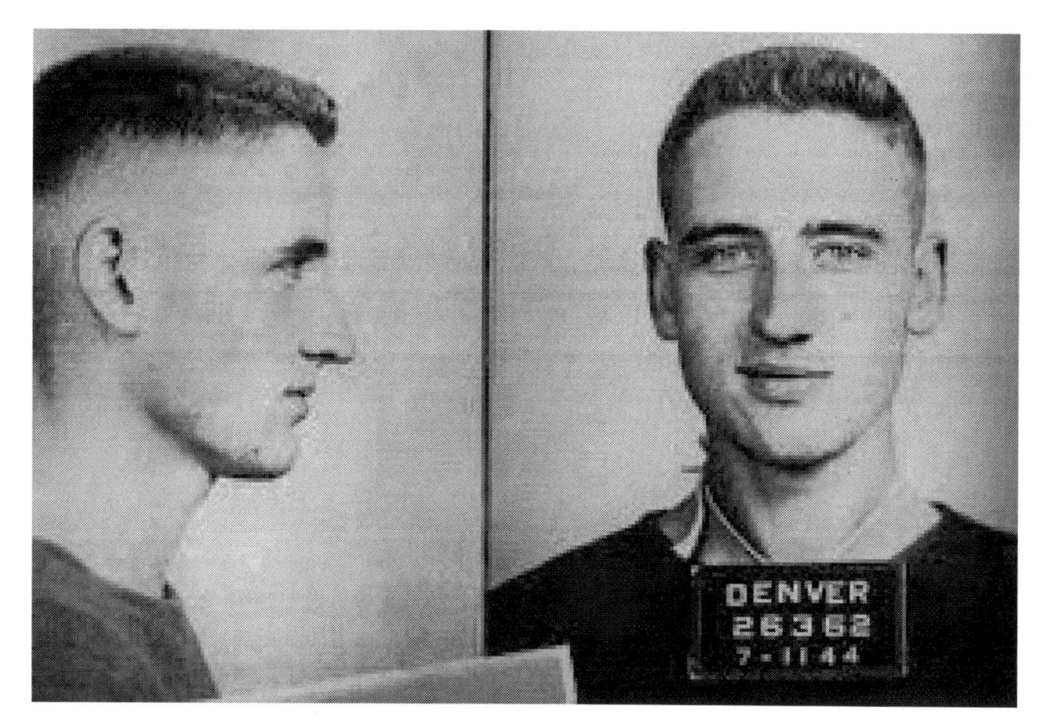

Mug shot of Neal Cassady, courtesy of the Denver Police Department

A darker case was that of Harvey Glatman, "The Glamour Girl Killer," who had a long life of violent crime. On May 4, 1945, Glatman, a senior at Denver East High School, bound, gagged, raped, and robbed three women in Denver's Capitol Hill neighborhood. Burke charged Glatman with the series of crimes. On July 15, 1945, while on bond in the Denver case, Glatman bound, gagged, raped, and robbed a woman in Boulder. He was subsequently charged with those crimes in Boulder. Glatman was committed to the Colorado Psychopathic Hospital for evaluation. On September 27, 1945, while out of the hospital and out on bond from both the Denver and Boulder cases, Glatman again bound, gagged, raped, and robbed two women in Denver's Park Hill neighborhood. He raped yet another Denver woman, who screamed and ran out of her house, resulting in Glatman's capture. Burke charged Glatman with the new assaults. Glatman pleaded guilty in Denver and was sentenced to one to five years in prison. Upon his release, Glatman moved to New York City, where he committed several more robberies and assaults on women. He was sentenced to Sing Sing prison for five years. Upon his release, he returned to Denver, and then moved to California where, between August 1957 and July 1958, he murdered three women: Judy Ann Dull, Shirley Ann Bridgeford, and Ruth Mercado. After his capture and conviction for murder, Glatman was sentenced to death. On September 18, 1959, he was executed at San Quentin.[323]

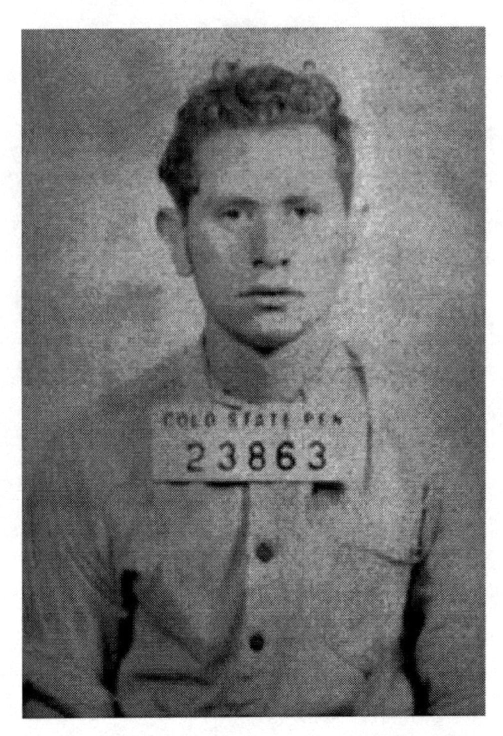

Harvey Glatman, "The Glamour Girl Killer," Colorado State Penitentiary mug shot

The only police officer to die on duty during Burke's tenure, Patrolman Virgil Hall was shot and killed after he and his partner, Robert LaVernway, stopped a vehicle that had just been stolen. The two suspects took off running and the officers split up to chase the thieves. LaVernway heard Hall's shotgun fire and when he went to investigate, he found both Hall and the suspect wounded. Hall died the next day. The suspect recovered, was convicted of murder, and sentenced to life.[324]

---

[323] Harvey Glatman. "Glamour Girl Slayer." Information researched and summarized by Heather Martin, Jeremy Bower, Tabatha Dobbins, Jacqueline Parker, Amanda Peacock, Martha Phillips, and Lauren Przepiora. Department of Psychology Radford University Radford, VA 24142-6946, https://web.archive.org/web/20180613201840/http://maamodt.asp.radford.edu/Psyc%20405/serial%20killers/Glatman,%20Harvey.pdf; *The Los Angeles Times*, 1959.

[324] Officer Down Memorial Page, https://www.odmp.org/officer/5946-patrolman-virgil-m-hall.

Patrolman Virgil Hall, photo courtesy of the Denver Police Museum

In a case presaging the Denver Police scandal to follow, Burke used the grand jury to indict three Denver Police officers in 1946; one for theft, one for obtaining money through false pretenses, and one for assaulting two Latinos with his night stick. Burke criticized Mayor Stapleton and the Denver Police Chief for "doing nothing to weed misfits out of the police department." Burke argued that "the policemen committed crimes ranging from murder to petty theft," and Stapleton did nothing about this behavior.[325]

Also in 1946, a fatal bar shooting took place in the famous Brown Palace Hotel in Denver. Dr. James K. Mullen was shot to death in the "Ship's Tavern" of the Brown Palace on October 1, 1946, by Ronald F. Smith. Smith, an ex-Marine and former Grand Junction police officer, fired at least four shots around the bar. He hit and wounded two other patrons. Smith was subdued after the shooting by a blow to the head with a bottle. Burke charged Smith with first-degree murder and assault to commit murder. The defense pleaded insanity, but the jury found Smith guilty on all counts and he was sentenced to life in prison.[326]

The following year saw the kidnapping and murder of a gas station attendant. Gas stations at this time handled large amounts of cash, making them vulnerable to robbery, and station attendants were frequent victims of violence. On September 20, 1947, Paul J. Schneider kidnapped Frank J. Ford from his service station on Brighton Boulevard in Denver. Schneider took a considerable sum of cash and checks and then abducted Ford. Schneider took Ford, who ~~was often locked in the trunk~~ of the car, more than one hundred miles out of Denver before

[325] *Enduring Legacies* by Arturo J. Aldama, Elisa Facio, Daryl Maeda, and Reiland Rabaka. University Press of Colorado, 2011.
[326] *Steamboat Pilot*, April 3, 1947, p 3.

killing him. A month later Schneider was arrested in Kentucky trying to cash a check known to have been in Ford's possession. Schneider confessed to killing three men over a period of 18 days, including two Detroit, Michigan filling station attendants, Donald Dusseau and James R. Hall. Based on Schneider's confession, Ford's body was discovered on October 24, 1947, 14 miles northeast of Brush, Colorado on Highway 6. He had been beaten with a tire iron and shot to death. Although the robbery and kidnapping were committed in Denver, it was determined that Ford was killed in Washington County, making it mandatory that the trial be held in Akron. Prosecutors in Michigan agreed to allow Schneider to be tried in Colorado first. The DA in Brush, Colorado filed first-degree murder charges against Schneider, who pleaded not guilty by reason of insanity but was convicted of first-degree murder and sentenced to death. On September 16, 1949, Schneider was executed for the murder of Ford. Approximately fifty people crowded around the gas chamber to watch his final moments.[327]

Late in his second term, Burke ran afoul of the popular reform mayor J. Quigg Newton. Burke's office sought medical records on a victim of a fatal traffic accident. When the newly appointed director of Denver General Hospital refused to turn over the records without a written authorization, Burke threatened to have him jailed. The mayor accused the district attorney of bullying, and the newspapers quoted Burke as yelling at the hospital administrator, "I am the district attorney" when demanding the records. Of the incident, Mayor Newton said, "The district attorney acted in an arbitrary manner. Instead of sitting down and discussing the matter sensibly, he threatened to throw my director of hospitals in jail."[328]

After leaving the district attorney's office, Burke returned to private practice and was active in local veteran's groups. In 1949, he volunteered to represent Joe Sam Walker on murder charges in Boulder, Colorado. Burke agreed to take the case out of concern for "fair play and justice." Walker was charged with the rape and murder of Theresa Catherine Foster, a first-year student at the University of Colorado, on November 9, 1948. The slaying touched off Boulder's most extensive murder investigation until the JonBenét Ramsey case, culminating in Walker being charged with first-degree murder. The *Denver Post* injected itself into all aspects of the case, including the investigatory process. Throughout the pretrial period and the trial, the *Post* distorted evidence, presented speculation as fact and dubious detective work as infallible, and

[327] *Brush News-Tribune*, Volume 53, Number 43, October 23, 1947, p 1; *Brush News-Tribune*, Volume 54, Number 4, January 22, 1948, p 1.
[328] Rocky Mountain News, October 17, 1947

described events that never happened, all to boost newspaper sales. Walker was tried and convicted of second-degree murder and sentenced to 80-years-to-life in prison. In 1969, the Colorado Supreme Court reversed Walker's conviction concluding that the *Post's* reporting was so prejudicial that it prevented Walker from receiving a fair trial. The Boulder district attorney chose not to try Walker again and he was released. A month later, Walker hanged himself.[329]

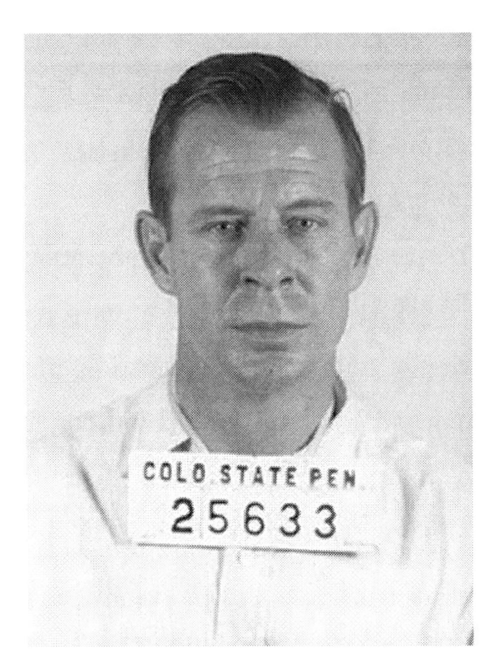

Joe Sam Walker, photo courtesy of the Colorado State Penitentiary

After an unsuccessful bid for a Denver county judgeship in 1952, Burke returned to his hometown of Minneapolis in 1955. That same year he founded the Wild Rice Run, a nature preserve of several hundred acres along the Willow River and Shovel Lake in Swatara, Minnesota. Burke died in Minnesota in 1961.

22. Bert Keating (1948–1967)

Bert M. Keating was the longest-serving district attorney in Denver's history; he served more than 18 years in the era before term limits for Colorado

[329] *Steamboat Pilot*, April 28, 1949, p 2; *Golden Transcript*, Volume 103, Number 174, September 23, 1969, p 1; *Someone's Daughter: In Search of Justice for Jane Doe* by Silvia Pettem, Taylor Trade Publishing, 2009, p 150.

district attorneys; he died in office during his fourth elected term. Keating was born June 1, 1904, in Chicago, Illinois. His father managed a chain of restaurants and the family moved frequently. In 1911 they came to Colorado and Keating remained there for the rest of his life. He attended high school in Denver, the University of Denver, and law school at Westminster Law School. Keating's son, Robert, served as a Denver city council member in the mid-1960s. In 1951, Keating founded the National District Attorney's Association (NDAA) and headed the organization. Presenting a posthumous award, the president of the NDAA stated that the honor was given to Denver's longtime DA for making "the greatest contribution to law enforcement and good government" in his community.[330]

Keating was active in Denver and Colorado Democratic politics for many years before his service as district attorney. In 1932 he was elected to the Colorado legislature and reelected in 1934. In 1936, he began his first of four successive terms on the Denver Election Commission. To remain in that office, Keating would resign two months before the end of each term, thus circumventing a Denver charter rule prohibiting a commissioner from succeeding himself. He was elected district attorney in 1948 and served until 1967. Like several Denver DAs before and after him, Keating ran for Denver mayor, losing by only 820 votes to Will Nicholson in 1955. In addition to gaining a reputation as a tough prosecutor, Keating became known for innovative juvenile justice initiatives, for prosecuting deadbeat fathers who owed child support, and for cracking down on check forgers. He worked nationally to get Congress to adopt reciprocal nonsupport laws enabling states to extradite non-supporting parents across borders.

Keating was known for his quick wit. When defense attorney Sol Cohen teased Keating, asking, "When are you ever going to win a case?" Keating responded, "When you are on the other side."[331] Keating was also known for smoking Pall Mall cigarettes all his life, and in 1954 smoking nearly killed him. While driving in the foothills west of Denver, he dropped his cigarette. When he reached down to retrieve it, he drove off the road and was thrown from his car and pinned under it for an hour. Keating was hospitalized and nearly died from his injuries. He recovered but still succumbed to cigarettes when he contracted lung cancer in 1967.

---

[330] *Six of the Greatest: A Tribute to Outstanding Lawyers in Colorado History: Bert M. Keating* by Theodore A. Borrillo and Zeke Scher Colorado Lawyer July 1992.
[331] *Six of the Greatest: A Tribute to Outstanding Lawyers in Colorado History: Bert M. Keating* by Theodore A. Borrillo and Zeke Scher Colorado Lawyer July 1992.

A later Denver district attorney, Dale Tooley, became known for pioneering ethnic and gender diversity in the Denver district attorney's office, but years earlier Bert Keating's staff represented a cross-section of the Denver community, including Italian, Irish, Greek, Jewish, Black, Hispanic, and women attorneys. Keating hired Orrelle R. Weeks and Dorothy Binder, both of whom went on to distinguished judicial careers. Binder was the first female deputy district attorney in the history of Colorado; she handled parental desertion and nonsupport cases from 1958 to 1963. Keating also hired Black attorneys James Flanigan and Gilbert Alexander, and Hispanic attorneys John Sanchez and Donald Pacheco, all of whom became Denver judges. James Flanigan was the first African American in Denver to be a deputy district attorney.[332] Flanigan left the district attorney's office in 1957 to become a Denver Municipal Court judge, the first African American judge in Denver history and perhaps the first African American judge in the state. He subsequently served as a Denver County Court judge, and in 1964 he became the first African American elected as a Denver District Court judge. In 2010, the new Lindsey-Flanigan Courthouse in Denver was named for Flanigan and Judge Benjamin Barr Lindsey.[333]

Keating's office was also ahead of its time in how they dealt with crimes against the gay community. In 1951, a group of young men attacked and robbed three young men who were in Cheesman Park after hours. Denver police rounded up the assailants based upon physical appearance and questioned them. After their arrest, the assailants told the officers the victims attempted to pick them up, and that so angered the defendants that they vented their anger by attacking the three young men. They also robbed them, believing there was no chance the victims would complain to police. However, the men did file complaints and Denver Police followed through with arrests. The willingness of the Denver police to arrest and DA Keating to prosecute assaults on gay men indicated a level of tolerance among the police force and prosecutor's office that was rare at that time in the United States. The young assailants in the park attack were prosecuted in Juvenile Court.

As district attorney, Keating oversaw the prosecution of two monumental cases that drew national and international attention: that of John Gilbert Graham, who blew up a United Airlines

---

[332] *Six of the Greatest: A Tribute to Outstanding Lawyers in Colorado History: Bert M. Keating* by Theodore A. Borrillo and Zeke Scher Colorado Lawyer July 1992.

[333]https://www.waymarking.com/waymarks/WMAHB5_Denver_Justice_Center_Lindsey_Flanigan_Courthouse_Denver_CO.

plane over Longmont, Colorado, and the infamous Denver police burglary scandal of the early 1960s.

Keating personally prosecuted John "Jack" Gilbert Graham, a case now largely forgotten but one of the most sensational criminal cases in Colorado's history. On November 1, 1955, Graham planted a homemade bomb in his mother's luggage. The bomb exploded minutes after United Airlines Flight 629 carrying his mother, Daisie King, and 43 other passengers and crew took off. All aboard died when the plane crashed in Longmont. Graham had planned on the plane exploding over the mountains where the wreckage would have been more difficult to recover, but a flight delay kept the plane on the ground longer than the murderer calculated. Graham's was the first airplane bombing in U.S. history. At the time of the bombing, there was no federal crime covering Graham's actions, therefore Keating had to charge Graham in state court. Keating chose to charge Graham with only one murder, that of his mother, even though 43 other people died by Graham's actions. On July 14, 1956, President Dwight D. Eisenhower signed the Airline Sabotage Bill into law in response to the Graham case. The bill allowed for the death penalty for anyone who was convicted of causing the loss of life by damaging an airplane.

Graham had been an underachiever. He was bright yet had accomplished little at the time of this crime. He had one prior run-in with the law in 1951 when he was arrested and convicted of forging $4,200 in bad checks. The bombing occurred as Graham's mother was on her way to visit her daughter in Anchorage, Alaska. Graham ultimately confessed to the killings but nevertheless the case went to trial. The pressures on Keating and his office were huge. Thousands of phone calls and letters from all over the world poured into the office. The district attorney's office received support and advice from the FBI under legendary J. Edgar Hoover, the Justice Department, and the U.S. Attorney's Office. National and international press covered the trial. The case was televised; this was the first time that television broadcasted a criminal trial in the United States.

Left: Graham being brought into court, photo courtesy of Prelinger Archives; Right: United Airlines Flight 629's tail was discovered on this Weld County farm – see lower right, photo courtesy of FBI.

The investigation into the bombing revealed that Graham's motive for the mass murder was to kill his mother and obtain a large life insurance payout. After planting the bomb in his mother's luggage, Graham took out $37,000 in flight insurance on her. Investigators determined that this was probably not the first time Graham had used an explosion to collection an insurance policy. In May 1955, Graham opened the Crown-A Drive-In that his mother had built for him to manage at 581 South Federal Boulevard in Denver. Shortly thereafter the restaurant was severely damaged in an explosion that appeared to be arson. Graham had insured the restaurant and then collected on the insurance following the mysterious blast. Although Graham was never prosecuted for the arson of the Crown-A Drive-In, evidence of the incident was allowed in the bombing trial.

On February 10, 1956, while he was awaiting trial, Graham attempted suicide in his jail cell. He fashioned a crude garrote by tying a pair of socks together and using a cardboard toilet roll to tighten the garrote and hold it tight with the knots in the socks on the pressure points of his neck. Jail guard James Martin discovered Graham unconscious but still alive and saved Graham's life. When word got out in the newspapers that Martin had saved Graham's life, however, the guard had to disconnect his home telephone because of the number of harassing calls he received from angry callers that thought he should have let Graham die.

Keating was meticulous. He collected all the recoverable portions of the wrecked plane and transported to Denver, where they were separately stored and securely guarded. He had Dr. J. William Magee, Assistant Chief of Physicists at the Chemistry Division of the FBI Laboratory in Washington, D.C., testify that the foreign substance adhering to the exhibits resulted from the explosion of dynamite manufactured by the DuPont Company. Dr. Magee identified part of a six-volt Eveready Hot Shot battery in the wreckage. Only dry cell batteries were used in United Airlines planes as part of emergency equipment, and they were one-and-a-half-volt single dry cell batteries. Joseph T. Grande testified that he sold Graham the timer that Graham used to set off the blasting caps and the 25 sticks of dynamite he placed in his mother's luggage. Keating had a six-foot model of United Airlines DC-6B Mainliner built by Douglas Aircraft Company at a cost of $1,200. The top of the model lifted off so jurors could investigate the passenger compartment and the cargo pit where the suitcase bomb was placed. Keating and his trial team used the model throughout the trial with various witnesses to demonstrate different aspects of their testimony.

The wreckage of the plane was carefully laid out in a Denver warehouse, helping investigators solve the case, photo from FBI website "Famous Cases and Criminals": https://www.fbi.gov/history/famous-cases/jack-gilbert-graham

During the trial, Keating offered two live sticks of dynamite into evidence. The courtroom became tensely quiet as Keating showed FBI explosives expert, J. William Magee, the sticks of dynamite. When Magee asked if he could offer a word of caution there was "nervous laughter" from the trial spectators. The judge asked, "Then this is not explosive?" and Magee answered, "Oh, yes it is." Assistant DA Max D. Melville responded from counsel table, "It shouldn't be thrown on the floor." The judge cautiously admitted the dynamite into evidence.

Dr. Earl J. Miller was called to testify because he had identified Daisie King's body after it was pulled from the wreckage of the airliner. Miller was a friend of King and had dined with her the night before the fatal flight.

The forensic evidence along with Graham's confession led to his conviction for first-degree murder, and he was sentenced to death. A man named LeRoy Leick shared death row with Graham. In 1953, Leick had murdered his wife to collect on a $7,000 insurance policy, a crime not unlike Graham's. Both murderers died in the gas chamber in Cañon City—Graham on January 11, 1957, less than a year after his conviction, and Leick on January 22, 1960. Graham's last words summed up his attitude: "As far as feeling remorse for these people, I don't. I can't help it. Everybody pays their way and takes their chances. That's just the way it goes."[334]

Six Denver police officers died in the course of duty during DA Keating's almost 19 years in office. Patrolman William Claassen was shot and killed as he and his partner were investigating a burglary-in-progress at a local pharmacy. When they entered the pharmacy, the suspect opened fire. Both Claassen and his partner were able to return fire and kill the suspect.[335] Patrolman Donald Seick was killed January 12, 1958, when he attempted to question a man at a service station. Seick was off duty at the time, but he had previous contact with the suspect and suspected that he had just robbed the business. As Seick intercepted the man, the suspect shot Seick in the chest with a gun hidden in his jacket pocket. The suspect was apprehended a few days later. After being convicted by Keating, he was sentenced to life. He was paroled in 1974.

---

[334] Scrapbook of various articles regarding the Graham case in possession of the Denver district attorney's office.

[335] Officer Down Memorial Page, https://www.odmp.org/officer/3076-patrolman-william-allen-claassen, https://www.odmp.org/officer/12009-patrolman-donald-l-seick.

Patrolmen William Claassen (left) and Donald Seick (right), photos courtesy of the Denver Police Museum

In the history of the Denver Police Department, two Denver officers died in the line of duty from inadvertent gunfire; one of those occurred during Keating's tenure. Patrolman Edward Smerdel was killed at the police substation while cleaning his weapon. He had been with the department for 12 years.[336]

Patrolman Edward Smerdel, photo courtesy of the Denver Police Museum

Two other Denver officers were killed by criminal gunfire in 1962. Detective Darrell Suer died March 11, 1962. He was off duty when three armed men entered the restaurant where Suer and his wife were dining. When the men pulled guns and attempted to rob the restaurant, Detective Suer engaged the criminals. In the ensuing gun battle, Suer and one of the suspects died. Four suspects were arrested the following day and two received life sentences.[337]

[336] Officer Down Memorial Page, https://www.odmp.org/officer/21452-patrolman-edward-h-smerdel.

Patrolman Carl Knobbe was killed in 1962 when he stopped a stolen car. As he was approaching the vehicle, the suspect opened the door and shot the officer. The suspect was convicted by Keating and sentenced to death. His sentence was later commuted to life, but he was shot and killed in a prison escape attempt.[338] In a similar case, patrol officer Paul Lewis Major died after he and his partner stopped a stolen vehicle on January 20, 1965. While chasing one of the suspects, Major was shot in the chest and head. The suspect was caught, convicted, and sentenced to life.

Detective Darrell Suer (left) and Patrolman Carl Knobbe (right), photos courtesy of the Denver Police Museum

In a surprising incident on December 24, 1954, patrol officer John Ford, Jr. was arrested for breaking into the Pink Lady, a stripper bar at 519 18th Street earlier that year. After his arrest, Ford admitted to a dozen burglaries he had committed since he joined the force in 1952. Keating charged Ford with second-degree burglary. He was convicted and sentenced to prison for one to five years.[339]

---

[337] Officer Down Memorial Page, https://www.odmp.org/officer/12960-detective-darrell-j-suer.
[338] Officer Down Memorial Page, https://www.odmp.org/officer/7640-patrolman-carl-b-knobbe.
[339] *Greeley Tribune*, January 20, 1956, p 7.

The Pink Lady Bar and Grill, photo courtesy of "Save the Signs" Facebook post

In a similar case, On December 20, 1959, Denver Police Patrolmen Bobbie G. Whaley, George Zellner, and Keith Hutton broke into the Flaming Pit Restaurant in Denver, busted into the safe, and stole $3,425 in cash. Keating charged the three patrol officers along with Officer Harold Bailey, who pleaded no contest to similar charges in the case and testified for the prosecution. The three men were convicted and sentenced to six to 20 years in the state penitentiary.[340]

These incidents involving police officers were only the beginning. During Keating's tenure, the Denver Police Department suffered it darkest days. During this time, approximately 050 Denver police officers were found to be involved in criminal activity or actively covering up crimes of fellow officers. Denver police officers burglarized businesses while other officers functioned as lookouts. Officers also burglarized businesses in Arapahoe and Adams County. Keating himself did not escape criticism. When the first Denver officer, Arthur Winstanley, was arrested, Keating convened the grand jury to look at official corruption. Though many observers felt that there was considerable evidence indicating otherwise, this grand jury returned no indictments against any Denver officers. (It did indict one Arapahoe County deputy sheriff.) Not until Winstanley was arrested by Aurora police officers for another burglary did the full extent of the scandal come to light. Winstanley made a deal and implicated several other Denver officers, and then the dominoes began to fall. At the end of three years of investigations, grand juries, and trials, 43 Denver officers pleaded guilty or no contest to criminal charges; six were acquitted at

[340] *Denver Post*, December 26, 1961.

trial. Many others quit the department either in disgust or out of fear for their own safety. In addition to Denver cops and an Arapahoe County deputy sheriff, the Adams County Sheriff, the highest-ranking police official in that county, was arrested and convicted of conspiracy.[341]

One of the police cases prosecuted by Keating occurred in 1960 when Denver police burglars broke into the Gano-Downs store on 16th and Stout streets in downtown Denver. Gano-Downs was a high-end clothing store that had a safe holding a reported $22,000. The burglars/cops removed the entire safe. After receiving a tip in October of 1961, the safe was recovered in more than 30 feet of water at the bottom of a mine shaft outside Central City, Colorado. The revelation that the perpetrators had been Denver police officers became known only after the burglary ring was uncovered.[342]

As the story unraveled of how almost 20% of the Denver Police Department was involved in one way or another in the burglary ring, it was investigative reporter Bill Gagnon from radio station KTLN who relentlessly kept the investigation in the public eye. Denver Mayor Richard Batterton and Manager of Safety John Schooley continually said, "It's just a few bad apples and we have caught them,"[343] but it was the crew at KTLN that would not let the mayor or the manager of safety sweep the growing scandal under the rug. Staff at the radio station received anonymous death threats because they continued to editorialize about the crimes and corruption; honest Denver police officers fed the team at KTLN the names of the bad cops and what they were doing. Getting this information out to the public played a significant role in Keating finally being able to prosecute the cops involved in the ring.[344]

---

[341] *Crime Buff's Guide to the Outlaw Rockies*, by Ron Franscell, Morris Book Publishing, 2011, pp 25–26.
[342] *Burglars in Blue*, by Art Winstanley, Author House, 2009, p 55.
[343] Madison Wisconsin State Journal, October 29, 1961, p 12.
[344] https://fadedsignals.com/post/101971224871/ktln-am-signed-on-from-denver-in-1948-at-990-khz.

Investigative reporter Bill Gagnon, photos from the KTLN/KTLK memory page
http://denverradio.tripod.com/ktlk.html

The other key player in bringing the burglary ring to light was Denver District Court judge George McNamara. In 1961, Judge McNamara inspired bad cops to talk to investigators when he sentenced one of the first police defendants to 30 years in prison for his part in the safe-cracking ring. At sentencing, Judge McNamara said, "It's an intolerable situation when a policeman hides behind his badge to commit a felony." Investigators credited the stiff sentence with getting others to talk about making deals and who else was involved.[345]

During the police burglary scandal, Keating used the testimony of fellow officers who had already been convicted and sentenced to win convictions against other officers. Keating referred to these officers as his "singing thieves." Jokes about the scandal began to be told around the city. One such joke involved a woman calling the police to report a burglar in her basement, being told to get his badge number and they would arrest him the next day at roll call. Another joke involved the kids of Denver playing "cops and cops" instead of "cops and robbers." The scandal was national news for months. Morale for the honest officers on the force was abysmal.

Keating's office prosecuted Denver police officers in other incidents as well. On December 20, 1950, Denver police officer Delmar Reed shot and killed 15-year-old Charles H. Wilson, who had escaped from custody after being arrested for drunkenness. Keating charged Reed with first-degree murder. Reed was represented by Fred E. Dickerson, a prominent defense attorney, and his law partner, former U.S. Attorney Tom Morrissey (grandfather of recent DA Mitch Morrissey, coauthor of this book). There was a significant amount of interest in the case

[345] *Burglars in Blue,* by Art Winstanley, Author House, 2009, p 136–137; *Denver Post*, December 26, 1961.

because Wilson was Black. At trial, Reed contended that he fired accidently when he shot and killed Wilson. Based on the evidence presented at trial, District Court Judge Henry Lindsley (son of former DA Henry A. Lindsley) ruled out possible verdicts of first and second-degree murder and instructed the jury to render a verdict on voluntary or involuntary manslaughter. The jury acquitted Reed on March 23, 1951.[346]

Keating also prosecuted white-collar criminals. For example, Fred Ward, an orphan, one-time rug peddler, and ex-convict who parlayed a used car lot into a multi-million dollar seven-state Hudson automobile distributorship. At one time, Ward sold more than $20 million in cars and was the number three car dealer in the nation. A lavish entertainer and spectacular promoter, Ward was a pal of Denver and Colorado leaders. He and his wife, Iva, entertained Denver society at their luxurious suburban 229-acre Broomfield, Colorado ranch, which included stables and a swimming pool. Ward would give away new cars to people who had done good deeds on his weekly "Biggest Heart" radio show. Because of fraudulent borrowing to support his lifestyle, however, Ward's regional automobile distributorship crumbled in bankruptcy in 1951. In 1952, Ward was indicted by the Denver grand jury; he was acquitted in the first trial. In the second case, Ward was indicted on four counts, including false pretenses, confidence games, and conspiracy to commit both in obtaining a loan for his automobile firm from the J. K. Mullen Corp. The jury found Ward guilty of all four counts of the indictment. He was sentenced to seven years in the state penitentiary and received an additional federal sentence for a conviction in federal court for mail fraud. When he went to prison, Ward was more than a million and a half dollars in debt. In prison, Ward invented a hand washer for nylon clothes and started a business selling them to pay back the debt.[347]

---

[346] *Denver Post*, December 22, 1950, p 3; *Denver Post*, March 23, 1951, p 1.

[347] "Forgotten Adams County," Volume 1, COGenWeb Project p 5–7; *Rocky Mountain News* April 5, 1952, p 5; *Denver Post,* April 5, 1952, p 7; *Denver Post,* November 13, 1952, p 1; *Denver Post,* February 18, 1954, p 17.

The Fred Ward, Inc. Hudson Sales and Service Center, Curteich Linen postcard

On October 10, 1952, Keating filed an economic crime case against Silas M. Newton and Leo A. GeBauer who fleeced Herman Flader out of $231,452 in a fraud and confidence game. Newton and GeBauer were "doodlebuggers," a term used in the oil industry for men with mysterious devices that were supposed to locate oil underground. Previously, the pair had manufactured a flying saucer hoax that was the basis for Frank Scully's best-selling book, *Behind the Flying Saucers,* which lauded Newton as a world-famous geophysicist who was an authority in locating oil. As a result of this endorsement, the con men got access to potential investors. Both Newton and GeBauer were convicted at trial. They faced 30 years in prison but were sentenced to probation on the condition that they pay restitution to Flader. GeBauer paid $3,000 upfront and started making small payments. Newton never paid a dime.[348]

[348] *The Flying Saucer Swindlers*, by J. P. Cahn, True Magazine August 1956, p 36.

Silas M. Newton (left) and Leo A. GeBauer (right), photos from True Magazine, 1956

A celebrity case during Keating's tenure involved the folk singer Bob Dylan. In the summer of 1960, Dylan lived in Denver and played music at the Satire Lounge at 1920 East Colfax Avenue. Dylan was befriended by Walt Conley, a singer who was managing and performing at the Satire. Later in the summer, Dylan was accused of stealing records from Conley's home by Dave Hamil, a musician who lived at Conley's house. Hamil confronted Dylan at his rented room next door to the Raylane Hotel, at 1999 Lincoln Street in Denver, and accused him of stealing the records. Dylan denied the charge and locked Hamil out of his room; Hamil called the Denver police. Dylan, who, in fact, did have the records, threw them out the third-floor window down into the alley below. Hamil retrieved the records from the alley and urged Conley to press charges. Conley declined and, although the district attorney's office reviewed the case, Keating did not file charges. Dylan left the city soon thereafter and summed up the incident as follows: "I was run out of Denver for robbing a cat's house."[349]

---

[349] *Westword*, June 15, 2016. "Passin' Through: Bo Dylan's Ill-Fated Summer in Denver." https://www.westword.com/music/passin-through-bob-dylans-ill-fated-summer-in-denver-8007398.

Bob Dylan, photo from National Archives and Records Administration from U.S. Information Agency. Press and Publication Service, Image by Rowland Scherman, 1963

In the history of Denver, two Catholic priests were murdered in their churches; during Keatings' tenure, however, a priest was charged with murdering a church intruder. On April 2, 1961, John Joseph Thorburgh and Robert Eugene Sanders burglarized the rectory of Saint Catherine's Church at 4200 Federal Boulevard in Denver. They were confronted by Monsignor Delisle Lemieux as they were attempting to rifle the poor box. Lemieux heard the racket and armed himself with a shotgun. The priest told the burglars to stand fast and not move or he would shoot. The two men lunged at Lemieux, and he pulled the trigger of the shotgun. The shot hit both men. Sanders was an ex-convict whose rap sheet covered three pages. He died later at the hospital while undergoing surgery. Lemieux told police that he did not mean to kill Sanders. He said he aimed low, but Sanders walked right into the shot. Only slightly wounded, Thorburgh fled the church. He was arrested in Fresno, California 11 days later. Keating charged Lemieux with first-degree murder, explaining that it was a legal formality to exonerate Lemieux and justify his actions in killing Sanders. The priest pleaded not guilty and was immediately acquitted by Judge Joseph Cook in a directed verdict. Cook ruled that a jury could come to no other decision. When he was returned to Denver, Keating charged Thorburgh with attempted burglary. He pleaded guilty and was sentenced to prison.[350]

In 1963, Keating presented evidence at the penalty phase of the murder trial of Luis José Monge. It was the first time in Colorado that a jury was convened for the penalty phase only. The penalty phase occurs after a guilty verdict in a death penalty case; this is when the jury determines the punishment for the defendant. Monge had pleaded guilty to the murders of his pregnant wife and three of the couple's 10 children, after his wife discovered his incestuous abuse of one of their daughters. After hearing the evidence, the jury deliberated just a few hours before recommending a death sentence. Monge was executed in 1967. Just before his execution by gassing, Monge asked the doctor overseeing the process: "Will that gas bother my asthma?" The doctor replied, "Not for long."[351]

A few years later, on August 17, 1967, two armed masked men entered the home of millionaire architect Temple Buell at 106 S. University Boulevard in Denver. The men woke up the four people in the house and stole more than $57,000 in money, jewelry, and traveler's checks. They bound Buell with tape and forced his wife to take them room to room, ransacking the entire house. Before the robbers left, they locked the occupants of the home in a closet and left in Buell's automobile. Denver police traced the abandoned car to a motel on Colorado Boulevard and Mississippi Avenue and believed that Francis L. Hohimer, an Iowa inmate, had been one of the robbers. Hohimer was the leader of a gang that pulled these types of home invasions across the country. After the robbery unit of the Denver police built their case, Keating charged Hohimer with burglary and robbery and, because he was "at large," Hohimer was placed on the FBI's Ten Most Wanted list. He was arrested in Connecticut and returned to Denver. He pleaded guilty and was sentenced to 10 to 30 years in prison. The other robber was never identified.[352]

During his time in office, Keating had a "flower fund," which was a voluntary system that encouraged district attorney employees to donate a percentage of their salaries to Keating for political purposes. On every election day, DA employees were given the day off to campaign for

---

[350] "The Fighting Priest." 2018. As Close to Crime blog. http://asclosetocrime.blogspot.com/2018/05/the-fighting-priest.html.
[351] Monge v. People 406 P.2d 674 (1965); *Time Magazine*, June 9, 1967.
[352] *The Springfield News-Leader*, November 26, 1973, p 2.

Keating or other Democrats. The employees understood that if Keating lost an election, they could lose their jobs. When Keating died in office in 1967, Governor John Love appointed Republican Mike McKevitt to fill the vacancy, and practically everyone in office got fired—down to the file clerk. It was not until the election of Dale Tooley that rank-and-file district attorney staff were given civil service protection.

23. Mike McKevitt (1967–1971)

James Douglas "Mike" McKevitt was born October 26, 1928, and grew up in Spokane, Washington. He attended the University of Idaho and served as a combat intelligence officer in the Air Force during the Korean War. He attended the University of Denver Law School and had a private law practice for several years before joining the Colorado Attorney General's Office as an assistant attorney general from 1958 to 1967. Republican Governor John Love appointed McKevitt to the Denver district attorney position in 1967 after Bert Keating's death. McKevitt won election for a full term in 1968 but left office to run for Congress, becoming the second former prosecutor to serve as a U.S. congressman for Denver. Republican McKevitt won the Denver congressional seat, defeating long-time Democratic representative Byron Rogers who had won the Democratic nomination in a fierce primary race. McKevitt was able to take advantage of a split Democratic vote, his reputation as a tough crime-fighting district attorney, and his anti-busing views to win the seat. McKevitt's conservative policies did not go over well with Denver voters, however, and he lost the district two years later in the next election when he was defeated in 1972 by Patricia Schroeder.[353]

Among the headline-grabbing activities during his short term were his closure of a movie theatre for playing the erotic film, "I Am Curious (Yellow)" and his threats to close restaurants that served hippies. His most notorious fight came against the café La Petite. The restaurant in the old Mayflower Hotel at 17th and Grant became known as a hippie hangout, and the police department, with the support of the district attorney, enforced curfews regularly there. McKevitt famously promised, "We're going to get those scumbags out of here."[354]

---

[353] History, Art and Archives of the U.S. House of Representatives, https://history.house.gov/People/Listing/M/McKEVITT,-James-Douglas-(Mike)-(M000513)/; Ralph Nader Congress Project. *Citizens Look at Congress: James D. McKevitt, Republican Representative from Colorado.* Washington, D. C.: Grossman Publishers, 1972; *Rocky Mountain News* September 29, 2000, p 14B.

His prosecution of hippies did not always involve anonymous restaurant patrons. On Saturday October 21, 1967, the rock and roll band Canned Heat was booked to play at the Family Dog at 1601 West Evans in Denver. The Denver police obtained a search warrant to search the band's rooms at the Ranch Manor Motor Inn at 1490 South Santa Fe Drive in Denver and found about an ounce of marijuana, a small amount of hashish, and a small-caliber handgun. All the members of the band were arrested after the search. A judge was not available to set bail until Monday, so the band members spent the weekend in the Denver city jail. McKevitt charged the band members with possession of narcotics and conspiracy to possess narcotics. The president of Liberty Records agreed to give the band $10,000 for their legal fees in return for the publishing rights to the band's music. Those rights would include the song "Going Up the Country," which became a rock anthem throughout the world and was adopted as the unofficial theme song for the film Woodstock. Because of the legal fees deal, the band never received a penny of the publishing rights for "Going Up the Country," nor for several other worldwide hit songs that were worth millions over the years. Band members Henry Vestine, Samuel Taylor, and Robert Hite pleaded guilty to conspiracy to possess narcotics, and the case against Frank Cook was dismissed. Vestine, Taylor, and Hite received probation. The fifth member of the band at that time, Allan Wilson, was outside when the police entered the room and was not arrested.

[354] *Denver Post*, September 29, 2000.

Canned Heat, Promotional photo from Canned Heat.com

The Denver bust was immortalized in the Canned Heat song "My Crime" with the following lyrics:

"I went to Denver late last fall
I went to do my job; I didn't break any law
We worked in a hippie place
Like many in our land
They couldn't bust the place, and so they got the band
'Cause the police in Denver
No they don't want long hairs hanging around
And that's the reason why
They want to tear Canned Heat's reputation down."

Turning to police deaths during McKevitt's tenure, Paul Wilson was the second Denver officer to die on duty through an inadvertent gunshot. On September 14, 1968, Wilson was shot and killed by another officer when he walked into the briefing room at the District One police station. The other officer was showing a gun to a third officer when it accidently discharged, striking and killing Wilson.[355] One other Denver officer died on the job in 1971—Patrolman William Wirtz died after his motorcycle was struck by a car at Lawrence and Speer.[356]

Patrolman Paul Wilson, photo courtesy of the Denver Police Museum

355 Officer Down Memorial page, https://www.odmp.org/officer/14354-police-officer-paul-d-wilson.
356 Officer Down Memorial page, https://www.odmp.org/officer/14394-patrolman-william-j-wirtz.

McKevitt's office oversaw several murder cases of note. On November 8, 1968, Tina Louise Lester shot and killed Ronald Schlatter at the Blue Chip Tavern on Arkins Court in Denver. Schlatter was playing pool in the bar. He and Lester scuffled after she distracted him while he was trying to make a shot on the pool table. During the fight, Schlatter made a racial slur toward Lester, who was Black, and she pulled out a pistol and shot him in the chest before fleeing. McKevitt charged Lester with first-degree murder and a nationwide warrant was issued for her arrest. She was not arrested until February 6, 2009, in Dayton, Ohio—living under the name of Agnes Ramey. Denver DA Mitch Morrissey reviewed the case before Lester was returned to Denver. The original detectives in the case had died; witnesses had also died or they could not recall what happened well enough to overcome Lester's claim of self-defense. Morrissey dismissed the case.[357]

On March 14, 1969, Dr. Thomas Riha, a professor of Russian history at the University of Colorado, vanished from his home in Boulder. A woman named Gloria Tannenbaum was the lead suspect in Riha's disappearance and was also suspected of poisoning her friends Gustav Ingwerson and Barbara Egbert with potassium cyanide. During a search of Tannenbaum's home, Denver police found Riha's passport and driver's license and a pound of potassium cyanide. There was insufficient evidence for indictment on the murders, but DA McKevitt charged Tannenbaum with forging Ingwerson's will, which named her as the sole beneficiary. The Boulder district attorney charged her with forging the deed of trust on the sale of Rhia's home. Tannenbaum was found not guilty by reason of insanity in both jurisdictions. She committed suicide by ingesting potassium cyanide at the state mental hospital in Pueblo.[358]

---

[357] The Dickinson Press, February 7, 2009, https://www.thedickinsonpress.com/news/1779909-woman-arrested-40-year-old-denver-slaying; Denver District Attorney and Denver Police Department Joint News Release, February 12, 2009.

[358] *New York Times*, January 19, 1970, p 27; "The Disappearance of Professor Thomas Riha," July 16, 2019, https://history.denverlibrary.org/news/disappearance-professor-thomas-riha.

Thomas Riha (left) and Gloria Tannenbaum (right), photo of Riha from the *Rocky Mountain News* on February 22, 1970, and photo of Tannenbaum from http://unknownmisandry.blogspot.com/2016/08/galya-tannenbaum-suspected-serial.html

Denver faced a series of bombings in 1970 during a period of racial unrest in the city precipitated by the Denver desegregation case of Keyes v. School District No. 1. One bombing was at the home of Dr. Wilfred Keyes, the lead plaintiff in the lawsuit against the Denver Public School system, which was intended to force school racial integration. He had not yet been called to testify in the case. On February 24, 1970, the front porch of his home at 2651 Ivanhoe Street in Denver was blown off by a pipe bomb. Keyes' wife found the bomb, and Keyes narrowly escaped injury when he tried to drench it with water. His wife and their two children, ages 8 and 9, were also unhurt, but the front porch was destroyed and many windows in the home were shattered. The Denver police bomb squad was unable to identify the bomber and McKevitt never charged anyone for the bombing.[359] Empty Denver school buses were also targeted, with twenty-four destroyed and 15 others damaged in February 1970.[360] Another bomb was thrown against the home of Judge William Doyle, who had decided the Keyes case. Again, the perpetrators were never caught.[361]

[359] *Rocky Mountain News*, February 25, 1970, p 9; *Denver Post,* February 25, 1970, p 1; "Denver after Brown v. Board: From Segregation to Integration (in theory)," by Martina Will, Ph.D., *Front Porch*, February 1, 2019.
[360] *Denver Times*. 1970. "Denver Blasts Destroy 24 School Buses."
https://www.nytimes.com/1970/02/07/archives/denver-blasts-destroy-24-school-buses.html.

McKevitt's office also prosecuted common street crime. On May 2, 1970, during a shootout in John's Lounge at 931 Santa Fe Drive in Denver, a patron killed the owner of the bar, George Meiter, and a patron, Alfonso Vigil. Another patron, Richard Javorsky, was wounded. The altercation began as an argument between two customers when one of them pulled a gun. Meiter, who was tending bar, also pulled a gun and ordered the armed man out of the bar. The patron shot Meiter in the neck and the abdomen and then started firing randomly around the bar. Vigil was struck in the head and Javorsky was shot in the hip. Other patrons chased the shooter out of the bar and began beating him on the street. He fired off two more rounds and was able to escape by running south on Santa Fe Drive. Although there were eyewitnesses to the shooting, none of the bar patrons knew the shooter and homicide detectives could not identify the man. McKevitt was never able to charge anyone involved in the double homicide.[362]

On July 12, 1970, Clifton Grady Ashley fatally stabbed his ex-wife, Robyn Flowers, outside a concert at the Denver Coliseum. Denver Detective Tom Lohr found witnesses who saw Ashley force Flowers down some stairs at knifepoint and then stab her three times during an argument. After the stabbing, Ashley disappeared into the crowd. McKevitt charged Ashley with first-degree murder. After Ashley pleaded guilty to a reduced charge of voluntary manslaughter, he threw an ashtray at District Judge Merle Knous, hitting him on the forehead. Knous recused himself from sentencing Ashley, and a six- to eight-year sentence was handed down by District Judge Robert Kingsley. Ashley was back on the streets in less than five years. Several decades later, on December 10, 1995, Ashley shot and killed his pregnant stepdaughter, Oraleita Goodloe, for not "respecting" him. Ashley shot Goodloe several times and although doctors delivered Goodloe's baby girl by Caesarean section, the infant died within 24 hours due to complications resulting from a lack of oxygen. Denver DA Bill Ritter charged Ashley with first-degree murder. The jury found Ashley guilty, and he was sentenced to life in prison.[363]

---

[361] Cody White. "Rediscovering Black History." https://rediscovering-black-history.blogs.archives.gov/2018/07/31/keyes-v-school-district-number-one-denver-colorado-eliminating-the-root-and-branch-of-school-segregation/.
[362] Denver Police Department's Cold Case Page: https://www.denvergov.org/content/dam/denvergov/Portals/720/documents/coldcases/70-407465.Mieter.pdf.
[363] *Rocky Mountain News,* December 14, 1995, p 36A.

Clifton Grady Ashley, mug shot courtesy of the Colorado Department of Corrections

Meanwhile, the Smaldone family—which had been involved in Denver organized crime since the 1930s—made a criminal appearance during McKevitt's tenure. On April 13, 1970, there was a gunfight at Darlene's Ice Cream Parlor at 3759 Navajo Street between bookmaker Joe Nuoci and gangster Eugene "Checkers" Smaldone and Checkers's henchman Joe "The Ram" Salardino. During an argument over money Nuoci owed Smaldone, Salardino went for a gun and Nuoci maced him, causing Salardino to drop the gun. Nuoci then pulled his own gun. Smaldone picked up Salardino's gun and shot Nuoci in the arm and armpit. Nuoci fired at Salardino three times but missed. McKevitt charged Smaldone and Salardino with assault with a deadly weapon, assault to murder, and two counts of conspiracy. At trial they were acquitted based on self-defense.[364]

In the famous "Nixon tapes," McKevitt was discussed by President Richard M. Nixon, Chief of Staff Bob Haldeman, and White House assistant Charles Colson and John Ehrlichman in the Oval Office. They were discussing who in Congress would be best to leak information to the press. At the time, McKevitt was a Republican representative from Denver. When Haldeman suggested McKevitt, Nixon said "He's been a prosecutor. The question is, is he conservative?" Haldeman replied that it was a great opportunity for a congressman to make "himself a senator overnight." Ultimately the president passed on using him; McKevitt did not know at the time that he had been considered for this job.[365]

---

[364] *Rocky Mountain News*, April 29, 1970, p 5; *Denver Post* April 29, 1970, p 23.

After losing his congressional reelection race, McKevitt served in the Nixon administration, both in the Attorney General's Office and as counsel to the Energy Policy Office in the White House. After that, he worked for many years in private practice as an attorney and as a lobbyist in Washington. The National Federation of Independent Business (NFIB) became particularly influential in the late 1970s under the leadership of McKevitt who served as the federal legislation director. Founded in 1943, the NFIB became the leading advocate for small-business owners in the United States and helped achieve major tax reductions (1981), tax reform (1986), and a significant reduction in the regulation of small businesses during the Reagan administration.

McKevitt is credited as the driving force behind the Korean War Memorial in Washington, D.C., guiding the legislation through Congress when he served as Denver's representative. President Ronald Reagan appointed him to sit on the advisory board to the war memorial. He also served as a trustee and vice president of the U.S. Capitol Historical Society.[366]

Part of the Korean War Memorial in Washington, DC, photo in the public domain

When McKevitt died on September 28, 2000, Senator Chuck Hagel made the following statement part of the congressional record: "Mr. President, few individuals ever touch the lives of

---

[365] *Abuse of Power, The New Nixon Tapes*, edited by Stanley Kutler, The Free Press, 1997, pp 11–12.
[366] Biographical Directory of the House of Representatives 1774-present, https://bioguideretro.congress.gov/Home/MemberDetails?memIndex=M000513.

people like the late Mike McKevitt did. Former Congressman and Assistant U.S. Attorney General James D. 'Mike' McKevitt passed away last week here in Washington, D.C. He was a remarkable man, a selfless public servant, and a loyal friend. He was always working on behalf of others to make the world better. His positive attitude, personal warmth and absolute sense of fair play were most unique in a far too often cynical, and mean-spirited town called Washington, D.C. For 30 years, he rose above the pettiness, nonsense and nastiness that often dominates the environment of the world's most powerful city. He made it more fun to be here. He made it all seem more noble than most of it is."[367]

[367] Congressional Record Volume 146, Issue 120 (October 2, 2000) page number range S9599-9599

24. Jarvis Seccombe (1971–1972)

JARVIS W. SECCOMBE
1971-1972

Jarvis Seccombe took office January 1, 1971. He was the second Denver district attorney appointed by Republican Governor John Love, this time because McKevitt left office early to run for Congress. Seccombe served as district attorney for only two years. He had been a chief deputy under McKevitt and, at age 33 when he was appointed, was said to be the youngest DA in any major American city at that time. Seccombe was born in Salt Lake City but raised in Colorado. He served in the U.S. Army, both active duty and as a reservist. Seccombe received his undergraduate degree from University of Colorado at Boulder and his law degree from the University of Denver in 1964. He had been a practicing attorney for only six years when he became district attorney.[368]

Seccombe launched several office initiatives in his short tenure. He created a special narcotics unit and a section to concentrate on commercial fraud schemes and white-collar crime. He actively advocated for legislation proposing measures to increase penalties for certain felonies and to allow confiscation of property used in organized crime and drug trafficking. These proposals were passed by the legislature and became law. By coordinating his organized crime unit with the Denver grand jury and the U.S. attorney, he effectively attacked the crime confederation. He proposed laws to control professional gambling and loan sharking, and his organized crime unit was nationally recognized for its effectiveness. He instituted a program of pretrial conferences that required defendants to choose between going to trial or pleading guilty. He proposed, helped draft, and was instrumental in the final passage of 60 vital changes to the Colorado Criminal Code and 30 vital changes in the Colorado Code of Criminal Procedures. He advocated for a comprehensive drug education program for Denver grade schools. Despite his impressive initiatives, Seccombe lost to the Democratic candidate Dale Tooley in a 1973 Democratic sweep of local and state elections.

One Denver police officer was killed in the line of duty during Seccombe's term. Patrolman Merle Nading was shot during an altercation when one of the two suspects he was trying to subdue grabbed the officer's revolver and shot him in the back. Seccombe charged one of the men for the murder, but he was acquitted at trial.[369]

---

368 Biography provided by his wife, Diane Seccombe.

369 Officer Down Memorial page, https://www.odmp.org/officer/9848-patrolman-merle-e-nading.

Patrolman Merle Nading, photo courtesy of the Denver Police Museum

On October 3, 1971, the same day Nading was killed, Denver police officer Daril Cinquanta attempted to speak to three people in a car parked in the 4400 block of Mariposa Way in Denver. Lawrence Pusateri and two women were in the car. As Cinquanta approached, Pusateri shot the officer point blank in the abdomen. Cinquanta, who had joined the Denver Police Department the year before, crawled to his patrol car and radioed for help. After the shooting, Pusateri fled to Mexico where he was arrested for a drug crime. Seccombe charged Pusateri and he was deported back to the United States to stand trial in Denver. At trial, the jury convicted Pusateri of shooting Cinquanta and he was sentenced to prison. Three years later, the 31-year-old Pusateri escaped from the Colorado State Hospital in Pueblo. Although he was traced to San Jose, California, Pusateri evaded capture.[370] That was until August 2020 when Cinquanta, who had pursued leads on Pusateri for more than 46 years, tracked him to Espanola, New Mexico. FBI and local authorities arrested Pusateri, age 77, and charged him with escape and unlawful flight. Pusateri had used several different aliases during his over four decades on the run and though he initially denied his identity, his tattoos gave him away.[371]

---

[370] *The Blue Chameleon: The Life Story of a Supercop* by Daril Cinquanta, Waldorf Publishing, 2017, p 1; FBI Law Enforcement Bulletin, January 1986, p 32; *Denver Post* May 26, 2012.

[371] *Denver CBS 4*, August 7, 2020. https://denver.cbslocal.com/2020/08/07/denver-police-daril-cinquanta-luis-archuleta-lawrence-pusateri/.

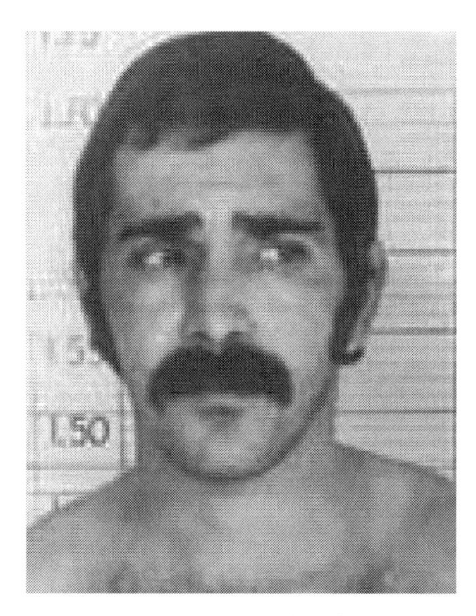

Lawrence Pusateri's 1974 mug shot from Soledad prison

A late-night gun fight occurred on December 5, 1971, between Elmore Brown and Richard Charles Williams in Cooks of Colorado Inc., an after-hours club at 3200 Downing Street in Denver. The fight was broken up and moved outside. Once outside, Brown pulled a pistol and shot Williams once in the chest, killing him. Bystander Katherine Young then pulled her pistol and shot Brown three times. Brown died from the gunshot wounds. Several other people watching the incident pulled out their weapons and fired them. Denver police arrested Young, but Seccombe refused to file murder charges against her, determining that she shot Brown in defense of Williams.[372]

On July 4, 1972, a bomb exploded in the faces of three Denver police officers as they tried to remove it from a car at 3915 Vrain Street, the home of Arthur Holman. All three officers were injured. The most seriously injured was bomb squad Sergeant Jack Burns. When the bomb blew up, Burns' right eye was blinded and his left eye was seriously damaged, leaving him legally blind. His right hand and two fingers of his left hand were blown off. Burns also suffered loss of hearing. Also injured were Detectives Clifford Stanley and John Garrison. Stanley lost his right hand, and his right leg was severely injured. He remained in the hospital for more than two years. The bomb, made up of two boxes of blasting caps, was discovered under the hood of a car owned by Holman, a janitor at Rust Sales Company, a bakery goods manufacturing plant in Adams County, Colorado. The car was parked at Holman's home when he discovered the bomb while checking his oil, but detectives believed the bomb was rigged while in the company

[372] *Rocky Mountain News*, December 6, 1971, p 5.

parking lot. On June 29, 1972, Claude Martin and two other Rust employees had been injured at the Rust plant when a similar device exploded in a car. Police found another bomb in a company truck at that time and were able to defuse it. Fingerprints of Loring O. Goodan were discovered on blasting caps used in both bombs. Goodan was the estranged husband of a woman who worked at Rust. Seccombe charged Goodan with first-degree assault, arson, and criminal mischief. He pleaded guilty to assault with intent to murder and was sentenced to nine to ten years in prison for the Vrain Street bombing. He was given an additional prison sentence for the Adams County bombing.[373]

On November 11, 1972, a three-way shoot-out erupted between Frank Granato, the owner of the Hinky-Dink Bar at 1719 Market Street in Denver, bartender Salvador Valles, and customer Larry Martinez. The trouble began when Martinez came in the bar and ordered a drink. Valles refused to serve him and told Martinez he appeared to have had enough already. Martinez pulled out a pistol and began firing; Valles returned fire with his own gun. Granato armed himself as well and began shooting. The patrons took cover under tables or exited the bar. Martinez shot bystander Daniel Leos to death when Leos and another patron tried to disarm him. There were up to 18 shots fired in the melee. The bartender Valles received a gunshot wound in the chest. Bar owner Granato suffered gunshot wounds to the chest and abdomen. Martinez had a gunshot wound in the leg and was arrested for investigation of murder. Seccombe charged Martinez with first-degree murder and two counts of attempted first-degree murder. He was convicted and sentenced to life in prison.[374]

Seccombe prosecuted NBA star Lucius Allen, after Allen was caught on October 4, 1972, smoking a joint in a car with fellow Milwaukee Bucks player and NBA superstar Kareem Abdul-Jabbar and two other men. Unfortunately for them, a Denver police officer pulled them over and they were arrested for possession of marijuana. They all spent a night in jail, and the arrest received national attention. As to Abdul-Jabbar, Seccombe said there was "insufficient evidence of any crime," and he was not charged. Lucius Allen was charged with possession of marijuana, but the charges were later dismissed, and he was cleared.[375]

[373] *Colorado Springs Gazette*, July 10, 1972, p 3.
[374] *El Paso Herald Post*, November 13, 1972, p 88.
[375] *Jet Magazine*, October 26, 1972, p 51.

Kareem Abdul-Jabbar as a Milwaukee Buck in the NBA, 1969–1970
Photo from Wikipedia

After leaving office in 1973, Seccombe went to work in the legal department of Mountain Bell Telephone where he was general counsel for Colorado. When Mountain Bell became Qwest, he was counsel for environmental health and safety/OSHA until he retired in 1997. Seccombe then became the oldest certified snowboard instructor in the country—by many accounts his favorite job. Seccombe died on August 2, 2010.[376]

[376] Interview with Diane Seccombe.

25. Richard Dale Tooley (1973–1983)

Richard Dale Tooley was born in Denver, Colorado on November 14, 1933. Known as Dale, he graduated from the University of Colorado at Boulder (CU) and was chosen by his classmates to be "Canebearer" at the 1957 commencement (the cane was a symbol of merit and honor; past Canebearers include the late U.S. Supreme Court Justice Byron White, former CU President Robert Stearns, and former Colorado Governor George Carlson). In 1958, Tooley joined the Colorado National Guard and served as a second lieutenant in the 124th Signal Battalion along with future U.S. Senator Bill Armstrong, also a second lieutenant. On more than one occasion the two future politicians discussed philosophy and politics.

Tooley was active in politics and served as chair of the Denver Democratic Party in the late 1960s. He successfully managed Mayor Tom Currigan's 1967 reelection campaign. After an unsuccessful campaign for CU regent and an unsuccessful bid for Denver mayor in 1971 against Bill McNichols, Tooley ran for district attorney in 1972 and easily defeated the Republican incumbent Jarvis Seccombe.

DA Tooley was known for a cool demeanor and was not easily thrown off his game. One morning at 5 a.m., Tooley received a threatening phone call at his home. The caller stated that he was going to "kill the DA." When Tooley asked the caller why he was calling at such an "ungodly hour," the caller apologized indicating that he was terribly sorry, but he did not have a phone easily available to call later.[377]

Tooley set an aggressive agenda for the DA's office. Known as a reformer, Tooley championed the passage of more than 100 pieces of legislation to bring about much needed change in the criminal justice system. He created prevention programs, such as neighborhood watch, rape prevention, juvenile diversion, and Colorado's first domestic violence unit. He modernized the office, setting up an on-call system for witnesses, a victim-witness program, as well as complex crime and consumer fraud units. He targeted striptease clubs and white-collar criminals for prosecution. Under his administration, the office support staff was brought under the City of Denver's merit system—the Career Service Authority. This change brought greater stability to the office and made it less blatantly political. The victim compensation program

[377] *I'd rather be in Denver: Dale Tooley's Own Story*, Legal Publishing Company, 1985, p 93.

started by Tooley helped lead to a statewide victims' compensation program. He granted his attorneys wide discretion to seek justice, not merely convictions. He increased minority staffing on the office from 3% to more than 50% during his 11 years' tenure.[378]

Three Denver police officers died on duty during Tooley's tenure. Police officer William Smith was killed on January 23, 1975, when he and his partner interrupted a robbery in progress at a bar on Federal Boulevard. Officer Smith was shot as he was entering the business and died shortly after. The two suspects were caught and prosecuted.[379] Detective Donald DeBruno died after being shot and killed while he and his partner attempted to serve warrants on a man wanted for murder in Canada. Detective DeBruno's partner, as well as the suspect, were also wounded in the shooting. The suspect was convicted by Tooley and sentenced to life in prison.[380]

Patrolwoman Kathleen Garcia was the first female Denver police officer killed in the line of duty. Garcia had been on the force for only six weeks when she was killed following her shift in District One. Officer Garcia was sitting in her patrol car in front of her house on South Galapagos Street at about 4:30 in the morning when someone approached the driver side door; after a struggle, the assailant shot her in the head. The suspect fled the scene as Garcia tried to reach her home. She collapsed in her yard and was taken to Denver General Hospital, now Denver Health, where she died later that day. Patrolwoman Garcia's gun was missing from the scene, and it is believed the suspect shot her at close range with her own service revolver. Tooley tried a neighbor, 27-year-old Steven Warren, for her murder, but he was acquitted.[381] Warren lived across the street from Garcia; his brother was a Denver police officer who had attended the police academy at the same time as Garcia. Warren had a couple of low-level criminal charges, but the case did not develop until a friend of Warren's, Ray Gardino, came forward a year later to say that he and Warren had been smoking pot and drinking beer early that morning and were sitting in his truck at 4 a.m. when Garcia came home. Gardino reported that Warren left the truck to go over to Garcia's vehicle. While he was doing this, Gardino "rested" his head on the steering wheel. The sound of two gunshots startled him awake and he said he took off, thinking that he was being shot at. When Gardino met up with Warren a week later and

[378] *I'd rather be in Denver: Dale Tooley's Own Story*, Legal Publishing Company, 1985.
[379] Officer Down Memorial page, https://www.odmp.org/officer/12501-police-officer-william-e-smith; "It Has Been 45 years Since That Tragic Night," Denver Police Museum Website, https://www.denverpolicemuseum.org/2020/04/30/it-has-been-45-years-since-that-tragic-night/.
[380] Officer Down Memorial page, https://www.odmp.org/officer/3953-detective-donald-lee-debruno.
[381] Officer Down Memorial page, https://www.odmp.org/officer/5270-patrolwoman-kathleen-garcia.

asked him what happened, Warren said he was trying to "get with that girl" but she would not have anything to do with him. In subsequent conversations, Gardino said that Warren admitted to him that he shot and killed Garcia, "Just for the hell of it."

Another witness told police that he overheard Warren in a bar telling someone else, "I killed a damn cop." But, when the DA filed charges against Warren, Gardino recanted, saying he was pressured by the police to give false information. And the witness who said Warren was bragging at a bar about killing a cop was unable to identify Warren. In all, forty prosecution witnesses testified at the trial prosecuted by chief deputy DA Jim Allison in September 1982. Defense attorney Scott Robinson told jurors that his client had a functional IQ of 74 and was incapable of taking the necessary actions described by the prosecution to have committed the crime. The jury deliberated for six and a half hours before voting unanimously to acquit Warren.[382]

From left to right: Officer William Smith, Detective Donald DeBruno, and Officer Kathleen Garcia, Photos courtesy of the Denver Police Museum

Early in Tooley's tenure as district attorney, Colorado Wildlife officers charged 20 cases against parents who brought their kids to the annual Huckleberry Finn Day at Washington Park. Dressed in costumes from the book *Tom Sawyer*, the kids fished in an irrigation ditch in the park. The children received prizes for the biggest and the most fish caught. Parents who helped the small children were cited by Colorado Wildlife officials with fishing without a license. Tooley dismissed the cases and refused to allow wildlife officials ever again to charge cases in Denver without his consent.[383]

---

[382] William Wilbanks. 2000. *True Heroines: Police Women Killed in the Line of Duty Throughout the United States 1916-1999*. Turner Publishing, p 45.
[383] *I'd rather be in Denver: Dale Tooley's Own Story*, Legal Publishing Company, 1985.

Sketch from *The Project Gutenberg EBook of Adventures of Huckleberry Finn, Complete* by Mark Twain

Also showing his discretion and judgment, in 1973 Tooley championed a bill that eliminated fornication from the statute and made adultery a misdemeanor. Ever since Colorado was a territory, adultery and fornication were crimes punishable by imprisonment—and the punishment increased for each subsequent conviction. During debate in House Judiciary Committee on the change, Tooley's assistant, retired Chief Justice O. Otto Moore, was asked the difference between adultery and fornication. Moore responded that he had tried both and he was unable to tell any difference.[384]

Tooley's office encountered a continued threat of bomb violence. On October 27, 1973, members of the Denver Police Bomb Squad were called to dispose of two bombs found within hours of each other. One was at the home of Robert Crider, a Denver school board member, and the other at the Denver Post Office address of police officer Carol Hogue. Then three days later, the Denver Police Department Bomb Squad disposed of a third bomb that had been mailed to the Two Wheeler Motorcycle Shop at 1443 E. 38th Avenue in North Denver. Captain Robert Nicoletti, a fingerprint specialist with the Denver Crime Lab, found Francisco "Kiko" Martinez's fingerprints on the envelope containing the bomb mailed to Hogue and on the envelope mailed to the motorcycle shop. Captain Robert Shaughnessy, head of the Denver Police Department bomb

[384] *Adultery* by Jerry Koppel, April 5, 2008, http://www.jerrykopel.com/2008/Adultery.htm.

squad, disposed of all three bombs. He found that the explosive devices sent to Hogue and Crider were similar in the packaging envelopes, first class label, and coil stamps, and in contents: 9-volt battery, electric blasting caps, and three sticks of Atlas Power Primer dynamite dated October 1967, containing 75% nitroglycerin. Shaughnessy found that the bomb sent to the motorcycle shop was packaged a little differently but contained similar contents including five sticks of Atlas Power Primer dynamite. The police lost the bomb mailed to Crider.

DA Tooley charged Martinez with attempted first-degree murder, attempted first-degree arson, second-degree assault, and unlawful use of explosives or incendiaries and conspiracy. Martinez also faced separate charges in federal court stemming from the Hogue incident. Eventually, Tooley dismissed the state charges against Martinez because of problems in the federal case and later Martinez was acquitted in federal court.[385]

On May 9, 1975, a visitor to the offices of Lieutenant Governor George Brown, Colorado's first Black lieutenant governor, left a shopping bag with a secretary. The bag contained a bomb. Two dummy bombs in similar packages were found outside the office of Attorney General J.D. MacFarlane in the Capitol building and in the Social Services Building across the street. The bomb in Brown's office contained a coffee can filled with explosives, cotton and rocks; it was left on a couch by a middle-aged Black woman who identified herself as Janie Guess, who told secretary Debbie Ortega, "Brown will know what to do with this." Brown became suspicious when he started to open the package and called security guards, who summoned the Denver Police Bomb Squad. The bomb was taken to an empty field in west Denver and detonated. The building was searched thoroughly following the incident, but no more packages were found. Tooley was never able to charge the would-be bomber because the person was never identified.[386]

On August 7, 1975, an explosion tore through the Champa Street entrance of the U.S. Courthouse in downtown Denver. There were no reports of injuries, although damage was extensive to the courthouse, a recreation center, a bar across the street, and an automobile in a garage beneath the blast site. The bomb contained more than thirty sticks of dynamite. A group calling itself the Continental Revolutionary Army took credit for the bombing. The group had previously claimed responsibility for bombing a Public Service Company facility in Adams

---

[385] *Denver Post*, October 31, 1973, p 1; *Rocky Mountain News*, November 10, 1973, p 48; *La Cucaracha*, Volume V, Number 34, November 28, 1980, p 1.
[386] *Greeley Daily Tribune*, May 12, 1975, p 12.

County; a warehouse owned by International Telephone and Telegraph Company in Denver; the offices of the Central Bank building in downtown Denver; the office of the U.S. Securities and Exchange Commission in Denver, injuring one person; and the American National Bank building in downtown Denver, injuring four employees. Tooley never prosecuted anyone for these acts because the person or persons responsible were never identified.[387]

The Byron G. Rogers Federal Building and U.S. Courthouse, photo Courtesy of the U.S General Services Administration

On April 8, 1977, Tooley's Chief Deputy Richard Spriggs moved to dismiss all charges against Anthony Quintana, an activist with the militant Chicano rights group "Crusade for Justice" Quintana was charged along with Juan Haro in a 1975 plot to bomb a Denver police substation. Spriggs dismissed the case against Quintana one week after Haro was acquitted of the charges by a jury, saying the prosecution's case had been seriously weakened when the government's star witness, Joseph Cordova Jr., failed to recognize Quintana during the preliminary hearing. Years later, Haro wrote a book admitting his and Quintana's involvement in the bombing plot. He wrote that he acted on orders from Corky Gonzales, leader of the "Crusade for Justice," and it was Gonzales who had supplied the dynamite for the bomb.[388]

---

[387] *Denver Post*, August 8, 1975, p 1, and August 9, 1975, p 3.
[388] *Rocky Mountain News*, December 24, 1973, p 8; *Westword*, "Smoke and Mirrors" by Harrison Fletcher, April 22, 1999.

According to *Westword* magazine, "In 1975 Denver had a higher incidence of bombings per capita than any other U.S. city. That year the Denver police bomb squad was called out 339 times, found 73 explosive devices and investigated 24 actual explosions. The targets included banks, restaurants, hotels, school buses, bridges, parks, electrical transmission centers, a radio station and even the home of the regional CIA chief. Tooley had no explanation for the bombings but other Denver officials theorized: 'Proportionally, there are more political radicals, malcontents or maniacs in Denver willing to vent their emotions by blowing something up.'"[389]

Turning back to organized crime, the Smaldone family made yet another appearance during the 1970s in Denver. An associate of the famous crime family, Ralph Pizzalato, was found shot to death in his Cadillac on January 28, 1974, while parked behind the Alpine Inn at 3551 Tejon Street in Denver. Pizzalato had a bullet wound to his temple and marks on his neck indicating that he had been choked. His killers had played tic-tac-toe on the sole of one of Pizzalato's shoes. His murder may have been connected to the shooting and attempted murder of Chauncey Smaldone's wife, Pauline, six months earlier. Detectives were never able to identify Pizzalato's killer, so Tooley was unable to charge anyone with the murder.[390]

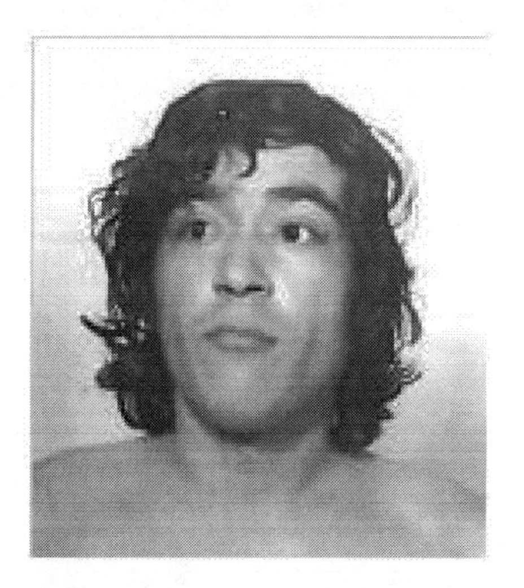

Ralph Pizzalato, photo courtesy of the Colorado Bureau of Investigations

During an attempted robbery, 19-year-old cashier Paula Rowe was shot to death on August 16, 1974, as she was closing her ticket booth at the front gate of the amusement park Elitch Gardens at 4655 W. 37th Avenue. As the shooter fled the scene, he also threatened a man

[389] *Westword Magazine*, April 22, 1999.
[390] *Denver Post*, November 3, 2006 Colorado Bureau of Investigations, Cold Case File, https://apps.colorado.gov/apps/coldcase/casedetail.html?id=930.

named Michael Martin with the gun. Although John Abercrombie Jr. became a suspect, the police department never showed Martin a lineup that included Abercrombie. Rowe's murder went unsolved, but Abercrombie was convicted of a similar robbery and murder of a young female clerk in Jefferson County, Colorado. When the Jefferson County murder conviction was overturned, Abercrombie pleaded guilty to robbery. In 1990 Denver homicide detective Joe Russell, with the help of detective Mike DeSanti, combed volumes of reports, talked to officers who had interviewed more than 30 witnesses, and, after a year of work, they found Michael Martin living in Florida. When shown a photo lineup, Martin immediately identified Abercrombie as Rowe's shooter. Investigators also found Ricky Ellis, an associate of Abercrombie, who contended that Abercrombie had told him he had committed the shooting. Denver DA Norman S. Early charged Abercrombie with first-degree murder and attempted aggravated robbery. The case went to trial three times, each time ending in a mistrial for varied reasons. Finally, Abercrombie pleaded guilty to manslaughter and was sentenced to a year in prison. After his release, Abercrombie was arrested on March 10, 2000, for robbing a bank in Aurora, Colorado. Nine days later, Abercrombie ended his 30-year criminal career, which had started when he was 18 years old, when he fashioned a noose from a laundry bag and hanged himself in the Arapahoe County jail.[391]

On November 18, 1974, Raymond A. Yost took a shotgun and killed his three napping children, 5-year-old twins Michelle and Michael and 3-year-old Julie, in their beds in their north Denver home. Yost left a cryptic scribbled note on a television set in the family home and fled in his station wagon with the 12-gauge shotgun still with him. The note said, "I'm going to leave you the same way I found you before we were married."[392] Yost was arrested near Buena Vista by the Colorado State Patrol about three hours after his wife, Carol, found the bodies of the three children. Mrs. Yost had received a telephone call at work from her husband telling her she should call the police and go home. The three victims were Mr. Yost's children by a previous marriage. Two other children, 9-year-old Jolm and 6-year-old Linda, were at school at the time of the shooting. Yost and his wife were having marital problems, and Mrs. Yost complained of frequent assaults by her husband. Tooley charged Yost with three counts of first-degree murder.

---

[391] *Rocky Mountain News*, August 17, 1974, p 6; *Colorado Spring Gazette Telegraph*, February 23, 1992; *Rocky Mountain News*, July 25, 1992, p 32.
[392] *Greeley Daily Tribune*, November20, 1974, p 14.

Yost pleaded not guilty by reason of insanity. He was found to be insane at the time of the murders and was sent to the Colorado State Hospital.

In 1974, when Tooley was running for mayor, he and Denver Police Chief Arthur "Art" Dill got into a debate over police using hollow-point ammunition. Dill confirmed that detectives had been using the controversial ammunition but denied that uniformed officers were carrying the bullets while on duty. Tooley said he believed "a significant number" of detectives and uniformed officers were using the bullets in violation of police policy. Dill's position was that this ammunition was safer because there was less chance of a ricochet and less chance of a bullet passing through one person and into an innocent bystander. Tooley was concerned that hollow-point bullets were more deadly than conventional solid-point bullets. The debate intensified after Denver patrol officer William Smith was gunned down by David Lee Bridges using hollow-point ammunition during a robbery on January 23, 1975. Bridges was shot and later died during the shootout. After Smith's funeral, scores of police officers marched on Tooley's mayoral campaign headquarters to protest his position against hollow-point ammunition for the police. The police vowed to work against Tooley becoming mayor. Tooley lost the mayoral election but continued working as district attorney.[393]

Denver Police Chief Arthur "Art" Dill, photo courtesy of the Denver Police Museum

[393] *Denver Post*, January 25, 1975, p 1; "It Has Been 45 Years Since That Tragic Night," Denver Police Museum, https://www.denverpolicemuseum.org/2020/04/30/it-has-been-45-years-since-that-tragic-night/.

David Lee Bridges, photo courtesy of the Denver Police Museum

In 1975, former New York police detective Michael Borelli plotted to murder his business partner, furniture store owner Hal Levine, a gambling addict who was embezzling from the business. Borelli and Levine were partners in businesses including Donato's, an Italian restaurant on the west side of Denver. Upon Levine's death, Borelli and his other partners stood to benefit from a $5.3 million life insurance policy taken out on Levine. Borelli had his friend and fellow New York cop Robert Davis carry out the hit. On September 7, 1975, Terry D'Prero, the bartender at Donato's, picked up Davis at the airport and drove him to Levine's home where Davis shot Levine and his wife multiple times. Levine died, but his wife survived. D'Prero helped Davis dump the murder weapon in the sewer and drove him back to the airport. Tooley charged Borelli and Davis with first-degree murder and attempted first-degree murder, solicitation, and conspiracy. D'Prero was granted immunity in exchange for testifying against Borelli and Davis. Both men were convicted in separate trials. Borelli was sentenced to death, and Davis received a 30 to 40 year sentence for conspiracy. Borelli's conviction was overturned on appeal and he was acquitted at a second trial.[394]

Also in 1975, James Datzman, the chief of the South San Francisco police department was shot twice while he was attending a conference of the International Association of Chiefs of Police in Denver. Chief Datzman was approached by two men, Marvin Gray and William Felder, as he walked to his hotel room. Gray began cursing and then pushed Datzman who continued to walk away. Felder shot twice, hitting Datzman in the right knee and buttocks. Datzman ran toward a nearby street where he flagged down a police car. Five minutes after the shooting,

---

[394] *Denver Post*, February 16, 1976, p 1; *Denver Post*, September 16, 1976, p 3; *Rocky Mountain News* September 16, 1976, p 6.

police arrested Felder and Gray. Tooley charged both men with attempted robbery and first-degree assault. Gray pleaded guilty to menacing and was sentenced to four years in prison. Felder was sentenced to 22 to 30 years for his conviction of first-degree assault.[395] Gray, a murderer and suspected serial killer, later gained notoriety due to his deviant behavior as well as his boasts of killing 41 people across eight states. He was convicted of three murders and suspected of several others, although his confessions to forty-one murders were discounted as bragging. While imprisoned in Colorado, Gray achieved incredible results in powerlifting, almost breaking world records. He also committed several rapes and murders of fellow inmates, which resulted in prison authorities taking exceptional measures—confining him to solitary confinement in Colorado's highest-security prison.

Racist violence continued during Tooley's tenure. On September 25, 1976, Clifford E. Santen shot Melvin Meadows in the back of the head in a Denver movie theater. Santen did not know Meadows—Denver police believed the motive for the murder was that Meadows was Black and his girlfriend, sitting beside him when he was killed, was white. Detectives investigating the bizarre killing found racist and American Nazi party literature in the gunman's apartment. Acquaintances of Santen said he was obsessed with race. Meadows had been a star athlete at Denver's Manual High School, played football at the University of Wyoming, and had been working as a sales representative for American Express since graduating. Tooley never charged Santen for the racially motivated killing because Santen killed himself outside the theater after the murder.[396]

An unsolved, high-profile case during Tooley's term was that of Dr. Zdenka Kalendovsky. On February 7, 1977, Dr. Kalendovsky was shot in the parking lot of a medical clinic located at 701 E. Colfax Avenue. Kalendovsky was on staff at the clinic and was also a research neurologist and assistant clinical professor at the University of Colorado Medical Center. After she had finished work, Kalendovsky walked around back of the building into the parking lot. It was just after 6:30 p.m. and it was dark. She had her purse, a medical bag, and a package of electroencephalogram records. As she approached her car someone stepped in front of the doctor and shot her point blank in the face with a .38-caliber handgun. No one in the area reported hearing the gunshot, but a witness saw a man dressed in a dark knee-length coat fleeing

[395] *Desert Sun*, September 16, 1975, p A2; *Greeley Daily Tribune*, September 17, 1975, p 18.
[396] *Jet Magazine*, October 28, 1976, p 29, *Colorado Spring Gazette*, September 29, 1976, p 8.

from the area. Kalendovsky was transported to a local hospital but died from her injuries. It appeared to be a robbery attempt, but nothing was taken from the physician. Kalendovsky had been a woman's amateur tennis champion in Czechoslovakia (now the Czech Republic). After escaping the communist country, she became a world-renowned research neurologist who was looking at the cause of strokes in young people and the cause of migraine headaches. Tooley was never able to charge anyone for the doctor's murder, and the identity of her killer remains a mystery.[397]

Photo of Dr. Kalendovsky, photo courtesy of Denver Police Department

An interesting case of criminal incompetence happened on June 15, 1978, when Richard Wisse was sitting on the front porch of his Denver home and two men and a woman drove up in a car. The men got out of the vehicle and shot Wisse five times. Investigators discovered a severed tip of a finger at the scene outside the front door—one of the shooters had shot off his own finger in the incident. Raymond T. Morgan was arrested the next day after he entered a Colorado Springs hospital complaining of an injury to his left index finger. The severed fingertip from the scene was taken to the crime laboratory, where it was photographed, a blood sample

[397] *Denver Post*, May 4, 2013.

was taken, and a fingerprint was obtained. A fingerprint examination of the print from the fingertip and a set of Morgan's fingerprints revealed that the fingertip belonged to Morgan. Tooley charged Morgan with first-degree murder and conspiracy to commit first-degree murder. The fingertip was stored in a refrigerator at the crime laboratory. Approximately one month after the last test had been performed, however, the police department destroyed the fingertip without consulting either the court or counsel for either party. After a pretrial hearing, the judge suppressed all evidence regarding the fingertip because its loss prevented the defense from verifying the police test results or conduct their own testing on the item. Prosecutor and future DA Norman S. Early prosecuted the case. Despite not being able to admit the fingertip evidence, Early obtained a guilty conviction on both counts, based on other evidence and witnesses. Morgan was sentenced to life with the possibility of parole.[398]

On July 13, 1979, Gregory Evans broke into the Denver home of Venice Justice and her daughter, Gigi. Evans stabbed Gigi 14 times, killing her. He also raped and then stabbed Venice in the side and chest and left her to die. Denver police arrested Evans, and Tooley charged him with first-degree murder, sexual assault, and first-degree assault. Venice survived to testify against Evans, who was subsequently sentenced to life in prison. Venice went on to spend many years working as a volunteer victim advocate in the district attorney's office. On April 16, 1984, President Ronald Reagan honored Venice Justice and three other victims during Crime Victims Week for outstanding service on behalf of fellow victims. During the White House ceremony, Reagan commended each victim for "turning your anguish into constructive action—by establishing programs to aid your fellow citizens who have suffered as you did at the hand of criminals."[399]

In December of 1979, paraplegic Lewis Roger Moore murdered his roommate, William Charles Kidd, and then used a rented power saw to cut the body into pieces. Moore then spread body parts around the housing development in which they lived. He kept Kidd's head in the refrigerator and packed other body parts in a suitcase to take with him to visit his parents for Christmas, but he was apprehended at Stapleton Airport. Tooley charged Moore with first-degree

---

398 People v. Morgan, 681 P.2d 907. 1984.

399 *Rocky Mountain News*, July 18, 1979, p 6; *Rocky Mountain News* November 7, 1980, p 5; National Crime Victim' Rights Week Archive Award Recipients, 1984–2002, https://www.ovc.gov/ncvrw/1984-2002_NCVRW_Honorees.pdf.

murder, and he was convicted at trial. Although eligible for parole, it has been denied as recently as 2018, and he remains in prison.[400]

Lewis Roger Moore, photos from AP and Colorado Department of Corrections

During the Iran hostage crisis (November 4, 1979, to January 20, 1981), a wave of anti-Iranian sentiment swept throughout the United States, including Denver. On November 11, 1979, three teenagers—Michael Lopez, Steve Roane, and Paul Morizky—used baseball bats to smash out a window and then threw beer bottles into the apartment of Afshin Shariati, an Iranian student. Shariati believed a bomb had gone off, so he exited his apartment armed with a rifle and fired into the car the teenagers were fleeing in, killing Morizky and injuring the two others. Tooley charged Shariati with second-degree murder and attempted second-degree murder and personally tried the case, which received international attention. The testimony showed that the boys had come to the apartment to hassle and beat-up Iranians. Shariati admitted to the shooting

[400] *Rocky Mountain News*, April 19, 1985, p 19.

but said he did so to protect his home from what he thought was a bomb attack. The jury found Shariati not guilty of all charges.[401]

This time period in Denver saw a substantial number of cases relating to sexual violence. On June 30, 1980, Joseph Michael Ervin forcibly took Jennifer Black from her home to his house where he raped and threatened her for five hours. Black contracted a venereal disease from the rape. Tooley charged Ervin with kidnapping and sexual assault, and although Ervin had a criminal history that included arrests for rape, robbery, burglary, assault, sexual assault on a child, and murder, his family was willing to post a $25,000 bond. On June 27, 1981, while out on bond, Ervin shot and killed Aurora Policewoman Debra Sue Corr during a traffic stop. Corr was arresting Ervin for DUI and when she got her handcuff on his left wrist, he attacked her and disarmed her. When a passing motorist, Glenn Joseph Spies, attempted to stop the attack, Ervin shot Corr twice and shot Spies in the back. Ervin fled the scene in his car. Aurora police found Ervin's vehicle registration in Corr's front shirt pocket and arrested him at his apartment. He was still wearing Corr's handcuffs on his left wrist. On July 1, 1981, he was found hanged by the neck in his cell at Adams County jail. He had torn a towel into strips and used it to hang himself. He left a note to his wife and family apologizing for killing Corr and confessing where he had hidden her gun, which police then recovered.[402]

Between July 1970 and July 1972, 965 cases of rape were reported in Denver. Of these 965 complaints, only 14 men were convicted of rape. In 1974, Denver had the highest rate of reported rape in the United States. The age range of rape victims in the city was from 2 to 84 years old, with the majority falling between the ages of 16 and 24. Most of these rapes were committed by previous offenders. To deal with these crimes, DA Tooley had his office draft five proposed bills concerning rape and victim compensation laws. The first proposal called for the abolishment of the "Lord Hale" instruction given to juries in rape cases (a legal relic from 17th century England) in which Colorado judges warned juries that the charge of rape "is one which is easily made and once made, difficult to defend against." It was widely believed that this instruction prejudiced the jury.[403] The second proposal created a "rape shield" that prohibited "admission into evidence in rape or sexual assault cases testimony relating to the victim's

[401] *I'd rather be in Denver: Dale Tooley's Own Story*, Legal Publishing Company, 1985, pp 75–79.
[402] *True Heroines: Police Women Killed in the Line of Duty Throughout the United States 1916–1999*, William Wilbanks, Turner Publishing, 2000, p 49.
[403] The Empirical, Historical and Legal Case Against the Cautionary Instruction: A Call For Legislative Reform, Duke Law Journal, Vol. 1988:154, p 154.

previous sexual conduct."[404] The third proposal ended the prohibition on charging a husband with raping his wife. The fourth proposal asked that evidence of the defendant's common plan, scheme, design, identity, motive, etc., be allowed as evidence in rape or sexual assault cases. The last proposal also provided for the state to pay necessary costs for emergency care and related medical care for victims of violent crimes. In the case of rape, these payments covered abortion costs, if necessary. All the changes proposed by Tooley became law.[405]

Tooley ran for mayor a second time in 1975. Again, Bill McNichols was the incumbent, again a run-off determined the winner, and once again McNichols prevailed. Tooley continued to serve as district attorney and easily won reelection in 1976 and 1980. He ran for mayor one last time in 1983. In his last attempt at the city's top slot, Tooley resigned as district attorney to concentrate full-time on the mayor's race. The primary election saw a three-way contest among McNichols, Tooley, and state legislator Federico Peña. This time, the aging McNichols finished third. The runoff between Tooley and Peña resulted in Peña winning to become Denver's first Hispanic mayor.

Denver Mayor Federico Peña

Tooley soon found himself fighting the toughest battle of his life when he was diagnosed with cancer in late 1984, just months after the mayoral campaign concluded. In his characteristic way and with unceasing energy, Tooley attended many public functions and completed an

[404] Colorado Revised Statutes Section 18-3-407.
[405] Sexual Assault Law Reform in Colorado Bill 1042, Elizabeth Lottman Schneider, 53 Denv. L.J. 349. 1976.

autobiography, *I'd Rather be in Denver—Dale Tooley's Own Story* in his remaining months. He received treatment at Johns Hopkins with negligible effect. Tooley's good friend, Jean Galloway, organized a cancer awareness campaign and Tooley agreed to serve as honorary chair.[406] Dale Tooley died on April 1, 1985, at the age of 51.

The Cover of Dale Tooley's book, photo from author's collection

Every St. Patrick's Day, the mayor of Denver changes the name of Wazee Street to Tooley Street for the day, to honor Irish Americans and the popular former district attorney.[407] On October 13, 2010, the main plaza at the new Denver Justice Center was dedicated as Dale Tooley Plaza.[408] Tooley's wife Mary Ann and their three sons, all well-respected Denver attorneys, were present at the ceremony to honor Tooley and the example he set for his family

---

[406] *I'd rather be in Denver: Dale Tooley's Own Story*, Dale Tooley, Legal Publishing Company, 1985, p 177–182.
[407] *Westword Magazine*, March 17, 2010.
[408] *Denver Post*, October 13, 2010.

and the legal profession in Denver. Two former Denver district attorneys, Norman S. Early and Governor Bill Ritter, along with then-current DA Mitch Morrissey also were present at the dedication ceremony.

From left to right: Bill Ritter, Norm Early, Mary Ann Tooley, and Mitch Morrissey at the dedication of Tooley Plaza
Photo courtesy of the Denver district attorney's office

26. Norman S. Early (1983–1993)

Norman S. Early became the first African American to serve as Denver district attorney. Governor Dick Lamm appointed Early to the office when Dale Tooley resigned to run for Denver mayor. Early went on to be elected three times and served as district attorney until 1993. Early was born and raised in Washington, D.C. He graduated from Calvin Coolidge Senior High School and although he got good grades, there was little money for college. The track coach at American University in Washington, D.C. recruited Early for the team; Early worked on the AU buildings and grounds crew to help pay tuition. After receiving his undergraduate degree, Early attended Illinois University College of Law. He moved to Denver and joined the district attorney's office in 1973 as chief deputy in charge of the Victims' Assistance Unit when he was appointed district attorney. Early's tenure as DA was marked by increasing gang violence in the city and by Early's emphasis on crime victims' rights.

A young Norm Early, photo courtesy of American University[409]

One of the first cases handled by Early's office was a corruption case against another elected district attorney. Nolan L. Brown was the district attorney for the First Judicial District, which includes Jefferson and Gilpin Counties. While district attorney, he asked an employee from the Colorado Department of Motor Vehicles in Denver to delete traffic convictions from his driving record. The Department of Motor Vehicles employee told his supervisor, and the supervisor instructed a subordinate to delete the two oldest tickets from Brown's driving record.

[409] American University, Washington DC Alumni page, https://www.american.edu/ucm/news/20171113-norm-early.cfm.

During an unrelated investigation at the Department of Motor Vehicles, DA Investigator Rick Johnson uncovered the Brown situation and brought it to the attention of Early. Early charged Brown, and Denver chief deputies Jeffrey Bayless and David Heckenbach tried the case. On October 9, 1985, a Denver jury convicted Brown of second-degree forgery, abuse of public records, and computer crime. He was sentenced to probation and lost his license to practice law as well as his position as district attorney.[410]

Nolan L. Brown, district attorney for the First Judicial District, photo courtesy of the Denver district attorney's office

Another noteworthy case prosecuted by Early's office at the start of his tenure also involved a law enforcement official, an Aurora police officer. On January 14, 1985, attorney Jeanne Elliott was shot four times and left paralyzed by off-duty Aurora police officer Gerald Utesch in the Arapahoe County courthouse. Elliott was an attorney representing Utesch's former wife in a child support dispute in the Arapahoe County District Court at the time of the shooting. Utesch was charged with attempted first-degree murder and first-degree assault. Because prosecutors from the 18th Judicial District were present in the courtroom and witnessed the shooting, the Denver district attorney's office was appointed as special prosecutor to the case. DA Early assigned future DA Bill Ritter to handle the case. At trial, the jury convicted Utesch of first-degree assault and attempted second-degree murder. He was sentenced to 32 years in prison.[411]

[410] People v. Brown, 726 P.2d 638 (1986).
[411] UPI Archives, August 15, 1986, https://www.upi.com/Archives/1986/08/15/Former-officer-convicted-in-

Early received significant criticism in 1984 for his failure to bring criminal charges against a group of neo-Nazis responsible for the murder of popular but acerbic radio talk show host Alan Berg, who was Jewish. An automatic weapons-wielding assailant gunned down Berg in front of his Capitol Hill apartment. The evidence eventually led to a right-wing white supremacist group known as "The Order." Even though the killers of Berg were convicted on federal charges and given long prison sentences, Early's reluctance, for fiscal reasons, to try the killers on state criminal charges was roundly condemned.[412] Early's office also received criticism for failing to take any action against penny stock underwriters, who swindled millions of dollars from investors. In particular, Early's office took no action against the penny stock king, Blinder Robinson & Co.[413]

Alan Berg, photo from Colorado Public Radio article, "Murder of Colorado radio man Alan Berg still resonates 30 years later" by Andrea Dukakis, June 18, 2014

Gang violence proliferated during this era of Denver's history. In 1985, Phillip Jefferson, Albert Jones, and Michael Asberry organized Denver's version of the Crips street gang, which had originated in Los Angeles. Over the next two decades, DAs Norm Early and Bill Ritter would charge all three men with numerous felonies. Jefferson was charged for two murders in a June 1986 shooting, for which he was convicted of two counts of manslaughter and sentenced to six years. Jones is serving life in prison in California for his role in the shooting death of a 63-

courtroom-shooting/2355524462400/.

[412] *Denver Post*, June 17, 2009, https://www.denverpost.com/2009/06/17/the-murder-of-alan-berg-in-denver-25-years-later/.

[413] *Rocky Mountain News*, November 10, 1987, p 14; *Denver Post*, June 17, 2009.

year-old store clerk. After numerous felony convictions and prison sentences, Asberry was shot several times in front of an Aurora apartment building during a non-gang related killing. Asberry died on May 17, 2008.[414]

The formation of the Crips gang was the beginning of years of gang violence in Denver. Early's office vigorously prosecuted a series of cases as gang crime in the city skyrocketed. One such incident occurred in the early evening on July 13, 1988, when Rory Franco Atkins, carrying a .22-caliber pistol, went with two friends to drive two teenage girls to their home. During the drive, he stated that he wanted to shoot a "crab," a pejorative slang term for a Crips gang member. After taking the two girls to their home, Atkins and his two companions noticed two other girls walking along the sidewalk and stopped their vehicle to speak with them. A young man was walking a few feet behind the girls with a blue bandanna in his back pocket, which in gang culture is a symbol of membership in the Crips gang. Without warning, Atkins called out to this young man, "Yo, blood, are you a crab?" And, without waiting for a response, he aimed his gun at the victim and shot him in the chest, killing him. Early charged Atkins with murder in the first degree, based upon both extreme indifference murder and murder after deliberation. The jury found him guilty of both counts and he was sentenced to life without parole.[415]

Rory Franco Atkins, photo courtesy of the Colorado Department of Corrections

[414] *Rocky Mountain News*, September 10, 1995, p 6.
[415] *Rocky Mountain News*, May 18, 1989, p 41; *Denver Post,* May 24, 1989, p 3.

Elliot "Hollywood" Raibon and his "Rollin' 30" Crips gang member friends were out looking for trouble on November 5, 1988, when Cameron Smith rode by on his bicycle wearing a red University of Oklahoma hat. Raibon mistook Smith, a college student who had just received a scholarship to the University of Oklahoma, for a Bloods member because of the color of the hat. Raibon confronted Smith and they got into an altercation. After Smith got the better of him, Raibon fatally shot him. Charged with first-degree murder by Early's office, Raibon was convicted and sentenced to life in prison.[416]

Elliot "Hollywood" Raibon, photo courtesy of the Colorado Department of Corrections

In June of 1989, while awaiting trial in the Denver County jail for robbing the Parkside Café on York Street in Denver, Roger "Roy" Young plotted the murder of the key witness, Parkside waiter Frank Magnuson, who was to testify against him. On June 6, 1989, just nine hours before Young's trial was scheduled to start, Kevin Fears and Roy's brother Joseph Young broke into the home rented by Magnuson. Two hours later, Magnuson and one of his roommates returned home, and both were shot to death. A third man was also shot but survived by pretending to be dead. Early charged the Young brothers and Fears with two counts of first-degree murder and attempted first-degree murder and sought the death penalty. The jury convicted Fears of all counts and he was sentenced to life imprisonment after the jury declined to impose the death penalty. Soon thereafter, prosecutors allowed Roy Young to plead guilty to two counts of first-degree murder in exchange for waiving the death penalty. He was sentenced to consecutive life sentences. In 1993, Joseph Young pleaded guilty to reduced charges and he was

[416] People v. Raibon, 843 P.2d 46. 1992.

sentenced to 24 years in prison for his role in the crimes. In 2005, Fears committed suicide in prison.[417]

In a related case, Darren Gene Smith shot Christa Schaeffer five times at point blank range of the night of February 25, 1991, as part of a witness murder plot. Although seriously wounded, Schaeffer survived the encounter with Smith which had been arranged by her husband Roger "Roy" Young. Schaeffer was set up by her husband because she had told authorities details of Young's plot to murder prosecution witness Frank Magnuson two years previously. Smith and Young were charged with attempted first-degree murder and additional habitual criminal charges were also added. Smith and Young were both convicted; Smith received a 50-year sentence, and Young was sentenced to prison for life.[418]

On September 9, 1989, 17-year-old Sean Taylor, a member of the street gang called the Lincoln Park Piru Bloods, gunned down 17-year-old Dean Rahim, who had no gang affiliations. The incident began when a car full of Bloods gang members drove through Crips territory near East Martin Luther King Boulevard and Fillmore Street in Denver. When the Bloods spotted Rahim, Rahim feared violence and fled to a nearby house, known to be a residence of Crips gang members. There the Bloods taunted the occupants, who came out onto the porch. Taylor fired a shot, which hit Rahim's arm and entered his chest, hitting a lung and his heart. He died almost immediately. Early charged Taylor with first-degree murder. At trial, based on the testimony of fellow Bloods gang members, Taylor was convicted of first-degree murder. He was sentenced to life with parole after 40 years. Taylor was given a second chance, however, because of his years of commitment to atone for his crime by counseling inmates and helping others to stay out of prison. In 2011, former DA Bill Ritter, while serving as Colorado governor, commuted Taylor's sentence, and he was paroled on July 1, 2011.[419]

In the early morning hours of July 2, 1987, Patricia Lynn Cannata was stabbed to death by her boyfriend, Lawrence Garcia -- in front of her two-year-old son, Matthew. Initially, Garcia claimed an intruder had broken into the home and stabbed Cannata, who was six and half months pregnant. Early charged Garcia with first-degree murder and his deputies Leslie Hansen and Todd Kettlekamp prosecuted the case. In September 1988, a jury convicted Garcia of second-degree murder and he was sentenced to

---

[417] People v. Fears, No. 93CA0720, August 7, 1997.
[418] People v. Fears No. 93CA0720, August 7, 1997; *Rocky Mountain News*, June 18, 1989, p 24; *Rocky Mountain News*, June 19, 1989, p 6; *Rocky Mountain News*, August 14, 1991, p 23; *Rocky Mountain News*, March 25, 1993, p 3; *Rocky Mountain News*, June 19, 1993, p 5; *Colorado Springs Gazette Telegraph*, March 3, 1991, p 22; *Colorado Springs Gazette Telegraph*, May 23, 1992, p 18.
[419] *Rocky Mountain News*, September 12, 1989, p 7; *Rocky Mountain News*, September 14, 1989, p 35.

24 years in prison. After serving 18 years of his sentence Garcia was paroled. Because of the callous indifference he experienced in the Colorado parole system, Cannata's father, Joe Cannata, founded the non-profit Voices of Victims to provide post-sentencing advocacy and support to victims of violent crimes. VOV provides information on the post-sentencing process, accompanies the victims to the hearings, and offers financial support when needed for travel, lodging, and meals to enable the victims and families of victims to attend relevant post-sentencing hearings.[420]

Patricia Lynn Cannata and Joe Cannata, founder of Voices for Victims.
Photos courtesy of Joe Cannata

Over the years, many Denver district attorneys had contact with celebrities, and Early's office was not an exception. In August of 1984, Otis Armstrong, former running back for the Denver Broncos, was indicted by a Denver grand jury for seven counts of illegally obtaining large quantities of the addictive painkiller Percodan. Early signed the indictment, which claimed that by "fraud, deceit, misrepresentation, subterfuge and concealment," Armstrong had obtained nearly 1,500 tablets of Percodan from nine doctors within a six-month period. Armstrong pleaded guilty to one count of illegally obtaining Percodan; the conviction was wiped off his record after a year.[421]

One of the most violent cases handled by the district attorney's office during Early's tenure occurred on November 14, 1984. Lorraine Martelli, a 54-year-old bookkeeper and former nun, was leaving work in the early evening when brothers Chris and Frank Rodriguez kidnapped her. Both men raped her, and then Frank tortured and stabbed Martelli to death with a knife. Early announced that his office would seek the death penalty for both brothers. Chief Deputy

[420] *Rocky Mountain News*, June 18, 2004; *Denver Post*, September 18, 2010

[421] *Rocky Mountain News*, August 11, 1984, p 5; *New York Times*, August 19, 1984, Section 5, p 1.

DAs Michael Little and Michael Kane prosecuted Chris. The jury convicted Chris and sentenced him to life in prison. Little and Chief Deputy Craig Silverman prosecuted Frank. The jury found him guilty and sentenced him to death on January 28, 1987. Both brothers died in prison, Frank from hepatitis.[422]

Early's office also had to deal with several cases involving attacks and killings of law enforcement officers. On September 6, 1987, inmate Timothy Vialpando killed Denver Deputy Sheriff Daniel Stillwell at Denver General Hospital. Vialpando had been taken to the hospital for treatment of a self-inflicted minor stab wound while in prison and was shackled to a bed in a room. Stillwell was on duty at the hospital, assigned to check on inmates who were not in the locked ward. When he entered Vialpando's room for a routine check, Vialpando attacked the deputy, got Stillwell's revolver, and shot him twice in the chest. Vialpando managed to remove his leg irons and fled. When he was captured in the hospital a few minutes later by Denver General Hospital security guards, he still had Stillwell's gun. Vialpando had a 15-year history of jail escapes, rapes, and assaults, and he had been on trial for raping a 12-year-old girl when he killed the deputy. Early charged Vialpando with first-degree murder, robbery, escape, possession of contraband, and being a habitual criminal, and sought the death penalty. There were two trials. In the second trial, Vialpando pleaded not guilty by reason of insanity. After a sanity trial, a jury found him sane at the time of the charged offenses. During a trial on the merits, the jury rejected his affirmative defense of impaired mental condition and convicted him on all counts. Vialpando was sentenced to life without parole.[423]

[422] People v. Rodriguez, 794 P.2d 965 (1990).
[423] People v. Vialpando 809 P.2d 1082 (1990).

Deputy Sheriff Daniel Stillwell (left) and Timothy Vialpando (right), photo of Stillwell courtesy of the Denver Sheriff's Department and photo of Vialpando courtesy of the Colorado Department of Corrections

Officer Patrick Pollack was killed on December 12, 1986, while chasing a robbery suspect. Officer Pollack and his partner were eating lunch at a restaurant when an armed robbery call came. The business being robbed was across the street from the restaurant. Pollack and his partner saw two suspects and gave chase. One of the suspects ambushed and shot Pollack as Pollack was going through a gate. Pollack's partner shot and killed the suspect.[424]

On June 3, 1987, Patrolman James Edward Wier was killed while responding to a man with a gun call in south Denver. Wier was hit by a shotgun blast as he stood to return fire at the suspect. As officers converged on the scene, the suspect shot himself. [425]

Officers Patrick Pollack (left) and James Wier (right), photos courtesy of the Denver Police Museum

On February 9, 1988, an incident in Denver drew national attention: one of the first police chases ever recorded on camera. It began when Phillip Hutchinson robbed a bank and fled the scene. He was chased by the police and a nearby news helicopter, which filmed the entire chase. At one point during the chase, Hutchinson ran down and killed Denver Police Detective Robert Wallis, who had served with the police department for 20 years. Hutchinson then wrecked the stolen car he was driving and took a hostage at gun point, forcing the man into his truck and making him drive Hutchison out of the area. Later, the news helicopter pilot lowered the aircraft in front of the truck to stop it. Police officers opened fire, freeing the hostage

[424] Officer Down Memorial page, https://www.odmp.org/officer/10742-officer-patrick-joseph-pollock.
[425] Officer Down Memorial page, https://www.odmp.org/officer/14156-patrolman-james-edward-wier.

unharmed and killing Hutchison. DA Early reviewed the shooting officers' conduct and ruled that their conduct in killing Hutchison was justified.[426]

Detective Robert Wallis, photo courtesy of the Denver Police Museum

On March 29, 1985, Denver police officers David Roberts and Gene Shaw went to an apartment at 198 South Clarkson Street in Denver to apprehend two men who had hijacked and robbed an airport shuttle bus near Stapleton Airport. When one of the arrestees, Russell Rogers, complained that his handcuffs were too tight, Roberts loosened them. Rogers slipped a hand free, grabbed a pistol from a nearby table, and shot Roberts in the mouth. Roberts lay in a coma for more than a month. Early charged Rogers with attempted first-degree murder in addition to the kidnappings and robberies. Rogers was convicted and sentenced to 80 years in the Department of Corrections. He will be eligible for parole in 2024. After Roberts came out of the coma he was paralyzed on the left side of his body. Although the injuries forced his retirement, Roberts became involved with training officers regarding traumatic incidents in the line of duty. Over time, Roberts's condition deteriorated and he died on May 27, 2011.[427]

---

[426] *Rocky Mountain News*, February 1989, p 7; Officer Down Memorial page, https://www.odmp.org/officer/13786-detective-robert-w-wallis.
[427] Officer Down Memorial page, https://www.odmp.org/officer/21166-patrolman-david-roberts; *Denver Post*, March 31, 2011.

Officer David Roberts (left) and inmate Russell Rogers (right), photo of Roberts courtesy of the Denver Police Museum and photo of Rogers courtesy of the Colorado Department of Corrections

In 1983, Early responded to six deadly clashes between police and civilians in six weeks, leading Early to write a letter to the police chief urging an overhaul of police training. His letter, Early urged expanded training on "strategic skills development: how to analyze situations, develop options, and select the option that minimizes the likelihood of a violent confrontation." He promoted the establishment of "periodic target course 'shoot-don't shoot' live training under street conditions, particularly for officers on the front line." It took 24 years for the city to put Early's suggestions in place—and a $1.3 million settlement in the federal lawsuit of the family of 15-year-old Paul Childs, a developmentally disabled boy shot to death by police in Denver on July 5, 2003, while wielding a kitchen knife. In the interim, more than 168 civilians were shot by Denver police officers, ranking Denver sixth among the fifty-one largest police agencies in the nation for fatal shootings by police per resident.[428]

A high-profile case handled by Early's office was the United Bank slayings in 1991. On Father's Day, four employees of United Bank were found murdered at the bank's downtown office. Suspicion fell early on James King, a former Denver police sergeant and United Bank security officer. King knew the bank's security system and owned a gun like the one used in the killings. His suspicious behavior included disposing of a gun he owned that was like the one used in the killings, renting a large safety deposit box the day after the killings, and shaving off his mustache when he found out he was going to be charged. King was charged and prosecuted

[428] *Denver Post*, April 23, 2007.

but acquitted of the murders. King's defense attorneys were Scott Robinson and local legend Walter Gerash. Jurors found the evidence against him "too questionable" and acquitted King. No other person was ever charged with the murders.[429]

James King, photo courtesy of the Denver Police Museum

Ten-year-old Jakeob McKnight was walking home alone after swimming with his older brother and friends at a swimming hole in a park on the Bear Creek beltway in Lakewood, Colorado on the evening of July 21, 1991. The other children had bikes and rode off leaving Jakeob to walk, but he never made it home. The next day, his body was found with two dozen stab wounds not far from his house. John Ramsey "Felix" Chinn was the lead suspect because he had interacted with the boys at the swimming hole. Chinn was obsessed with Jakeob's blue eyes and said he wanted to photograph the boy the next day. Earlier in the year, Early had charged Chinn with sexual assault on a 9-year-old boy in Denver. One of the conditions of Chinn's bond in the case was that he have no contact with children. When the Lakewood investigation showed he had contact with the boys at the swimming hole, the Denver DA charged Chinn with violating the conditions of his bond. On December 10, 1991, however, Denver Chief Deputy DA Karen Steinhauser dismissed the earlier molestation charges against Chinn, explaining that the 9-year-old victim was not willing to testify because of the publicity. The prosecutor did not pursue the charges against Chinn for violating conditions of his bond release, and the Jefferson County district attorney never charged anyone for the murder of Jakeob McKnight. In a different case in

[429] *Denver Post,* June 10, 2013, https://www.denverpost.com/2013/06/10/james-king-key-figure-in-mystery-of-denver-fathers-day-massacre-dies/.

April of 2016, Chinn pleaded guilty to sexual exploitation of a child after being caught with sexual videos of children. He was sentenced to four years in prison.[430]

Jakeob McKnight (left) and John Ramsey "Felix" Chinn (right), photos courtesy of Lakewood Police Department

Early's office dealt with a particularly deadly domestic violence case in 1992. On March 5, Patricia Ruiz came home to find her ex-boyfriend Jeffery Alexander waiting inside her home at 895 King Street in Denver. Ruiz had ended her relationship with Alexander a couple of months previously. Since then, he had been harassing her, warning that Ruiz "wouldn't get away with this without paying." After a violent argument, Alexander was arrested on domestic violence charges. Later, Ruiz found her mother Elva Castro, her brother Antonio Robles, and her two cousins Nohemi and Jose Alvarado shot and lying in pools of blood in two bedrooms. Castro, Robles, and Nohemi were dead from gunshot wounds in the head from a .380 semiautomatic pistol. Six-year-old Jose survived but was paralyzed. Early charged Alexander with three counts of first-degree murder, attempted first-degree murder, and burglary. Alexander pleaded not guilty by reason of insanity but changed his mind and pleaded guilty to the five charges because Early planned to seek the death penalty if Alexander was convicted. Alexander was sentenced to three consecutive life terms in prison plus 80 years.[431]

---

[430] "Felix" Chinn Saga (page 225) *Denver Post*, July 18, 2014.
[431] *Rocky Mountain News*, March 9, 1992, p 7.

Jeffery Alexander, photo courtesy the Colorado Department of Corrections

Pent up hostilities surrounding the Ku Klux Klan protest of the Martin Luther King Jr. parade in Denver turned violent near the Colorado State Capitol on January 18, 1993. Neoal Hayes, a young Black man, attacked two white bystanders, Colleen Kelly and Aaron Bagully. Hayes was wearing gloves with metal in them when he stuck Kelly in the face, fracturing several bones in her face. A local news team covering the protest and paraded captured the attack on video. It appeared from the video that he attacked Kelly and Bagully simply because they were white. Early charged Hayes with two counts of first-degree assault and ethnic intimidation with injury. Early also charged Hayes as an adult due to the violence of the attacks and the fact that he was 37 days away from his 18th birthday. A jury found Hayes guilty of both counts of first-degree assault and he was sentenced to 24 years in prison.[432]

[432] *Rocky Mountain News*, August 21, 1993, p 5A.

Colleen Kelly (left) and Neoal Hayes (right), photo of Kelly courtesy of the Denver district attorney's office and photo of Hayes courtesy of the Colorado Department of Corrections

On September 6, 1989, 18-year-old Donnie Russell attempted to rob a neighbor in the Montbello neighborhood in Denver. Russell became enraged when the neighbor had only $3 and a credit card to give him. He then raped and beat her, tied her up, and sealed her in the crawl space of her home. Russell then set the home on fire. After he fled, the neighbor was able to kick her way out of the crawl space. While in the crawl space she wrote Russell's name on a wall, using her own blood, so investigators would know who had killed her if she died. The victim had to undergo surgery but survived. Early charged Russell with kidnapping, burglary, aggravated robbery, rape, first-degree assault, and arson. Russell was convicted by a jury of all counts and was sentence to 94 years in prison.[433]

Early initiated innovative programs to fight crime or to address specific crimes. In 1984 he started a drinking and driving awareness program called "It's Just Not Worth It" for high school students. Early was joined in the program by Barry Dosh, Barry's mother Gladys Dosh, and a deputy district attorney who prosecuted DUI cases. Barry Dosh would talk to the students about the car crash he was involved in while he was driving drunk. Dosh was paralyzed as a result of the crash. His mother, an employee of the district attorney's office, was there to assist her son. The deputy district attorney would explain the legal consequences of a DUI conviction,

[433] *Rocky Mountain News*, September 9, 1989, p 7; *Rocky Mountain News*, June 26, 1990, p 7.

and Early would emcee the event. Dosh's story was so compelling that often when he finished there was not a dry eye in the auditorium.[434]

Early also developed a program to vigorously investigate and prosecute street gangs. The COBRA unit was started in December 1989 to confront the changing landscape of street gangs and crack cocaine. The plan was to implement a vertical prosecution model, where most aspects of a gang case were handled by one division in the office as opposed to relying on other units or external resources. The COBRA unit's duties included confiscation and targeting gangs and crack cocaine trafficking organizations as well as career predators and white-collar criminals. Eventually the COBRA Division was divided into its different component units, many of which continue to exist in the office today.

On January 25, 1990, Denver police Metro/SWAT team technician Ronald Relf was one of several officers who executed a search warrant at 3139 Zuni Street. Armed with a flashlight and a 9-mm semiautomatic pistol, Relf opened a bedroom door and spotted Jesus Delgado, also known as Jesus Gandara, lying on a bed, and a woman walking toward Relf with her 2-year-old son in her arms. Delgado fired two shots that struck the door jamb within inches of Relf's head, spraying debris against his face. Relf reached with his left hand to push the woman and child out of the line of fire and returned fire at Delgado. Relf fired seven shots, and Delgado fired three from his .22-caliber revolver. Delgado was shot in the chest, abdomen, arm, and leg, and his shoulder was grazed. The woman and child were not injured. Delgado was taken to Denver General Hospital where he survived his wounds. Early charged Delgado with attempted first-degree murder, second-degree assault, and possession of cocaine. Drug paraphernalia, weapons, and ammunition were found at the house. Early also found that Relf was legally justified in wounding the drug dealer. Delgado was sentenced to 12 years in prison after he pleaded guilty to second-degree assault on a police officer. Relf received the Denver Police Department Medal of Honor for protecting the woman and her baby and was named the Colorado Police Protective Association's Police Officer of the Year.[435]

---

[434] *Denver Post* Archives, November, 18, 1984.
[435] Soldier of Fortune Magazine, October 1990.

Ronald Relf, photo courtesy of the Denver Police Museum

Early ran for Denver mayor in 1993 against City Auditor Wellington Webb. The race pitted two popular African American politicians. Early received the backing of outgoing mayor Federico Peña and much of the Denver political establishment. Despite significantly outraising his opponent and being the front-runner for much of the campaign, Early lost to Webb.[436]

Shortly after losing the mayoral election, Early left the district attorney's office to take a position as senior vice president of Lockheed Martin IMS, Criminal Justice Services, where he worked until 1997. Early was a founder of the National Black Prosecutors' Association and was awarded their Distinguished Service Award. He was a founding member of the Sam Cary Bar Association, established to support African American attorneys. Early received a multitude of achievement awards and recognitions, including from the U.S. Department of Justice, the National College of District Attorneys, the Anti-Defamation League, the National Organization for Victim Assistance, and the National Commission Against Drunk Driving in Washington, D.C. In 2000, Early coauthored the book *Step Ball: A Child's Book About Feelings and Differences*. Early continued to practice law and appear in the media as a legal analyst.[437] Early died May 5, 2022 at the age of 76 from complications due to diabetes.

[436] *Rocky Mountain News*, June 17, 1987, p 7.
[437] American University, Washington DC Alumni page, https://www.american.edu/ucm/news/20171113-norm-early.cfm.

27. Bill Ritter (1993–2005)

BILL RITTER, JR.
1993–2005

August William "Bill" Ritter was born September 6, 1956, in Denver, Colorado. He was raised on a farm in eastern Aurora with his eleven brothers and sisters. Ritter attended Gateway High School in Aurora and St. Anthony Seminary High School in San Antonio, Texas, from 1970–1972. At 14 years old, Ritter worked full-time summers in the construction industry and joined a local labor union. He continued to work in the construction field, which financed his college education. He completed a bachelor's degree at Colorado State University and pursued a law degree at the University of Colorado in Boulder. After graduation from law school in 1981, he worked as a deputy district attorney under Denver DA Dale Tooley. Ritter was a chief deputy in the district attorney's office when he left in 1987 to volunteer as a Catholic missionary and run a food and nutrition center in Mongu, Zambia. He returned to Denver in 1990 and took a position in the U.S. attorney's office. In 1992, he returned to the Denver district attorney's office as a chief deputy under DA Norm Early. In 1993 when Early left, Ritter was appointed Denver District attorney by Governor Roy Romer. Ritter was term limited in 2005 and stepped down. In 2006, he was elected Colorado's 41st governor and served from 2007 to 2011, becoming the second Denver DA to be elected governor. Ritter chose not to run for a second term and has been the director of the Center for the New Energy Economy at Colorado State University since February 2011.[438]

During his time as district attorney, Ritter continued and expanded victim involvement in the prosecution of cases. His office, under special programs' director Steve Siegel, developed the Victim Services Network, which integrated both public and private victim services to minimize the duplication of victim contact and enable crime victims greater access to assistance. Ritter also emphasized community involvement and initiated several innovative programs during his decade in office. He created a community justice program that assigned prosecutors to work directly with different communities in high crime areas. He expanded the juvenile diversion program, making it the largest in Colorado, and he started one of the first and largest drug courts, with the goal of providing alternatives to the criminal justice system.[439] Budget cuts at the end of

---

[438] Ballotpedia. https://ballotpedia.org/Bill_Ritter.
[439] Colorado Public Radio, June 23, 2014. https://www.cpr.org/2014/06/23/denver-drug-court-survives-near-death-experience-reaches-20th-anniversary/.

Ritter's service resulted in retrenchment in several programs, although his programs were so well-regarded that when the state cut its funding to the juvenile diversion program, the U.S. attorney general's office committed $250,000 to keep the program running at full staff.

An early controversial case handled by Ritter's office involved the shooting death of Jeffrey Truax in 1996 by several Denver Police officers moonlighting as nightclub security.[440] Truax was involved in a nightclub fight, and then was shot and killed as he backed his vehicle out of the nightclub parking lot and refused officer orders to stop. The officers reported that the vehicle posed a deadly threat to their safety, but critics of Ritter's decision to not file criminal charges against the officers believed that the officers were not justified in using deadly force in the incident.[441] As a result of this incident, Ritter put together a commission to examine the investigation of those shootings. Retired Colorado Supreme Court Justice William Ericson headed the commission. One of the recommendations from the commission was to keep most police shooting investigations out of the grand jury. This would ensure greater public access to the investigation as opposed to the secrecy implicit in grand jury proceedings.

Another notable case pursued by Ritter's office was the death penalty trial of neo-Nazi skinhead Nathan Thill. Thill killed West African immigrant Oumar Dia at a downtown Denver bus stop after taunting him and asking, "Are you ready to die?"[442] When Dia responded, Thill shot the Denver cab driver. During the same incident, Thill shot and critically wounded a bystander, Jeannie VanVelkinburgh, who had intervened to try to stop Thill. She later died from the injuries she sustained in the attack. Thill's trial was moved from Denver to Pueblo because of extensive pretrial publicity. Thill was found guilty, but the jury would not give the death penalty.[443] During Ritter's term, seven cases were tried under the death penalty statute, but no capital sentence was handed down by a Denver jury.

---

[440] *Denver Post,* November 21, 2003.
[441] *Westword Magazine*, March 18, 1999; *Denver Post*, October 31, 2000.
[442] Associated Press, November 21, 1997, https://apnews.com/article/ba345c4d93adc1a7edf2ad326e94ae1e.
[443] People v. Barum Colorado Court of Appeals No. 99CA1582, January 18, 2001; *New York Times*, November 22, 1997, Section A, p 7.

Left: Oumar Dia, photo courtesy of the Denver district attorney's office
Right: Nathan Thill, photo courtesy of the Colorado Department of Corrections

Ritter's office also presided over the controversial case of Lisl Auman, convicted of felony murder and sentenced to life in prison for a 1997 murder of a Denver police officer. The felony murder statute allows for the prosecution of anyone involved in the commission of a felony crime in which a murder occurs. This means a person can be charged with felony murder even if they did not participate in the physical act of murder. In Lisl Auman's case, she had asked Mattheus Jahning, a local skinhead, to assist her in stealing from a storage unit in Jefferson County. During the burglary of the storage unit, police responded, and a chase occurred involving several police departments. Jahning shot at the pursuing police. The chase ended in southeast Denver where Jahning attempted to hide in an apartment complex while Auman remained in the car. When Denver Police took Auman into custody, she refused to answer any questions. During the search for Jahning, he shot and killed Denver officer Bruce VanderJagt and then himself. Auman was handcuffed and in police custody when Officer VanderJagt was killed, but because of her participation in the crime, Auman was charged with felony murder. When she refused a plea offer to a lesser charge, she was tried and convicted on the felony murder charge and sentenced to life in prison. Her case became a cause célèbre, garnering a *Vanity Fair* article and support from the likes of journalist Hunter S. Thompson and others. The murder conviction was overturned in 2005 for improper jury instruction and Auman agreed to plead to burglary and accessory to murder charges. She was sentenced to 20 years in community corrections and given credit for the eight years prison time she already had served.[444]

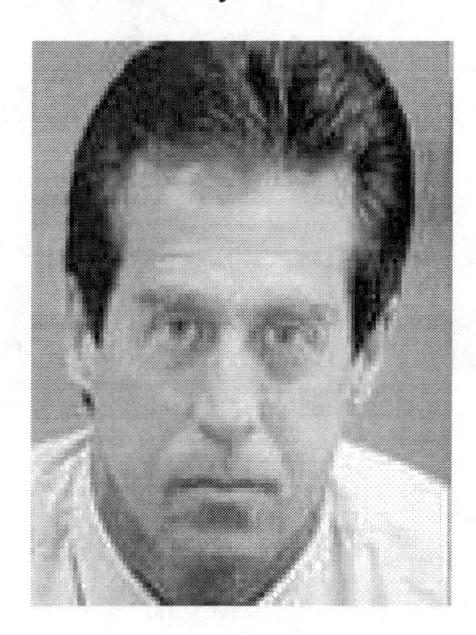

Denver Officer Bruce VanderJagt, photo courtesy of the Denver Police Museum

Ritter's office continued to confront street gang violence. On March 27, 1992, Michael Quezada, a California gang member, came to Denver and shot three local men in the parking lot of the Temptations nightclub, killing Kenny Knox, Donald Scott, and Ennis Evans. Ritter's office charged Quezada with three counts of first-degree murder but did not seek the death penalty because of a lack of aggravating factors. The death of multiple victims was not an aggravator until Ritter successfully lobbied to change the law because of the Quezada case. Although Quezada had killed someone in Los Angeles before the Denver murders, he had not gone to trial, so the California case could not be used against him as an aggravating factor. Prosecutors Tom Clinton and Craig Silverman took the triple homicide case to trial. Quezada was convicted of all counts and sentenced to three consecutive life sentences.[445]

In 1993, three Denver homes were the headquarters of a crack cocaine marketing empire run by Edith Cobb, who had a day job as a 911 dispatcher for Denver police. The investigation showed regular crack cocaine sales by Cobb or her tenants at the three locations. In the fall of 1993 Denver police vice and SWAT units conducted a raid on the three homes, discovered narcotics, and Cobb was arrested. One neighbor described calling 911 about a fight and loud argument at one of the locations while Cobb was working as a dispatcher. Cobb responded, "Oh,

---

444 *New York Times*, December 13, 1997, Section A, p 8; *5280 Magazine*, April 25, 2006; Officer Down Memorial Page, https://www.odmp.org/officer/15002-police-officer-bruce-vanderjagt.
445 *Rocky Mountain News*, September 26, 1994, p 5A; *Rocky Mountain News*, December 21, 1994, p 14A.

honey, that's my place," and no police officers showed. DA Ritter was able to use the civil confiscation law to confiscate the houses, and he charged Cobb with distribution of cocaine. She was convicted and sentenced to 14 years in prison.[446]

In November of 1996, Ritter indicted 10 leaders of Denver's Bloods street gang, accusing them of running an "illicit enterprise" and engaging in a pattern of racketeering that involved murder and drug trafficking. This trial was the first time in Denver that prosecutors and the Denver grand jury had used the state's racketeering statute—known as the Colorado Organized Crime Act—to go after a street gang. Many of those indicted pleaded guilty to racketeering, attempted racketeering, or drug charges. The convictions and long prison sentences for the leadership of the Bloods gang greatly reduced their impact on the illegal gang activities in Denver.[447]

The general violence in the city had a deadly impact on Denver police officers as well as the public. During Ritter's time in office, five Denver officers were killed in the line of duty. In addition to Officer VanderJagt, Officer Shawn Leinen was shot and killed by a juvenile named Raymond Gone in 1995, after engaging in a foot chase when Leinen observed the youth breaking into a car. While being chased, Gone turned and shot at Leinen, hitting him in the chest. The officer's bulletproof vest stopped the bullet, but the impact knocked Leinen to the ground. As he was on the ground, Gone came up to the officer and shot him in the head. Witnesses heard Leinen shout at the youth, "Don't do it man!" Gone was tried by Ritter's office and convicted of first-degree murder.[448] On December 23, 2020, current DA Beth McCann filed a notice of agreement that "extraordinary mitigating circumstances" warranted a reduction in Gone's sentence, vacating his first-degree murder conviction. His new sentence of 40 to 48 years in prison will allow Gone the possibility of parole.[449]

---

[446] *Denver Post*, October 26, 2007. https://www.denverpost.com/2007/10/26/san-rafaels-neighborhood-salvation/.
[447] *Denver Post*, December 7, 1999.
[448] *Rocky Mountain News*, February 26, 1995, p 4A; Officer Down Memorial Page, https://www.odmp.org/officer/783-officer-shawn-leinen.
[449] *Denver Post*, December 23, 2020. https://www.denverpost.com/2020/12/23/raymond-gone-denver-police-officer-shawn-leinin-murder/.

Officer Shawn Leinen (left) and Raymond Gone (right), photo of Leinen courtesy of the Denver Police Museum and photo of Gone courtesy of the Colorado Department of Corrections

Police officer Dennis Licata died September 6, 2000, in a motorcycle accident while responding to an accident. Officer Licata had received four department citations in his four years with Denver Police.[450]

Officer Dennis Licata, photo courtesy of the Denver Police Museum

In 1997, Officer Ron DeHerrera became the newest police officer in Denver history to be killed in the line of duty—he had graduated from the police academy the day before the accident that took his life. Officer DeHerrera's patrol car collided with the stolen vehicle that DeHerrera and his partner were looking for. The suspect's vehicle was traveling through the intersection at an estimated 95 mph at the time of the accident with DeHerrera and his partner. DeHerrera, in

[450] Officer Down Memorial Page, https://www.odmp.org/officer/15445-police-officer-dennis-michael-licata

the passenger seat, suffered massive injuries; his partner, though injured, made a full recovery. The driver, Gil Webb, was prosecuted, convicted and imprisoned.[451]

Officer Ron DeHerrera and the cars after the collision, photo of DeHerrera courtesy of the Denver Police Museum and photo of the cars courtesy of the Denver district attorney's office

Also in 1997, Detective Michael Dowd died from injuries he had sustained in a shooting that had occurred 28 years earlier on November 28, 1969, when he was shot by an escaped cop-killer, James "Mad Dog" Sherbondy. Sherbondy had been convicted of killing an Eagle County deputy sheriff in 1937. He was serving a life sentence when he escaped from a work farm. Dowd and his partner saw the wanted stolen vehicle and gave pursuit. During the car stop and subsequent foot chase, gunfire was exchanged. Detective Dowd was shot six times and suffered significant injuries but was still able to return fire, killing Sherbondy. Dowd had lifelong complications because of the injuries he sustained, and his death was a result of his line of duty injuries.[452]

[451] Officer Down Memorial Page, https://www.odmp.org/officer/14898-police-officer-ronald-leon-deherrera
[452] *Denverite*, March 29, 2017, https://denverite.com/2017/03/29/denver-cops-death-certificate-said-diabetes-partner-knew-wasnt-right/; Officer Down Memorial Page, https://www.odmp.org/officer/22510-detective-michael-e-dowd.

Top: A young and older Detective Michael Dowd. Bottom: James "Mad Dog" Sherbondy, photos of Dowd courtesy of the Denver Police Museum and photo of Sherbondy courtesy of the Eagle County Historical Society

Early in his tenure, Ritter found himself in the uncomfortable position of investigating one of his own employees for criminal behavior. Between August 12, 1991, and June 23, 1992, Linda Marie Chavez, also known as Linda Sandoval, received more than $7,000 in unemployment checks while working for the district attorney's office. Chavez came under suspicion when Denver vice and narcotics officers executed a search warrant in April 1994 on properties belonging to her and man who was the focus of a drug investigation. Authorities scrutinized Chavez's bank accounts and found that Chavez had approximately $120,000 deposited into accounts with the Colorado National Bank. The investigation uncovered checks from the Colorado Department of Labor and Employment. Denver Detective Gregory Faciane found that between July 30, 1991, and May 1992, a total of 15 unemployment checks were issued to Chavez, totaling $7,696. Two additional unemployment checks, each for $416, came through CNB on June 23, 1992. Ritter charged Chavez with felony theft and misdemeanor abuse of public records and recused himself from prosecuting Chavez. A special prosecutor from another district was appointed to pursue the case. Chavez went to trial and was convicted of all charges. She was sentenced to probation supervision.[453]

One of the more bizarre cases Ritter's office saw began to unfold on January 28, 1994, when a female graduate student at the University of Denver found a quarter-inch hole drilled into her bathroom floor of her apartment. Robert Bell, maintenance supervisor of the apartment complex, discovered plywood and concrete missing below the woman's bathroom vanity, enabling someone to see out of the vanity if the vanity doors were open. Bell also discovered the hole in the crawl space and while he was checking it, he heard someone else in the crawl space. Bell turned off his flashlight and seconds later turned it on to find Stephen Gordon, a tenant in the apartment complex.

Gordon had been relentlessly stalking the graduate student since meeting her at a shopping mall in the fall of 1992 in Scottsdale, Arizona. Gordon was so obsessed with the woman that he followed her when she relocated to Colorado and moved into her southeast Denver apartment complex. Ritter charged Gordon with eleven charges, including criminal trespassing,
harassment, attempted third-degree sexual assault under the so-called "peeping Tom" statute, and violating a restraining order. Prosecutors Marley McClintock and Curt Alfrey handled the case. At trial, apartment manager Laurie Daniels and Bell testified that they knew the woman was afraid of Gordon. The woman testified that Gordon had inflicted so much unwanted attention on her in Scottsdale that she had obtained a restraining order against him. Gordon admitted that he had followed the woman from Arizona to Denver and moved into the same apartment complex where she lived, but he denied tunneling through the crawl space into her bathroom. The jury convicted Gordon of all eleven charges, and he was sentenced to five years in jail.[454]

On December 7, 1994, a real estate agent and ex-cop named Robert Coleman shot 18-year-old Jeffrey Nowman after Nowman and another man tried to break into the Capitol Hill

---

[453] People v. Chavez, No. 96CA1199, August 21, 1997.
[454] Deseret News, March 21, 1995; *Westword* Magazine, December 14, 1994.

home of State Senator Pat Pascoe, a neighbor of Coleman. The two would-be burglars were running away from the home when Coleman, a former San Diego police officer, warned them to stop and then fired his handgun at them, hitting Nowman in the back and paralyzing him. The other man escaped. Ritter charged Coleman with first-degree assault. Ritter explained, "There is no justification articulated in the statutes of Colorado that specifically allows an individual to shoot at a person committing a property crime in their presence, particularly when that person is fleeing from them." Prosecutor Tom Clinton oversaw the case. Coleman pleaded not guilty, alleging that he suffered from post-traumatic stress and had momentarily reverted to his former identity as a San Diego police officer when he fired the shot that struck Nowman. The parties stipulated to the facts and the three doctor reports, and Coleman was sent to the state hospital. The paralyzed Nowman was charged with attempted burglary and a special prosecutor handled the case. Nowman pleaded guilty and received probation. Six months later, Nowman was charged with aggravated robbery for pulling a stickup from his wheelchair.[455]

In 1996, the district attorney's office had to come to terms with a violent crime committed by a former prosecutor within their office. On April 20, 1996, attorney Duncan Cameron killed his estranged wife, Debra A. Cameron, and a bystander, Nathan Clarke, in a downtown parking garage adjacent to her loft apartment. Duncan beat, stabbed, and then shot Debra, and then shot Clarke, a part-time waiter and student, when Clarke came to Debra's aid after hearing her screaming. When contacted by police the next day, Duncan provided an alibi and was not arrested. He fled the state and a few days later when he was pulled over for a traffic infraction in Barstow, California, he shot himself to death. Denver police continued the investigation, and forensic testing showed that a droplet of blood on Duncan's watch band matched Debra's blood type. Moreover, other blood found in the parking garage matched Duncan's type, particularly a blood stain that was found away from the scene of the murders but in the path that witnesses said the shooter had used to flee. Cameron had cut himself during the stabbing. Denver Police Chief David Michaud defended the department's not arresting Cameron by comparing it to the O.J. Simpson case. He said the major criticism of the Los Angeles police and the district attorney's office was that they "rushed to judgment." Denver DA Bill Ritter said moving too quickly against Duncan could have created problems if the case had gone to trial. It was clear from the evidence that Duncan was the killer, so the case was closed.[456] In a separate

[455] Associated Press, December 13, 1994, https://apnews.com/7d3c946bb23076d9f826b7109d5e67a5

incident in July 2006, another ex-Denver DA prosecutor, Jason Dotson, killed his wife and himself in their Aurora home with their three children present.

Another high-profile murder handled by Ritter's office occurred on the night of August 10, 1995, when Jon Morris lured five-year-old Ashley Gray out of her home at 2811 Stout Street, Denver. Less than 12 hours later, her body was found in a dumpster near Coors Field. "Uncle Jon" Morris was considered a member of the Gray family, having lived on and off for six years with Paul and Sharon Gray and their five children.

Morris had led Ashley to a loading dock near Coors Field where he raped and strangled her to death. Later, Ashley's older brother saw Morris walking alone near Curtis Park, about four blocks from the Gray home; Morris had a blood stain on his jeans, which DNA confirmed was Ashley's blood. At trial, forensic pathologist Dr. Werner Spitz testified that Ashley was alive when she was raped, and that she was strangled so violently with her T-shirt that an imprint was left at the base of her throat—the outline of a heart. In a videotaped interview with police after his arrest, Morris claimed he did not remember anything after leaving the Gray house, until he found Ashley naked at his feet.

According to his statements, Morris was heavily into crack cocaine at the time, and may have also killed 33-year-old Susan Boston, a prostitute and crack addict, by cutting her throat. He claimed that he woke up covered in blood with a piece of broken glass in his pocket. Boston's body had been found on February 3, 1995, propped against a fence in the 2300 block of Glenarm Place. On August 5, 1995, the body of Morris's sometime housemate Norma Fisher had been found in the backseat of a burning 1977 Cadillac; the cause of death was listed as smoke inhalation. The case was reopened as a possible homicide after Ashley Gray's murder.

Ritter charged Morris with first-degree murder after deliberation and felony murder, kidnapping, and sexual assault of a child and decided to seek the death penalty. Chief Deputy DAs Mitch Morrissey and Sheila Rapport handled the case. Initially Morris pleaded not guilty by reason of insanity, but no doctor found him to be insane, so he changed his plea to a simple not guilty. The defense filed hundreds of motions in the case—an unprecedented number—in an effort to ensure a death sentence was not obtained. After a lengthy trial, Morris was found guilty of first-degree felony murder, but the jury also found Morris not guilty of deliberate murder or any lesser form of homicide, so the prosecutors could not proceed with the death penalty. Morris

---

[456] *New York Times*, April 25, 1996, Section A, p 22; *Westword Magazine*, November 26, 2006.

was sentenced to life in prison without parole and within a few years died in prison. He was never charged with the murders of Boston or Fisher.[457]

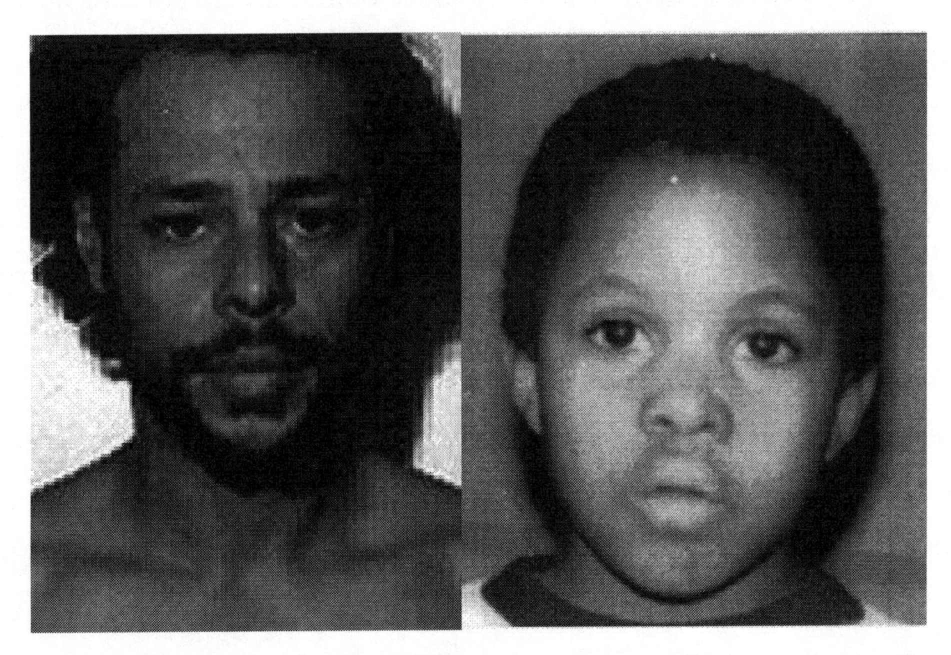

Photos of Jon Morris and Ashley Gray, courtesy of Denver district attorney's office

Perhaps the most famous case in Colorado happened on Christmas night 1996, when JonBenét Patricia Ramsey was murdered in her home at 749 15th Street in Boulder, Colorado. On September 5, 1999, chief deputy DA Mitch Morrissey was "loaned" to the Boulder County district attorney's office by DA Bill Ritter to be sworn in as a deputy DA for Boulder to provide aid in the 13-month-long grand jury investigation into the death of JonBenét. Morrissey joined Bruce Levin, chief trial deputy with the Adams County district attorney's office, and grand jury specialist Michael Kane in laying out the evidence for the grand jury looking into the six-year-old Boulder girl's slaying. Morrissey, a DNA and forensics expert, admitted that the case had run into trouble from the start. The coroner had used the same clippers to clip the fingernails of several corpses, including JonBenét's, rendering the fingernail clippings useless as evidence. In addition, the crime scene was contaminated, in part when the Ramsey family and their friends wandered around the house while the girl was missing. JonBenét's father, John Ramsey, disturbed the crime scene even more by carrying his daughter upstairs from the basement where she was found. Morrissey and Levin continued to advise the ongoing investigation until 2003.

---

[457] *Rocky Mountain News*, Aug 12, 1995, p 5A; Aug 14, 1995, p 4A; Oct 24, 1995, p 4A; Dec 18, 1997, p 19A; *Denver Post,* Aug 13, 1995, p A19; Aug 15, 1995, p B1; *Westword*, Feb 27, 1997; Nov 20, 1997.

Early in the investigation, celebrity forensic scientist Dr. Henry C. Lee was hired as a consultant by Boulder DA Alex Hunter. Lee had his own cable TV show, his testimony attracted courtrooms full of spectators, and he was hounded for autographs.[458] Lee's presence added to the intense media attention that surrounded the grand jury proceedings. To this day, the public remains entranced by the sad story of the little beauty queen. No one has ever been charged with the killing of JonBenét.

Six months after JonBenét's death, Jacques Richardson, the "Capitol Hill Rapist," was arrested after police saw him jump from Janey Benedict's apartment window. Benedict was found dead from oxygen deprivation, hog-tied with rope and a telephone cord so tight thatt her body bowed backward. DNA evidence tied Richardson to three other rapes. Ritter charged Richardson with the crimes and sought the death penalty for Benedict's murder. Chief deputies Marty Egelhoff and Bonnie Benedetti prosecuted the cases. Richardson was convicted by a Denver jury of two of the rapes before he was found guilty of killing Janey Benedict in a separate trial. A three-judge panel sentenced him to life without parole. Richardson was then convicted of the third rape. Chief deputies Benedetti and Mitch Morrissey prosecuted this trial. Richardson was sentenced to life without parole plus 236 years for all the Denver crimes.[459]

Jacques Richardson, the "Capitol Hill Rapist," photo courtesy of the Colorado Department of Corrections

---

[458] *Denver Post*, October 14, 1999.
[459] People v. Richardson, No. 99CA1230, February 14, 2002.

Also during this time, DA Ritter was criticized by community activists for not prosecuting Denver police officers. Denver officers were involved in more than 60 violent incidents during his time in office. A dramatic example was Daniel Pollack, Sr. On December 29, 1997, officer Pollack pulled over a woman in a traffic stop. He was on duty and in full uniform. He searched her purse and upon finding marijuana, handcuffed her. Pollack then asked what she would do to avoid being taken to jail. Pollack drove the handcuffed woman to a secluded location where he fondled her and forced her to perform oral sex on him. On January 4, 1998, Pollack approached a second woman and asked for identification near East 33rd Avenue and Downing Street in Denver. He asked to search her car and claimed he found marijuana. He told her she was in trouble, but they could work it out and again drove her to another secluded location and forced her to expose herself. On January 7, 1998, Pollack pulled over yet another woman in a traffic stop. He told the woman he could not let her go, handcuffed her, and fondled her. After the women came forward to police, Pollack resigned and Ritter charged him with seven counts, including kidnapping and sexual assault. Pollack pleaded guilty to sexually assaulting one woman and attempting to kidnap the other two. He was sentenced to 12 years in prison.[460]

On May 17, 1999, Reynaldo Flores kidnapped an 11-year-old girl who was walking to school in northeast Denver. Flores grabbed the victim by her sweatshirt hood and pulled her through the window into his car. The little girl bit Flores on his right side through his purple Rockies t-shirt. He drove her to a parking lot near old Stapleton Airport, raped her and threw her out of his car. She got help and was able to give Denver detectives a description of Flores's car. Adams County sheriffs located the car, and Flores was arrested. A search warrant was executed on his apartment and the Rockies t-shirt was recovered. DNA from the victim was found on the t-shirt, and DNA from Flores was found on the victim during a rape examination.

Ritter charged Flores with kidnapping and sexual assault on a child. Flores also was charged with kidnapping and sexual assault on a child in Adams County after DNA connected him with another crime as well. Chief deputy Mitch Morrissey and Adams County chief deputy Bruce Levin presented evidence at extensive pretrial hearings on the admissibility of the new short-tandem-repeat DNA testing that was utilized in the two cases. This trial was the first time in both Denver and Adams County where judges ruled the new DNA technique was generally

[460] McConnell v. Pollack, Civil Action No. 99-WM-159, October 13, 2000, Denver Post, July 21, 2000.

accepted in the scientific community and therefore admissible in these and future trials. The jury found Flores guilty of all counts and he was sentenced to 146 years in prison. Flores was also convicted of all counts in Adams County and was sentenced in that case as well.[461]

Reynaldo Flores, photo courtesy of the Denver district attorney's office

DNA also came into play for solving the murders of Anita Boatner and Stephanie Ashley. Serial murderer Ned Pace Jr. raped and strangled the women in 1999 and dumped their bodies in alleys in Denver. The murders went unsolved until 2001, when DNA from Pace was linked to DNA he left on the victims. Ritter charged Pace with both murders, and chief deputies Mitch Morrissey and Tim Twining tried the case. The evidence in the murders of Boatner and Ashley, along with evidence that in 2000 Pace was caught raping and strangling a woman in Adams County, was presented to the jury. Pace was convicted on all counts and received two life sentences without parole. It was the first time DNA was used in Denver to solve a cold case and bring a serial murderer to justice.[462]

---

[461] *Rocky Mountain News*, April 7, 2001, p 5B.

[462] *Denver Post,* April 8, 2001, p B-2; *Rocky Mountain News*, October 24, 2002, p 6A.

Serial murderer Ned Pace Jr., photo courtesy of the Denver district attorney's office

Denver DA Bill Ritter was asked by the Denver police to join them in responding to Columbine High School's mass shooting on April 20, 1999. At the time, the shooting was the deadliest school massacre in history. Ritter watched as the students were evacuated from the school. Later, he helped deliver death notifications to the families of students who were shot and killed. Ritter served as a member of the Columbine Review Commission, which conducted a review of the tragedy for Colorado governor Bill Owens. Ritter pointed out the significant role that crisis management can play in responding to a tragedy. He believed that the terrible events that day were exacerbated by the Jefferson County Sheriff's unfortunate decisions.[463]

Yet another high-profile tragedy happened on July 5, 2003, when Denver police responded to a call on 5550 East Thrill Place in Denver. Family members at the home reported that teenager Paul Childs was threatening his mother and sister with a knife. At the front door of the home, Childs did not respond to orders by officers to drop the weapon but instead slowly advanced on officer James Turney holding the knife up in front of himself with both hands. As Childs approached Turney with the knife, the officer shot the young man four times, killing him. The investigation revealed that Childs was developmentally disabled, and police had responded to the home on other occasions when Childs was out of control. Turney had never responded to

[463] The Report of Governor Bill Owens, Columbine Review Commission, May 2001. https://schoolshooters.info/sites/default/files/Columbine%20-%20Governor's%20Commission%20Report.pdf.

the home and had no knowledge of Childs at the time of the shooting. The officer said that he fired his weapon because he feared for his life. Ritter cleared Turney of any criminal charges. In the clearance letter Ritter stated that although many people would be concerned that the officer did not use a less lethal alternative, the district attorney makes the prosecution decision based upon the facts before him.[464]

Paul Childs and Officer James Turney, photos courtesy of the Denver district attorney's office

Also in 2003, six people were shot in a Denver duplex by Edward Herrera and his adult son. Instead of stealing crack cocaine and cash as they had planned, the men bound the six victims with duct tape and Herrera shot them in the back of the head, while the three-year-old daughter of one of the victims watched. One of the victim's was Herrera's former girlfriend. Four of the six victims died. Ritter charged Herrera with four counts of first-degree murder and two counts of attempted first-degree murder. Herrera pleaded guilty to all counts to avoid the death penalty. He was sentenced to four consecutive life sentences plus 48 years in prison.

[464] Ritter's letter to Whitman, October 16, 2003. https://www.denverda.org/wp-content/uploads/decision-letter/2003/East-Thrill-Place.pdf.

Edward Herrera, photo courtesy of the Colorado Department of Corrections

During his four-year term as Colorado governor, former Denver DA Bill Ritter issued forty-two pardons. The most dramatic pardon Ritter granted was to Joseph "Joe" Arridy, who had been convicted of raping and killing 15-year-old Dorothy Drain with a hatchet in Pueblo in 1936. Arridy was put to death by the state in 1939 despite considerable doubt about his guilt. Arridy, who had an I.Q. of 46, was said to have given a detailed confession, but it was never corroborated by any witness. Furthermore, Drain's sister, who survived the attack, identified another man as the killer—Frank Aguilar. The hatchet was found in Aguilar's home, and he later confessed, claiming that he did not know Arridy. Aguilar was also executed by the state.[465]

[465] Governor Ritter's press release, January 7, 2011, https://files.deathpenaltyinfo.org/legacy/documents/ArridyPardon.pdf.

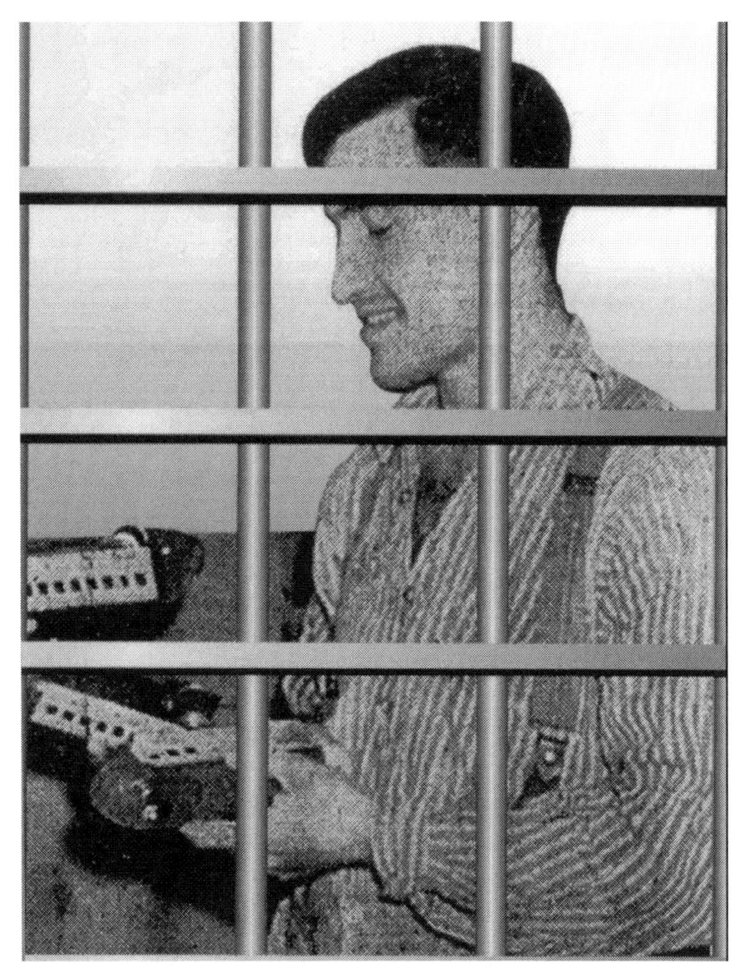

Joseph Arridy in his jail cell in Cañon City, photo from "Justice Story: The happiest man on death row," by Mara Bovsun, New York Daily News, April 28, 2019

Although Arridy probably was not even in Colorado at the time of the murder, he was framed by infamous Cheyenne County sheriff George Carroll, who obtained the confession from him. Initially, Carroll claimed Arridy confessed that he killed Drain on his own. When the hatchet was discovered in Aguilar's home, however, Carroll got Arridy to change his detailed confession to say they committed the crime together. After his conviction, Arridy played with a toy train on death row and smiled as he entered the gas chamber. He requested only ice cream for his last three meals. When Ritter issued the full and unconditional pardon, he said, "The facts surrounding Arridy's execution were nothing short of appalling." The governor went on to say that "pardoning Mr. Arridy cannot undo this tragic event in Colorado history."

28. Mitchell R. Morrissey (2005–2017)

Mitchell R. Morrissey was born in 1957 in Denver, Colorado. His father, Michael F. Morrissey, was an attorney who served in the Colorado House of Representatives. His grandfather Thomas J. Morrissey was the U.S. attorney for the 10th district for 16 years under Franklin D. Roosevelt and Harry S. Truman. Mitch Morrissey went to public schools, Mullen High School and the University of Colorado. Morrissey studied law at the University of Denver as had his grandfather, father, and brother. He started in the Denver district attorney's office as a legal intern in 1983 and was sworn in as a deputy under DA Norman S. Early. For the next 20 years, he served as a deputy and then as a chief deputy district attorney. His primary responsibility as a trial lawyer was to prosecute violent criminals in Denver. Morrissey had experience in the investigation and prosecution of serial murderers and sex offenders. Morrissey immediately recognized the potential of the science of DNA for law enforcement and tried the first DNA case in Denver. An expert in presenting DNA evidence in court, Morrissey worked with scientists and other prosecutors to ensure that different types of DNA technology were found to be admissible in Colorado courtrooms. In 2002, Morrissey was sworn in as a special assistant U.S. attorney to assist in the prosecution of federal cases involving DNA evidence. Morrissey is a member of the faculty of the American Prosecutors Research Institute and regularly addresses groups of prosecutors from all over the United States on forensic DNA issues. Morrissey is internationally recognized for his expertise in DNA technology, applying that technology in criminal prosecutions. He has trained law enforcement officers and prosecutors on DNA technology in the Middle East, Canada, and Central America as well as the United States.

As DA, Morrissey spearheaded several important civic capital campaigns, including building the Denver Crime Laboratory, which opened in 2013, and the Rose Andom Family Justice Center, which opened in 2015. He also campaigned for and helped lead the bond campaign to build the new courthouse and jail.[466]

Under Morrissey, the Denver district attorney's office vastly increased its use of DNA evidence. DNA was used for current cases as well as assisting in solving old cases, some decades

[466] Wikipedia, https://en.wikipedia.org/wiki/Mitchell_R._Morrissey

old. One such case occurred on August 12, 1985, when the body of 15-year-old Tracy Lynn Wooden was discovered in an alley behind Fox Supply Co. at 2229 Blake Street by an employee of the plumbing company—the same employee had been there at 3 a.m. and her body had not been there. Wooden had been treated for an injured knee and released from the hospital early on the morning of her death. After her discharge, Wooden vanished. The case went unsolved for 30 years until DNA from Daniel Fellovert matched DNA found on Wooden. In May of 2015, DA Morrissey announced that the Wooden murder was solved, although he could not bring charges because Fellovert, a convicted rapist, had died in prison in 2006.[467]

Tracy Lynn Wooden and Daniel Fellovert, photos courtesy of the Denver district attorney's office

On the morning of August 21, 2004, Denver Police responded to 1735 Lafayette Street in Denver, where the body of Gina Gruenwal was discovered in a breezeway by a house. Gruenwal was lying on her back with blood under her head and a stained pocketknife on the ground nearby. Her pants were unzipped and slightly pulled down. Police also found a black duffle bag near her body. Gruenwal was last seen by friends the night before when they dropped her off in the area. At the autopsy, the pathologist found bruising on the victim's thigh and a bite mark on her left wrist. Investigators from the Denver Crime lab collected saliva from the bite mark to preserve any possible DNA evidence. A male DNA profile was developed by DNA analyst Greggory LaBerge at the Denver Crime Laboratory, and the profile was entered into the national DNA database. The case went cold until April 11, 2011, when there was a match in the DNA database

[467] *Denver Post,* August 28, 2011; *CBS News*, May 5, 2015, https://www.cbsnews.com/news/da-killer-idd-in-1985-cold-case-murder-of-denver-teen/.

to Billy Jene Wilson, because he had been arrested in California. Additional DNA testing on items from the black duffle bag also matched Wilson. Denver homicide detective Mark Crider interviewed Wilson who admitted that he had been with Gruenwal. Morrissey charged Wilson with first-degree murder and kidnapping. The jury found Wilson guilty and he was sentenced to life without parole.[468]

In 2004, DA Morrissey, along with members of the Denver Crime Lab and Denver Police Department, started Denver's Integrated Cold Case Project. As part of this program, DNA was tested from an abduction and rape that occurred in the 3100 block of West 14th Avenue in Denver in November 1996. The DNA results showed that serial rapist Wayne Glasser had been the perpetrator. Glasser had grabbed the woman as she walked home from work and raped her after forcing her into his van at gunpoint. Morrissey charged Glasser with kidnaping and sexual assault. At trial, prosecutors not only presented the facts of the 1996 case, but the jury also heard from a girl that Glasser had molested when she was 14-years-old as well as a woman with Down syndrome that he had raped. Glasser was convicted of all counts and received 54 years in prison. This sentence was ordered to be served consecutively to a 16-year sentence from Arapahoe County. In a prior psychosexual evaluation, Glasser claimed that he had raped more than one hundred women, that he would defile dead bodies while he worked at a mortuary, and that he raped his family's pets.[469]

---

[468] *Denver Post,* August 11, 2011, https://www.denverpost.com/2011/08/02/man-charged-in-2004-denver-homicide-case/.

[469] *Denver Post*, January 22, 2009, https://www.denverpost.com/2009/01/22/sixty-year-sentence-in-denver-rape-kidnap/.

Wayne Glasser, photo courtesy of the Colorado Department of Corrections

On March 21, 2014, Governor John Hickenlooper signed into law a bill that eliminated the statute of limitations on non-sex offenses that occur in conjunction with sexual assaults that are proven with DNA evidence. Under the prior law there was no statute of limitations for sexual assaults proven with DNA, but other violent crimes like armed robbery and assault had a statute of limitations that would prevent prosecution of those offenses in cold cases. Morrissey championed the change in the law allowing the prosecution of other acts of violence a rapist was responsible for during a sexual assault.[470]

[470] Statute of limitations Reform, http://sol-reform.com/2014/03/sex-crime-statute-limitations-bill-among-10-signed-colorado-governor/.

Signing ceremony for the bill that eliminated the statute of limitations on non-sex offenses that occur in conjunction with sexual assaults that are proven with DNA evidence, photo courtesy of the Denver district attorney's office

On January 26, 2005, Morrissey filed the first "John Doe" DNA cases in Colorado. Denver police recovered DNA evidence in two burglaries, one in 2002 and one in 2004, where the intruder had masturbated while smelling the feet of women sleeping in their homes. The name of the offender was unknown and the statute of limitations on the 2002 burglary was running, so the cases were filed using the name John Doe with the offender's DNA profile. Eventually, Terre Jefferson was identified as the suspect after he was convicted on another burglary that required him to submit a DNA sample to the DNA database. That DNA sample matched the DNA profile from the John Doe cases. Jefferson pleaded guilty to burglary and indecent exposure in the John Doe cases and in an additional Denver burglary case. He was sentenced to 27 years in prison.[471]

[471] "Guilty by DNA," April 1, 2010, https://thecrimereport.org/2010/04/01/guilty-by-dna/.

Terre Jefferson, photo courtesy of the Colorado Department of Corrections

On July 11, 2005, a disabled Denver woman named Carol Colaiano was beaten and fatally stabbed in her apartment on the 1200 block of Galapago Street in Denver. The case remained unsolved for three years until Gerald Cooper's DNA was matched with DNA evidence found in Colaiano's apartment. In 2008, Morrissey charged Cooper with first-degree murder, two counts of felony murder, first-degree burglary, and sexual contact with force. Cooper had an extensive criminal history including an arrest in 1978 for sexual assault. When Morrissey charged Cooper, he was serving a prison term for an attack on another woman in Colaiano's apartment complex. Because of this conviction, Cooper's DNA was entered into the DNA database, leading to the match to Colaiano's murder. Cooper pleaded guilty to second-degree murder in Colaiano's killing and was sentenced to 48 years in prison consecutive to the sentence he was serving.[472]

Another case centered on Kristen Swanson, who was working as a waitress on October 28, 1980, at Summerfield's disco lounge located at 3737 Quebec Street in Denver. She was last seen alive leaving work at the end of her shift. Swanson was later found stabbed to death in her vehicle, which was parked at East 38th Avenue and Oneida Street in a Denver alley. Swanson had been raped and stabbed once in the chest. Homicide detectives spoke to her boyfriend and ran down every lead, but the case remained unsolved. Decades passed before DA Morrissey was

---

[472] *Denver Post*, February 1, 2008, https://www.denverpost.com/2008/02/01/man-charged-in-05-slaying-of-disabled-woman/.

asked by Randy Ricks, a friend of Swanson, if there had ever been a cold-case analysis of her murder. After Morrissey asked the Denver Cold Case Unit to review the case, a DNA profile of her rapist led detectives to Roderick Elias, who had been arrested in Topeka, Kansas in 2010. Elias was a career criminal who detectives could put in Denver at the time of Swanson's murder. When he denied knowing Swanson or ever having sex with her, Morrissey charged Elias with first-degree murder and, three decades after Kristen Swanson's rape and murder, a jury found him guilty. Elias was sentenced to life in prison.[473]

Kristen Swanson and Roderick Elias, photo of Swanson courtesy of the Denver district attorney's office and photo of Elias courtesy of the Colorado Department of Corrections

On July 8, 2008, at around 1:30 a.m., near 13th and Decatur Street in Denver Manuel McGee came across a woman who had gotten lost walking home. The woman said she needed to get to Federal Boulevard, and McGee offered to help. Once they arrived at a park, however, McGee grabbed her by her neck and threw her to the ground. The woman was choked to the point where she nearly lost consciousness, and McGee raped her. Male DNA evidence was recovered from the victim. The case went unsolved for three years until McGee was arrested for felony auto theft and his DNA was taken under a new law called Kate's Law that allowed authorities to take DNA upon arrest—rather than after conviction of a crime. Morrissey had proposed Kate's Law in Colorado and it was passed in 2010. After McGee's DNA matched the assault and rape at 13th and Decatur, Morrissey charged McGee with attempted murder and

[473] *Westword Magazine*, June 20, 2011.

sexual assault. He pleaded guilty to first-degree assault and attempted sexual assault and was sentenced to 25 years in prison.[474]

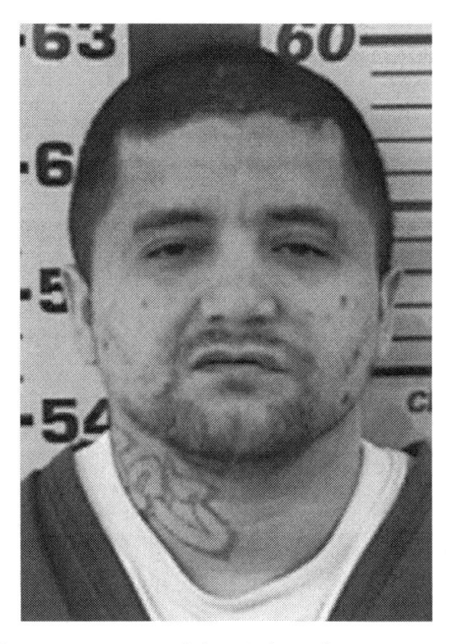

Manuel McGee, photo courtesy of the Colorado Department of Corrections

DNA evidence can also be used to free those wrongly prosecuted. In 2010, the Colorado Justice Review Project, created by Morrissey and Colorado Attorney General John Suthers, began reviewing some 5,100 Colorado cases where offenders were convicted of homicide and sexual assault to determine if DNA evidence could exonerate any of them. As part of the work of this project, in April 2012, Robert Dewey was exonerated for a 1996 rape and murder conviction in Grand Junction where he had served 17 years in prison.[475]

---

474 *Westword Magazine*, November 3, 2011, https://www.westword.com/news/manuel-mcgee-allegedly-got-away-with-brutal-rape-for-3-years-until-his-dna-betrayed-him-5849217.

475 Colorado Department of Law Attorney General John W. Suthers press release, October 1, 2009. https://www.denverda.org/wp-content/uploads/news-release/2009/Justice-Review-Project.pdf.

Robert Dewey, photo courtesy of the Colorado Department of Corrections

On March 26, 1979, 25-year-old Emma Jenefor was found raped and strangled to death in the bathtub of her Denver apartment in Cherry Creek. Police found a radio in the tub, which made it appear as if Jenefor had electrocuted herself. Jenefor's on-and-off boyfriend, who went by the nickname "Hook," was a suspect, but there never was enough evidence for an arrest. Denver DA Dale Tooley was unable to charge anyone with Jenefor's murder. In 2010, the Jenefor murder was reviewed as part of the Denver Cold Case Project. An unknown male DNA profile developed in the Jenefor murder matched unknown male DNA from the rape and murder of a woman named Peggy Cuff. 20-year-old Cuff had disappeared after her shift at a collection agency in Denver. Her partially nude body was discovered on November 3, 1979, five miles from her office in an alley; she had been raped and strangled. The same unknown male profile also emerged in the rape/murders of Joyce Ramey and Pamela Montgomery. Vincent Groves had been the primary suspect in the Ramey and Montgomery murders—Groves was a serial murderer who had been convicted of three murders but had died in prison before DNA screening became mandatory. Detective Mylous Yearling tracked down a decades-old DNA report with Grove's profile from a Lakewood, Colorado police investigator. That profile matched the DNA profiles from the Jenefor, Cuff, Ramey, and Montgomery murders. The families of the victims were notified that the cases were solved and on February 9, 2012, Morrissey cleared all four murder cases. Including his previous convictions, Groves was officially connected to seven murders and holds the distinction of being Colorado's most prolific serial killer. Cold case investigators throughout the Denver metro area believe Groves was responsible for as many as 20 additional murders, but there was no DNA in those cases to test.[476]

Not all the cold cases solved under Morrissey involved DNA. On May 18, 1999, two neighbors Malaika Tamu Griffin and Jason Horsley got into an argument in the 2300 block of Humboldt Street. Griffin went inside, got her 9mm handgun, and shot Horsley in the back, killing him instantly. Griffin disappeared after stealing a friend's car. Denver authorities found an assault rifle and grenades in her house, and her journals presaged racial violence against white people. Her story was profiled seven times on the TV show "America's Most Wanted" to no avail. But during the eighth airing on June 4, 2005, co-workers in El Cajon, California recognized Griffin and called the police. Morrissey charged her with first-degree murder, aggravated robbery, and aggravated motor vehicle theft. On March 5, 2006, she was convicted of all charges and sentenced to life in prison without parole.[477]

Jason Horsley and Malaika Tamu Griffin, photo of Horsley courtesy of the Denver district attorney's office and photo of Griffin courtesy of the Colorado Department of Corrections

[476] Daily Summit, March 7, 2012, https://www.summitdaily.com/news/denver-authorities-dead-inmate-killed-up-to-20/.
[477] Murderpedia, https://murderpedia.org/female.G/g/griffin-malaika.htm.

DNA evidence can be used in novel ways to hold individuals accountable. In the mid-1990s, Karen Stillman abandoned her children, Kristen and Will Stillman, at the home of Eric Torrez in Denver. Torrez held the Stillman children hostage for over a decade, subjecting the twins to psychological, sexual, and physical abuse, and fathering four children with Kristen. Torrez's wife, Linda, and son, Patrick, were also involved in the sexual abuse, and even the twin's mother, Karen Stillman, was aware of the abuse. When Linda would take the pregnant Kristen to the doctor, she told staff that son Patrick was the father of the babies. Eric would handcuff Will and hang him from a chain in the basement. Once he put him in an open sewage pit in the backyard for days. Karen, who was visiting, turned the hose on Will and laughed. In January 2004, the 15-year-old Kristen was forced to marry Patrick; her mother signed the form that allowed a juvenile to marry. In 2008, Will and Kristen, now adults, were able to escape the Torrez home and reported the abuse. Denver Police Detective Phil Stanford was assigned to investigate the case. DNA testing showed that Eric was the biological father of all four of Kristen's children.

DA Morrissey charged Eric, Linda, and Patrick Torrez with multiple counts of child abuse and sexual assault on the children, and he charged Karen Stillman with child abuse. Patrick Torrez pleaded guilty to second-degree assault and contributing to the delinquency of a minor and was sentenced to a sex offender program for eight years. Karen Stillman pleaded guilty to child abuse resulting in serious bodily injury and was sentenced to 16 years in prison. A jury trial for Eric and Linda Torrez began in 2010 but in the face of Kristen's devastating testimony, Eric Torrez pleaded guilty to five counts of sexual assault on a child; eight counts of sexual assault on a child by a person in a position of trust; two counts of sexual assault on a child, pattern of abuse; one count of sexual assault; and one count of sexual assault, position of trust and pattern of abuse. He was sentenced to the maximum 300 years to life in prison. Linda pleaded guilty to sexual assault on a child by a person in a position of trust. Initially, she was sentenced to an indeterminate-to-life probation sentence with a minimum of 20 years. Her probation was later revoked, and she was sent to prison for 20 years to life.[478]

[478] *Glamour Magazine*, June 29, 2011; *Westword Magazine*, September 7, 2011.

Kristen and Will Stillman, photos courtesy of the Denver district attorney's office

From left to right: Eric Torrez, Linda Torrez, Patrick Torrez, and Karen Stillman, photos courtesy of the Denver district attorney's office

An attempt on the life of the Colorado governor was also investigated by the Denver district attorney's office during Morrissey's tenure. On July 16, 2007, Aaron Snyder entered the west door of the State Capitol Building. Within five minutes he had reached the temporary offices of former district attorney and then-governor Bill Ritter. Snyder was dressed in a black tuxedo and carrying shooting earmuffs in his left hand. He stated, "I am the Emperor, and I am here to take over the State of Colorado." Colorado State Patrol Agent Jay Hemphill, assigned to protect the governor, intercepted Snyder in the reception area of the office, and diplomatically got him back out the door. They were standing immediately in front of the glass-windowed door to the governor's office, speaking at arm's-length. During the discussion, Snyder's comments became increasingly challenging. Snyder unexpectedly opened his tuxedo coat to show a large firearm protruding from his pants pocket and said, "No police are going to stop me." Hemphill drew his service pistol. As Snyder started moving toward him, Hemphill commanded loudly: "Stop—State Patrol—or I will kill you." Snyder ignored the commands and continued to move at Hemphill. Hemphill fired four shots. Snyder fell backward to the marble floor of the Capitol and died. Denver police responded to the scene, as did DA Morrissey. After investigation, Morrissey concluded that Hemphill's actions were legally justified.[479]

Aaron Snyder, photo courtesy of the Denver Police Department

Morrissey handled another case dealing with the assassination of a government official. On March 17, 2013, white supremacist gang member and recent parolee Evan Ebel used a payphone at a truck stop in Denver to order a pizza to be delivered. Nathan Leon, who delivered pizzas in addition to his job at IBM, arrived at the truck stop with the pizza. Ebel forced him into the trunk of Ebel's 1991 Cadillac DeVille and drove him to a remote location at 151 Rooney Road in Golden, Colorado where he shot Leon in the head and took his uniform. Two days later, Ebel, posing as a pizza delivery man, gunned down Colorado prisons' chief Tom Clements at his home outside Colorado Springs. After killing Clements, Ebel fled the state in the Cadillac.

Denver homicide detectives located the bank of payphones Ebel used to order the pizza. A surveillance camera showed which phone Ebel used to make the call. The Denver Crime Lab

[479] Morrisey's Letter to Peter A. Weir and Colonel Mark V. Trostel, August 3, 2007.
Denver Post, July 17, 2007. https://www.denverpost.com/2007/07/17/aaron-snyders-rise-and-fall/.

found Ebel's fingerprint on the receiver and his DNA on the mouthpiece. Another surveillance camera in Applewood, Colorado, where Leon's cellphone was recovered, showed Ebel alone driving Leon's car. DA Morrissey's office filed first-degree murder and kidnapping charges against Ebel and a nationwide at-large arrest warrant was prepared for his arrest.

On the run, Ebel shot Deputy James Boyd three times when the deputy tried to stop him for speeding in Montague County, Texas on March 21, 2013. Boyd survived the gun shots because of his bulletproof vest. Ebel then got into a high-speed chase, shooting at officers from his car window. The chase ended when the Cadillac he was driving slammed into an 18-wheel truck. Ebel got out of the car shooting and was in turn shot by officers. He died later in a Texas hospital. A ballistic comparison proved that Ebel's gun, recovered in Texas, was the same weapon used to kill both Leon and Clements.[480]

From left to right: Nathan Leon, Tom Clements, and Evan Ebel
Photo of Leon courtesy of the Denver district attorney's office and photos of Clements and Ebel courtesy of the Colorado Department of Corrections

Several shocking cases occurred during Morrissey's tenure that were emotionally difficult even for long-time professionals. On December 13, 2005, Czech citizen Martin Novotny broke into the home of his Brazilian ex-girlfriend, Ana Elisa Toledo, who worked as an au pair for a Denver couple. Novotny had plotted Toledo's murder for weeks before going to the Denver

[480] Morrisey's Letter to Peter A. Weir and Colonel Mark V. Trostel, August 3, 2007; *Denver Post*, July 17, 2007.

home in the 2500 block of South Cook Street, where Toledo was caring for the children. He was armed with a hunting knife, duct tape, and shoelaces, and had already dug a grave for Toledo near Castle Rock. Although she did her best to fight him off, Novotny stabbed Toledo 74 times. After the murder, Novotny turned himself in and gave a 45-minute confession to Denver Detective Shane Webster. Novotny said he had stabbed Toledo "many, many times." Morrissey charged Novotny with first-degree murder and burglary, and personally tried the case with Chief Deputy DA Verna Carpenter to draw attention to the issue of domestic violence. Novotny was convicted of all counts and immediately sentenced to life in prison without parole.[481]

Ana Elisa Toledo and Martin Novotny, photo of Toledo courtesy of the Denver district attorney's office and photo of Novotny courtesy of the Colorado Department of Corrections

On November 10, 2006, the Bingham family went downtown to have hot cocoa at a Larimer Square bakery. The couple was pushing four-year-old Macie and two-year-old Garrison in a tandem stroller when Lawrence Trujillo, driving a construction truck, roared through a red light at 15th and Lawrence Streets—mowing down the family. Rebecca Bingham and the two children were killed, and Frank Bingham injured. The stroller was dragged down the street under Trujillo's truck, knocking loose the license plate that would link him to the crime. Trujillo and his passenger Eric Snell sped away without stopping. Trujillo and Snell had spent much of the day drinking at strip clubs and continued to drink after trying to cover up evidence of the crime. Trujillo was later arrested and his blood alcohol content at the time was 0.226, more than twice

[481] *Summit Daily*, Associated Press, September 8, 2006.

the legal limit for driving while intoxicated. Morrissey charged Trujillo with three counts of vehicular homicide—DUI; three counts of vehicular homicide—reckless driving; two counts of child abuse resulting in death; three counts of leaving the scene of an accident resulting in death; and one count of leaving the scene of an accident resulting in serious bodily injury. Morrissey also charged the passenger Eric Snell with being an accessory to the crimes. Morrissey and Chief Deputy Lamar Sims handled the case. Trujillo pleaded guilty to all the charges, and Snell pleaded guilty to accessory to vehicular homicide. Trujillo was sentenced to 48 years in prison, and Snell received a six-year suspended sentence, a 90-day jail term for the DUI, and two years of probation; probation was later revoked, and the sentence imposed.[482]

The Bingham family, courtesy of the Denver district attorney's office

[482] *Denver Post*, October 2, 2007; *Denver Post*, April 2, 2008, https://www.denverpost.com/2008/04/02/passenger-in-bingham-case-sent-to-prison/

Lawrence Trujillo, photo courtesy of the Colorado Department of Corrections

A lethal case of witness intimidation occurred on December 6, 2006, when Willie Clark and Shun Birch broke down the door of Kalonniann Clark's Denver home, chased her outside, and shot her in the head as she ran down the sidewalk. Kalonniann was murdered on the orders of Brian Kenneth Hicks to prevent her from testifying against Hicks in an upcoming attempted murder trial. Hicks, the leader of one of Denver's largest drug-dealing gangs and had tried to shoot Kalonniann outside a Denver nightclub in 2005. Willie Clark was a member of the gang, and Birch was paid in money, cars, and drugs for his part in the murder. Hicks was in custody at the Denver County Jail at the time of the killing, so Detective Joel Humphrey listened to thousands of hours of recorded phone calls from the jail to decipher Hicks's calls to his fellow drug dealers and gang members planning the killing. DA Morrissey asked the Metro Gang Taskforce for help investigating the individuals involved in Hicks's drug operation. Many members of the gang were indicted by the U.S. attorney, and they agreed to cooperate in the murder case. The Denver grand jury indicted Hicks, Clark, and Birch for first-degree murder, solicitation to commit first-degree murder, conspiracy to commit first-degree murder, and aggravated intimidation of a witness or victim. Each man was convicted of all counts in separate trials and each are serving lengthy sentences that include life without parole.[483]

[483] *Denver Post*, October 2, 2007; *Denver Post*, April 2, 2008; *Associated Press*, November 19, 2008; *Westword*

Kalonniann Clark, photo courtesy of the Denver district attorney's office

From left to right: Brian Kenneth Hicks, Willie Clark, and Shun Birch, photos of Hicks and Clark courtesy of the Denver district attorney's office, photo of Birch courtesy of the Colorado Department of Corrections

Another crime involving the same gang occurred on January 1, 2007, when Denver Broncos cornerback Darrent Demarcus Williams was killed during a drive-by shooting. Williams and two other passengers were shot when a vehicle pulled beside Williams's rented limousine near 11th Avenue and Speer Boulevard. Williams sustained a single gunshot wound to the neck,

---

Magazine, February 7, 2011.

killing him instantly. The two other passengers injured in the shooting were both released from the hospital the following day. There was a total of 17 people in the vehicle. Williams had been attending a New Year's Eve party/birthday party held for and by Denver Nuggets basketball player Kenyon Martin at a nearby nightclub. The shooting was preceded by an argument and altercation at the nightclub between Crips gang members and other patrons, one of whom was Broncos teammate Brandon Marshall. Williams was not part of the altercation. The Denver police impounded a Chevrolet Tahoe in connection with the shooting. The vehicle was registered to Brian Hicks, a Crips gang member, who was already incarcerated awaiting trial for attempted murder and drug charges.

Morrissey enlisted the assistance of the Metro Gang Task Force which was investigating major narcotics operations involving the Crips. After the federal indictments of associates of Hicks came down, those members of the gang who had knowledge of the murder of Williams cooperated in the murder investigation. They named Willie D. Clark as the shooter. On May 30, 2008, the *Rocky Mountain News* obtained a signed confession letter by Crips gang member Clark, in which he admitted to firing the shot that killed Williams. After an extensive investigation, the grand jury indicted Clark on one count of first-degree murder and 16 counts of attempted first-degree murder. Chief deputies Bruce Levin and Tim Twining prosecuted the case. At trial, gang member Daniel Harris testified that he had been in the backseat of the Tahoe that Clark was driving. He said he saw Clark lean over the center console and fire shots out the passenger-side window. Harris testified that he did not know who, if anyone, was the second shooter. At the close of a lengthy trial, the jury found Clark guilty of all counts. Clark was sentenced to life in prison for the murder of Williams plus 1,152 years for the attempted murders of the other passengers in the limousine.[484]

On September 21, 2007, Miriam Gallegos called the Denver Police to report that her 3-year-old daughter, Neveah, had been kidnapped. Although she had not been able to see the driver, she was able to provide a description of the car. Police searched for the car and child without success. Later, Gallegos changed her story. She told detectives that her boyfriend, Angel Ray Montoya, called her at work and told her she needed to come home immediately. When she

[484] *Denver Post,* October 8, 2008, https://www.denverpost.com/2008/10/08/indictment-in-slaying-of-bronco-darrent-williams/; *New York Times*, December 31, 2016, https://www.google.com/amp/s/www.nytimes.com/2016/12/31/sports/death-darrent-williams-resonates-10-years-later.amp.html.

arrived at her apartment, she found Neveah unconscious and not breathing. Gallegos and Montoya put the toddler's body into a duffel bag; Montoya left with the duffel bag while Gallegos called 911 with her false story. Montoya was arrested but authorities were unable to locate Neveah's body, despite a widespread search. Montoya's attorney contacted DA Morrissey and indicated that if Morrissey would not seek the death penalty, Montoya would show police where he had hidden the little girl's body. Three days after the missing child report, Montoya took detectives and Morrissey to the Lakewood Dry Gulch in the 1100 block of Perry Street in Denver where he had disposed of the body, covering it with debris. At the time of the autopsy, the cause of Neveah's death was undetermined, but after consulting an expert on child deaths it was determined to have been asphyxiation. The Denver grand jury indicted Montoya on one count of first-degree murder and child abuse resulting in death and Gallegos on one count of child abuse resulting in death and being an accessory to a crime. Prosecutors Michelle Amico and Christine Washburn handled the case. Montoya was convicted at trial of first-degree murder and abuse of a corpse and sentenced to life without parole. Gallegos pleaded guilty to child abuse resulting in death and was sentenced to 12 years in prison.[485]

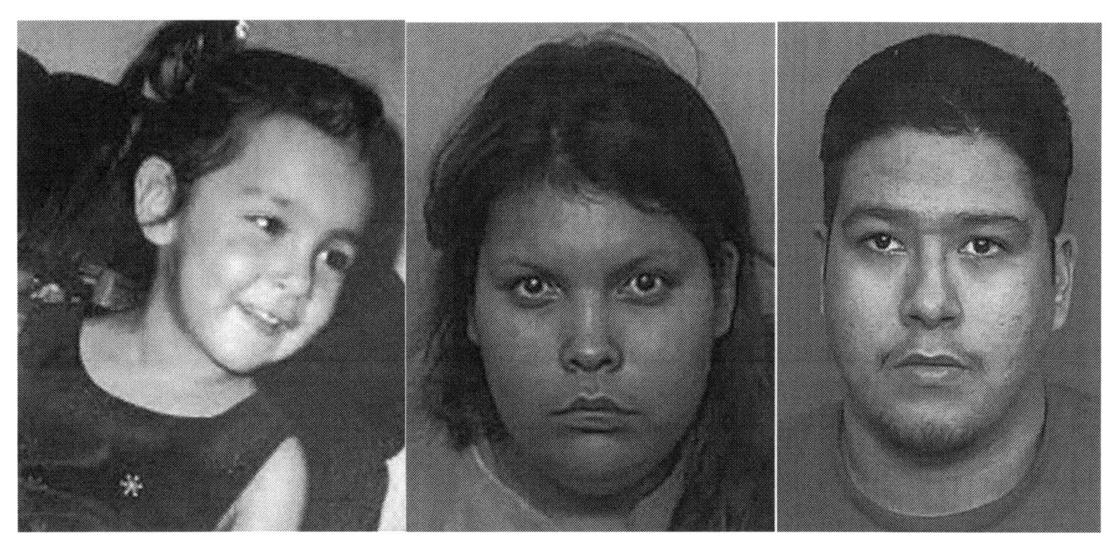

Neveah Janey Gallegos, Miriam Gallegos, and Angel Ray Montoya, photos courtesy of Denver district attorney's office

Morrissey's office handled corruption cases as well. On May 16, 2010, Denver police officer Hector Paez arrested a woman and ran a background check on her, finding an outstanding warrant for her arrest. He took the woman to an isolated area and coerced her into performing a

[485] *Channel 7 News Denver*, September 24, 2007; *CBS4 Denver*, May 6, 2009; *Denver Post*, January 7, 2011; *Denver Post*, May 15, 2012.

sexual act to avoid being taken to jail. Morrissey charged Paez with kidnapping and sexual assault. The trial was handled by chief deputy Doug Jackson. Paez denied the sexual assault and claimed that he took the woman to the secluded location to question her as part of an investigation. The jury found him guilty of sexual assault, kidnapping, and filing a false report. Paez was sentenced to eight years in prison.[486]

Hector Paez, photo courtesy of the Denver district attorney's office

Domestic violence cases continued to claim considerable resources in the office, as they have since the district attorney's office was established. One case charged by Morrissey illustrates how domestic violence can come in different forms. On November 17, 2014, Andres Sanchez-Luevano came home "extremely intoxicated" and when his girlfriend confronted him about his boozing, he began yelling at her and shoved her after she refused his demand to give him money. When she picked up the phone to call the police, Sanchez-Luevano grabbed her kitten, a one-month-old named Mickey, and slammed it against the floor, killing it. As he fled the scene, he said That's what you get, bitch." DA Morrissey charged Sanchez-Luevano with one count of aggravated cruelty to animals. He pleaded guilty and initially received two years' probation which was later revoked, and he was sentenced to a year in jail.[487]

Another common type of crime during Morrissey's tenure related to the burgeoning marijuana industry. The decriminalization of marijuana as well as the legalization of recreational

[486] *Westword*, November 12, 2018, https://www.westword.com/news/hector-paez-the-eight-year-ordeal-of-denver-police-officers-sexual-assault-victim-10983675.

[487] *Westword Magazine*, December 12, 2014.

marijuana use through Amendment 64 brought unique problems to Colorado, including crimes against marijuana businesses. Because marijuana use and cultivation remained against federal law, banking institutions refused to do business with marijuana establishments, forcing the businesses to handle all transactions in cash. This situation proved too tempting for criminals, and Morrissey's office often dealt with the aftermath.

One example happened on January 25, 2011, when Dominic Chee Marks and Cody Richison forced their way into the home of Susan Wiggs, a marijuana dealer, in search of money and marijuana. The robbery was interrupted by the arrival of Wiggs's husband and son. As Wiggs's husband struggled with Richison, who was carrying a shotgun, Marks fired his handgun. One of the bullets struck Wiggs and killed her. The robbers fled. By late 2012, Denver homicide detectives had statements from a group of witnesses who had driven with the robbers to Wiggs's home. Richison was arrested and confessed to his involvement in the crimes. Morrissey charged Marks and Richison with first-degree felony murder, aggravated robbery, and burglary. Marks was found guilty at trial of first-degree murder, aggravated robbery, and first-degree burglary. He was sentenced to life without parole. Richison pleaded guilty to attempted murder and was sentenced to prison for 20 years.[488]

Dominic Chee Marks (left) and Cody Richison (right), photos courtesy of the Colorado Department of Corrections

On March 23, 2011, five people were shot during a medical marijuana robbery at the Windsor Court Apartments at 900 South Quince Street in Denver. Amara Kamoh Sayon and

[488] People v. Marks, No. 14CA0030, December 3, 2015.

Cherise Houston died from their wounds—Sayon of a gunshot wound to the chest and Houston of a gunshot wound to the head. Morrissey was never able to charge anyone for these crimes because a week later, the shooters, Jovan Rivers and Darrell King, were killed attempting to rob a medical marijuana caregiver in Aurora, Colorado. Rivers and King were wielding the same weapons that killed Sayon and Houston when they were gunned down by a woman with an assault rifle during the attempted robbery.[489]

Robert Young and Mark Rubinson committed one of the more bizarre crimes of the last decade. On August 27, 2011, Young arrived at the home of his friend Jeffrey Jarrett in Denver and found Jarrett dead. Instead of calling authorities, Young went to find his friend Rubinson. The duo returned to Jarrett's home and—like the movie "Weekend at Bernie's"—they put Jarrett's body into Rubinson's SUV and headed to a nightspot, where they spent more than an hour drinking, leaving Jarrett's body in the vehicle. Young used Jarrett's credit card to pay for the drinks. Rubinson and Young then drove to another restaurant to hang out. Jarrett's body was still slumped in the back of the car. They then returned to Jarrett's home, carried him in, and put him in bed. From there they went to get gas and made a stop at a burrito joint, again using Jarrett's credit card. To cap off the evening, they then went to a strip club and used Jarrett's card to take out $400 from an ATM. Eventually they flagged down a police officer to tell him they thought their friend was dead. Police went to Jarrett's home and found the body. Young told the police Jarrett was obviously dead while they were at the first stop of the night. Morrissey charged both men with abusing a corpse, identity theft, and criminal impersonation. Young was convicted of all charges and sentenced to four years' probation, and eventually prison. Rubinson pleaded guilty to abuse of a corpse and received two years' probation.[490]

---

[489] *Westword Magazine*, March 28, 2011; *Westword Magazine*, April 4, 2011, https://www.westword.com/news/jovan-rivers-harrell-king-killed-in-alleged-aurora-medical-marijuana-burglary-5831045.
[490] *Westword Magazine*, January 20, 2012.

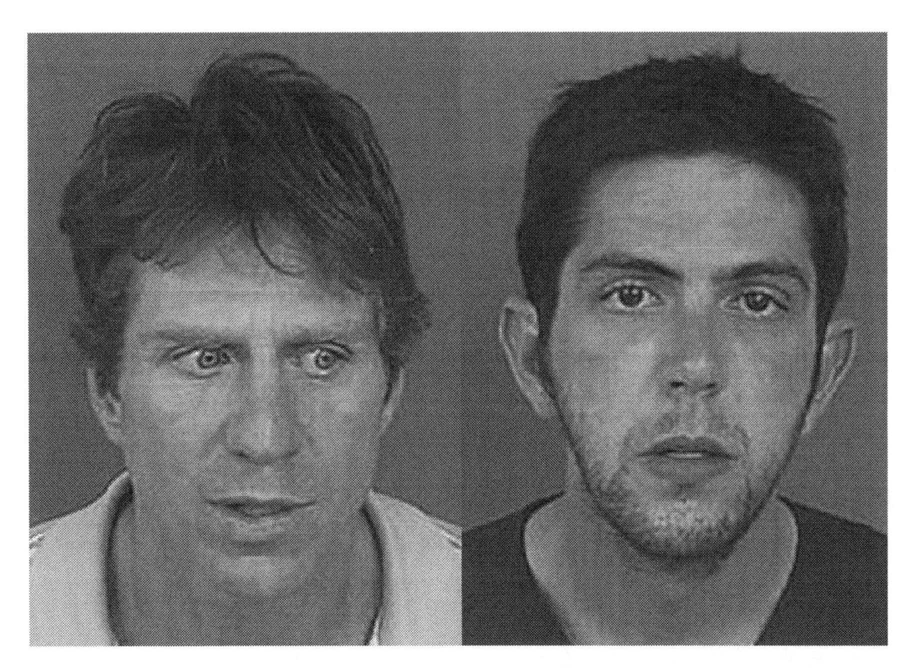

Robert Young and Mark Rubinson, photos courtesy of the Denver district attorney's office

Two Denver officers died in the line of duty during Morrissey's time in office. Detective Donald "Donnie" Young was killed May 8, 2005, while working off-duty at a private event. Young and another officer were approached from behind by a man who opened fire on them. Young was hit three times and died. The other officer was wounded, and the suspect fled the scene. A massive international fugitive hunt resulted in locating the killer, Raul Gomez-Garcia, in Mexico about one month later. Extradition to the U.S. proved problematic because Mexican law prohibited extraditing individuals if they would face the death penalty or life without the possibility of parole. Murder of a law enforcement officer in Colorado is usually a capital offense. Morrissey decided to charge Gomez-Garcia with second-degree murder to procure his extradition. Gomez-Garcia was tried, found guilty, and sentenced to 80 years in prison.[491]

[491] People v. Gomez-Garcia, No. 06CA2556, September 3, 2009.

Detective Donald "Donnie" Young (left) and Raul Gomez-Garcia (right), photo of Young courtesy of the Denver Police Museum and photo of Gomez-Garcia courtesy of the Colorado Department of Corrections

The second Denver officer to die during Morrissey's term of office was also the second female Denver officer to die in the line of duty. Officer Celena Charise Hollis became another victim of gang violence when she attempted to break up a fight among several people on June 24, 2012, at a jazz festival at Denver City Park. A purported gang member fired several shots during the melee in a dispute between two rival gangs, striking officer Hollis and killing her. Rollin Oliver was convicted by Morrissey of second-degree murder and sentenced to the maximum term of 26 years.[492]

---

[492] Officer Down Memorial page, https://www.odmp.org/officer/21309-police-officer-celena-charise-hollis.

Officer Celena Charise Hollis and Rollin Oliver, photo of Hollis courtesy of the Denver Police Museum and photo of Oliver courtesy of the Colorado Department of Corrections

The first Denver crime laboratory was established in 1947. The lab was in a single room in the Denver Police Headquarters Building at 1313 Champa Street. The first instrument in the lab was a comparison microscope for the examination of bullets and shell casings. It was purchased by ballistic and firearms expert, then police lieutenant Joseph Moomaw, with his own funds. Forensic sciences continued to develop throughout the 1950s and 1960s. During this time Denver police recruit classes were instructed in fingerprinting, firearms, crime scene preservation, and blood alcohol determinations. Moomaw was featured in a 1960 article in the *Denver Post* demonstrating how to handle a revolver to avoid damage to fingerprints. In 1978 when Denver police headquarters moved to a new building at 1331 Cherokee Street, the crime lab was located on the sixth floor. In 2007, DA Morrissey spearheaded the bond issue campaign to build a new crime lab. In 2012, a state-of-the-art, 60,000-square-foot crime lab was opened at 1371 Cherokee Street; the four-story building was designed to oversee Denver's forensic workload for the next 50 years.[493]

In 2005, Morrissey began conducting tours of the Denver Police Crime Laboratory to help nonprofits in metro Denver fundraise for their organizations introducing thousands of

[493] "New Lab Opening Day Booklet," June 5, 2012. www.denvergov.org/content/dam/denvergov/Portals/720/documents/News/CrimeLab_Booklet.pdf.

people to the work of the lab in solving the worst crimes in Denver. Originally the tours were in the antiquated facility on the sixth floor of Denver Police Headquarters wow desperately Denver needed a new crime lab. After the successful bond issue campaign, Morrissey continued donating tours of the new lab to charity throughout his tenure as district attorney, helping a variety of nonprofits raise tens of thousands of dollars and giving the public the opportunity to see one of Denver's finest civic and scientific assets.

Denver Crime Lab at 14th and Cherokee, completed in 2012 under the leadership of Crime Lab Director Dr. Gregg LaBerge and DA Morrissey

Morrissey instituted many initiatives focused on his expertise in DNA including the Denver Cold Case DNA Project where detectives review unsolved sexual assaults and murders to determine if they can be solved with new DNA technologies. In 2005, Morrissey, together with the Denver Crime Laboratory and the Denver Police Department, launched the Denver Burglary DNA Project using a grant from the National Institute of Justice. The DNA Burglary Project was designed to identify biological evidence at burglary crime scenes and develop DNA profiles that would help catch and later convict these criminals. The project proved that using DNA to solve and prosecute burglaries was not only cost-effective but had a positive impact on the quality of life in Denver. Once the project was implemented, hundreds of habitual burglars were arrested and convicted after their DNA was found at burglary scenes. As a result, the burglary rate in Denver was reduced by 11% each year for four consecutive years. The Denver Burglary DNA Project was part of a report by the National Institute of Justice and was implemented in other communities across the country.

The Denver Burglary Project flyer, photo courtesy of the Denver district attorney's office

Not all the new programs under Morrissey involved DNA. In 2006, along with Denver City Attorney Cole Finegan, Morrissey created the Denver Domestic Violence Triage Review Team. This team included a Denver police detective and staff from the Denver police department's domestic violence and victim's assistance units, representatives from the district attorney's office and the city attorney's office, and community advocacy groups to review domestic violence cases the day after they happened. The program continues today.

Denver Domestic Violence Triage Review Team Logo, photo courtesy of Denver district attorney's office

Identity theft was another of the white-collar criminal areas focused on by Morrissey's office. An article written by Morrissey entitled, "Identity Theft Prosecution a High Priority" in the September 2005 issue of the *Colorado Lawyer* discussed the proactive approach the Denver district attorney's Economic Crime Unit taking in the investigation and prosecution of identity theft rings working throughout Colorado. Morrissey gave examples of how the judges in Denver recognized the seriousness of identity theft crimes as evidenced by lengthy prison sentences for identity thieves. He also discussed the Economic Crime Specialists he employed to help scores of victims negotiate the steps necessary to prove their victimization and seek financial restitution. Morrissey explained how the district attorney's office provided identity theft prevention seminars throughout the Denver community so people could protect themselves.

On August 19, 2016, Morrissey announced the implementation of a paperless electronic system between the Denver police and the district attorney's office that would save about $1 million in staff time and paperwork yearly. Relying on video conferencing instead of in-person meetings, police were able to give prosecutors quicker access to investigative materials so they could determine whether criminal charges were warranted and, if so, file them faster. With more than 9,000 cases reviewed annually, the process removed mountains of paperwork that typically had congested storage shelves. Morrissey had already implemented a misdemeanor system that had been paperless for nearly two years. This final move made the criminal justice system in Denver nearly all electronic. Previously, cases were manually entered into two different systems, once within the police department and the other into the district attorney's computers. After implementation, material such as driver's license data and police body-worn cameras could be downloaded automatically into the prosecutor's system. The process also cut down on human errors that occurred with information that had been entered manually.[494]

Arson fires in Denver have long been investigated by specially trained investigators from the Denver Fire Department, not detectives from the Denver Police Department. Shortly after being elected, DA Morrissey assigned a deputy district attorney to be on-call 24 hours a day to assist fire investigators. Morrissey recognized that arson investigators need a go-to deputy who is an expert in arson cases, and he made sure that the deputy received training in arson and bomb investigations. This program received national recognition from arson investigators and fire departments across the country and Morrissey was asked to address a conference of the National Fire Protection Association.[495]

DA Morrissey at the Denver Fire Department "Fire Ops. 101 Course, photo and logo courtesy of the Denver Fire Department; Masonic building 1614 Welton Street 1996 arson fire. Photo courtesy of the Denver Fire Journal and Western Fire History, Dec. 9, 2014

Morrissey received several awards and recognitions during his long prosecutorial career. In 2001, he was named Colorado's "Prosecutor of the Year" and received the "Award for Prosecution Excellence" presented annually by the Colorado District Attorneys' Council. He received the Association of Prosecuting Attorneys' Lifetime Achievement Award for Innovation and Community Engagement. Morrissey was recognized for his work developing programs involving juvenile diversion, treatment courts, and witness protection.[496]

Morrissey championed alternatives to the criminal justice system for drug and alcohol abusers by kick-starting Drug Court and Sobriety Court. Denver's Drug Court is an innovative and humane approach to the area's drug problem. The treatment court once had served as a model for the nation, but in 2002 it became a casualty of judicial controversy, overcrowded criminal dockets, financial constraints, and apathy. Morrissey launched the new Drug Court on February 1, 2007, with the help of others in the city and funding from Denver's Crime

---

494 *Denver Post*, August 19, 2016.
495 Dialogue: Denver DA, August 2016, https://www.youtube.com/watch?v=uZR5XJZntGw.
496 Wikipedia, https://en.wikipedia.org/wiki/Mitchell_R._Morrissey.

Prevention and Control Commission. The new Drug Court included funding for mental health treatment.[497]

Denver's Sobriety Court was a special treatment court in Denver County for misdemeanor offenders. It was developed to reduce the rate of drunk driving in Denver. When Colorado passed a felony DUI law in 2015, Morrissey spearheaded the creation of the RESTART program in the Denver District Court. The RESTART (Recognizing and Establishing Smart Treatment Alternatives for Recovery and Transition) Program was an innovative program for individuals arrested on their fourth or subsequent DUI, DWAI or DUI Per Se offense. Because of his interest in finding creative approaches to the problem of domestic violence, Morrissey and his wife Maggie championed, both politically and financially, the establishment of the Rose Andom Center. Opened in 2015, the Center offers one safe place where domestic violence victims can obtain a variety of services. Morrissey and Denver mayor Michael Hancock met twice with then Vice President Joe Biden to obtain his support for the Center, which they received.

After three terms, Morrissey stepped down as district attorney in 2017 due to term limits. He continues to consult and train on the use of DNA in the criminal justice system both nationally and internationally. He also still works to solve cold cases using familial DNA searching and genetic genealogy analysis through his company United Data Connect.[498]

---

[497] Colorado Public Radio, June 23, 2014, https://www.cpr.org/2014/06/23/denver-drug-court-survives-near-death-experience-reaches-20th-anniversary/.
[498] United Data Connect Success stories, https://www.uniteddataconnect.com/successstories.

Flyer with the first four cases solved by Morrissey's United Data Connect team, photo courtesy of United Data Connect

29. Beth McCann (2017–Present)

BETH MCCANN
2017-

Beth McCann is Denver's current district attorney and the first woman elected to the post. Beth McCann assumed office January 10, 2017. Prior to her election as district attorney, McCann was a four-term state representative from northeast Denver where she worked on juvenile justice, human trafficking, and gun control legislation. McCann was born in Radford, Virginia and attended college at Wittenberg University and Georgetown University law school. Before entering private practice for eight years, she completed a clerkship for Colorado's U.S. District Court judge Sherman G. Finesilver and worked for seven years in the Denver district attorney's office as a deputy and chief deputy.

McCann was appointed the Manager of Safety by Denver mayor Wellington Webb; her term covered the 1993 riots and unrest called The Summer of Violence. McCann also worked as the Deputy Attorney General for Civil Litigation and Employment Law in the Colorado Attorney General's Office. An active leader in state and city politics, McCann is a founding member and former president of the Colorado Women's Bar Association and has served on transition teams and search committees as well as legal associations and the Board of Governors of the Colorado Bar Association.

One of the first serious crimes during McCann's first term occurred on January 31, 2017. Two women were asking an armed security officer named Scott Von Lanken about light rail routes when Joshua Cummings approached from behind and shot Lanken in the neck. The shooting happened just after 11:00 p.m. at 16th and Wynkoop streets on Union Station Plaza, one block from Union Station. One of the women heard Cummings say something like, "Do what you are told," just before he opened fire and ran away. Cummings was found later hiding on the terrace of an apartment building with the handgun. Cummings had joined the Army in 1996 but never saw combat and had pledged his allegiance to ISIS. He later told a reporter that he shot Lanken, "For the pleasure of Allah." DA McCann charged Cummings with first-degree murder. McCann and Chief Deputy Bonnie Benedetti prosecuted the case. The case was strong, eye-witness testimony, surveillance video of the shooting, and the 9-mm pistol found on Cummings was tied to the shell casing found at the scene through ballistic comparison. Cummings was convicted of first-degree murder and sentenced to life without parole.[499]

Scott Van Lanken (left), and Joshua Cummings (right); Van Lanken photo from OfficerDown.US, Cummings photo courtesy of the Colorado Department of Corrections

Later that same year, on June 2, 2017, Jason Brown was driving his truck "at an unknown speed," and ran over Kimberly Macey and another pedestrian as they walked through a Broadway alley near Ellsworth Avenue in Denver. Brown proceeded to step on the gas and flee the scene. Macey was killed and the male pedestrian suffered serious injuries. Brown was later arrested at his Lakewood home. McCann charged Brown with vehicular homicide, vehicular assault, careless driving resulting in death, careless driving resulting in injury, and two counts of leaving the scene of an accident. He was also charged with habitual criminal counts. After a four-day trial, Brown was convicted as charged and was determined to be a habitual criminal. He was sentenced to 108 years in prison.[500]

---

[499] Associated Press and Dailymail.com, January 25, 2018.
[500] *Street Blog Denver*, January 8, 2018.

Jason Brown, photo courtesy of the Colorado Department of Corrections

In another murder that summer, Delian Stamps went on a violent rampage on Curtis Street near 24th Avenue in downtown Denver. The attacks left 62-year-old James Farmer dead and three others, including a police officer, injured. Denver police officers responded to a call of a fight at 4:00 a.m. on June 16. When they arrived, they found a teenage boy and girl who had been injured. The boy had serious injuries and had to be hospitalized. A witness pointed police officers in the direction the attacker had fled. Officers found Stamps standing over Farmer, striking him repeatedly in the chest. Stamps was reported as saying, "I did it. I did it," as he continued to hit Farmer, killing him. As officers approached, Stamps charged toward them, and one of the officers was injured in the struggle. Stamps was taken into custody. The investigation revealed that Stamps had attacked and killed Farmer when Farmer tried to stop Stamp's attack on the two teenagers. DA McCann charged Stamps with first-degree murder, first-degree assault, two counts of second-degree assault, and third-degree assault. Stamps was convicted as charged and sentenced to life without parole plus 24 years.[501]

[501] *Denver Post*, March 5, 2019.

Left: James Farmer, Jr., photo courtesy of Chandra Banks. Right: Delian Stamps, photo courtesy of the Colorado Department of Corrections

Not every case investigated by the district attorney's office is blatantly violent, nor necessarily criminal. In the summer of 2017, McCann reviewed a controversial case in which members of the East High School cheerleading team were forced to perform splits, resulting in several of the team members crying out in pain. Denver police investigated and interviewed staff, cheerleading students' families, and the students themselves before presenting the case to the district attorney's office for review of criminal charges. The cheerleading team coach, who was accused of physical and emotional intimidation, was fired as a result of the investigation. The East High School principal retired and the assistant principal resigned. McCann described the video of the exercise as painful to watch but not a situation that rose to the level of criminal charges.[502]

Meanwhile, the murder of Caden McWilliams in 2018 by his parents Leland Pankey and Elisha Pankey is one of the most disturbing cases ever handled by the Denver district attorney's office. The seven-year-old suffered a fractured skull, a broken arm, and weighed only twenty-seven pounds when he died. After beating the child to death, his parents wrapped the second grader in garbage bags, put his body in a dog crate, and then entombed him in concrete before hiding the body in a storage shed. Caden's sister, who was four years old at the time of his death, heard his screams when he was being beaten and told authorities she "fed her starving brother

[502] *Denver Post,* October 14, 2017, https://www.denverpost.com/2017/10/14/former-east-high-cheerleading-coach-will-not-be-charged/.

cereal through the gaps in the dog kennel."[503] The kennel was a place where his father would sometimes make the boy sleep and where he had been found dead the morning after his fatal beating. Both parents pleaded guilty to child abuse resulting in death and tampering with a deceased human body. Leland Pankey was given a 72-year sentence; his wife, who pled butt first and cooperated with law enforcement, was given a 32-year sentence.

On March 24, 2019, Jerome Lucas broke into a woman's home and attacked her. The woman had returned home from the gym around 1:20 p.m. and then showered and took recycling items outside. She left the front door to her home open but closed her screen door. When she returned to her house, Lucas rushed up to her and punched her in the head several times, causing her to fall to the ground. Lucas demanded money and her "good jewelry." He then tied her up, gagged her, and sexually assaulted her. Afterwards, he barricaded her front door with her couches then stole her car and fled. The victim went out her back door and got to a friend's house to call police. She was taken to Denver Health Medical Center for treatment. A DNA profile was obtained from evidence taken from the scene and a CODIS (the DNA database) hit resulted in a match to Lucas. DA McCann charged 34-year-old Lucas with sexual assault, kidnapping, burglary, and assault. Police in Portland, Oregon and U.S. Marshals arrested Lucas and he was extradited back to Denver. Lucas was convicted and sentenced to 43 years in prison.[504]

[503] *Denver Post*, February 28, 2020.
[504] Denver district attorney's office, arrest affidavit, https://www.denverda.org/wp-content/uploads/news-release/2019/052119-Jerome-Lucas-Arrest-Affidavit-REDACTED.pdf.

Jerome Lucas, photo courtesy of the Colorado Department of Corrections

While in office, McCann has focused on improving relations between the community and the justice system as well as race relations. She was featured in the ABA Journal on June 1, 2019, as one of the "Prosecutors Changing the Paradigm." The article describes her as one of the "district attorneys of all political stripes [who] are reforming their offices to reflect a data-driven and more humane approach to criminal justice." She crusades nationally for "prosecutorial reform, advocates are urging change at the legislative level through aggressive decriminalization efforts and winnowing down chargeable offenses."[505] In 2021, The Denver DA website announced that McCann was part of a group that sent a letter to President Joseph Biden encouraging him to abolish the federal death penalty. McCann has also focused on domestic violence issues. Her office is represented on the Rose Andom Center's board and was also the first in Colorado to have a firearms relinquishment investigator.

Unfortunately, McCann also had to deal with both management and personal controversies during her first term. While McCann was a state senator, her husband, Christopher Linsmayer, was responsible for starting several fires in Grand County, in the Colorado mountains. Linsmayer pleaded guilty to a petty offense violation. "We fear for our lives and that of our property because this individual has been allowed to repeatedly commit the same acts of arson with no punishment," one neighbor said in a letter to authorities.[506] In 2020, Linsmayer started additional fires on their property. This time, the Grand County DA took a harsher stance, and Linsmayer was charged with twelve felony counts of fourth-degree arson[507] and pleaded guilty to both felony and misdemeanor charges in the summer of 2021.

In addition to her husband's legal issues, McCann had office controversies. Her second-in-command was forced to resign three years into her first term after he allegedly bullied other office staff. *Colorado Politics* reported that Assistant DA Ryan Brackley resigned after "bullying other staffers and intimidating another top prosecutor with a baseball bat."[508] Brackley, along with two other staff members, either disciplined or forced to resign, and were paid a total of $237,000 in settlement and severance pay by the DA.[509] Despite these challenges, McCann easily

[505] ABA Journal, June 1, 2019. https://www.abajournal.com/magazine/article/change-agents-reform-prosecutors.
[506] *Sky-Hi News*, February 9, 2020.
[507] *Grand Gazette*, November 3, 2020.
[508] *Colorado Politics*, July 19, 2018. https://www.coloradopolitics.com/denver/denver-das-2nd-in-command-to-resign-following-bullying-intimidation-complaints/article_a6c10dba-b192-11e9-8d1c-eb8c6c961fdd.html.
[509] Colorado Politics, September 7, 2019. https://www.coloradopolitics.com/news/premium/denver-district-attorney-

won her second term as district attorney in November 2020 and continues to bring Denver criminals to justice.

mccann-gave-237-000-in-settlement-and-severance-pay-to-employees-leaving/article_5147dba8-d176-11e9-801d-0b4fd83f0c92.html.

Conclusion

The history of the Denver district attorney's office reflects the changing society that it serves. As Coloradans' values evolved and the wider community became aware of issues like mental health, attitudes moved from the primarily law enforcement focus of the frontier to the criminal justice focus of today. Short trials and lynchings are long in the past; today's legal processes are intentional, careful, and transparent as befits a system that embraces a modern worldview. Law enforcement at all levels responds to the expectations of citizens. From body cameras to the public posting of formerly internal decisions, the actions and motivations of police officers and investigators are available for scrutiny like never before. The Denver district attorney's office leads the way in balancing the demands of justice with the needs of both victims and offenders.

We, the authors, encourage lawyers new to the profession or looking for a change to consider the public arena. District attorneys and public defenders work hard, deal with tough realities, and have the satisfaction of making a profound difference every day. New attorneys usually start in County Court and progress through levels until they reach District Court, where nearly all cases are at the felony level. County Court deputies handle less serious cases, but their efforts can be far-reaching—they can prevent the homicides of the future through early intervention in a defendant's trajectory. Criminal trials at all levels are challenging and thrilling. They inevitably change the lives of both defendants and victims. To lose a trial after weeks of work evaluating evidence, interviewing witnesses, enduring delays, agonizing over jury selection, and practicing opening and closing arguments is a disappointment so deep that it is hard to describe. Winning at trial is exhilarating, but not a reason for celebration, because someone's life or liberty will never be the same.

In prosecution and public defense, lawyers face the dark side of life but have the important opportunity to be part of a cohort dedicated to justice. The district attorney's office is where idealism and realism meet, and anyone lucky enough to work there will have indelible memories and great stories to tell.

Bibliography

Aldama, Arturo, Elisa Facio, Daryl Maeda, and Reiland Rabaka. 2011. *Enduring Legacies: Ethnic Histories and Cultures of Colorado.* University Press of Colorado.

Alt, Betty, and Sandra Wells. 2008. *Mountain Mafia: Organized Crime in the Rockies.* Cold Tree Press: Nashville, Tennessee.

Barber, John and Henry Howe. 1865. *Before and Since: Being an Encyclopedia and Panorama of the Western States, Pacific States and Territories of the Union.* F.A. Howe: Cincinnati, Ohio.

Bell, J.v.L. "1860 Denver City Turkey War." Frontier Colorado Historical Mysteries. http://jvlbell.com/1860-denver-city-turkey-war/.

Biography of Colorado. 1901. The Century Publishing Company: Chicago, Illinois.

Bricklin, Julia. 2018. *Polly Pry: The Woman Who Wrote the West.* TwoDot Books.

Carlino, Sam. 2019. *Colorado's Carlino Brothers: A Bootlegging Empire.* The History Press: Charleston, South Carolina.

Cinquanta, Daril. 2017. *The Blue Chameleon: The Life Story of a Supercop.* Waldorf Publishing: New York.

Correa, Thomas. 2020. *The American Cowboy Chronicles: Old West Myths & Legends: The Honest Truth,* Page Publishing.

Colorado and Its People; A Narrative and Topical History of the Centennial State. 1948. Lewis Historical Publishing Co: New York.

Cook, David, J. 1897. *Hands Up; Or Thirty-Five Years of Detective Life in the Mountains and on the Plains.* W. F. Robinson Printing Company: Denver, Colorado.

Goodstein, Phil. 2006. *In the Shadow of the Klan, When the KKK Ruled Denver 1920-1926.* New Social Publications: Denver, Colorado.

Goodstein, Phill. 2004. *Robert Speer's Denver 1904-1920.* New Social Publications: Denver, Colorado.

Goodstein, Phil. 1993. *The Seamy Side of Denver.* New Social Publications: Denver, Colorado.

Gove, Aaron, Reuben Hatch, Barrett McWhirter, Nathan Coy, Henry Burnside Smith, and William Barnard Mooney, ed. 1894. *The Colorado Law School Journal*, Volume 10.

Hall, Frank. 1895. *History of the State of Colorado.* Blakely Printing Company: Chicago, Illinois.

Herman, Ben and Hannah Bretz. 2008. "The First Horse Thief Vigilante Justice and Lynching in Golden." http://goldencemetery.blogspot.com/

History of Colorado – Biographical. 1927. State Historical and Natural History Society. Linderman Co., Inc.: Denver, Colorado.

Holbrook, Stewart Hall. 1956. *Rocky Mountain Revolution*. Published by Henry Holt.

Horsely, Albert. 1907. *The Confessions and Autobiography of Harry Orchard*. S.S. McClure Company.

Hosakawa, Bill. 1976. *Thunder in the Rockies*. William Morrow & Co.

Jackson, Kenneth T. 1967. *The Ku Klux Klan in the City, 1915-1930*. Oxford Press.

Johnson, Charles A. 1969. *Denver's Mayor Speer*. Green Mountain Press: Denver, Colorado.

Kania, Alan and Hartman, Diane. 1993. *The Bench and the Bar: A Centennial View of Denver's Legal History*. Windsor Publishers.

King, Jeffrey S. 2013. *Kill Crazy Gang: The Crimes of the Lewis-Jones Gang*. The Frank Manley Publishing Company: Washington, D.C.

Kipling, Rudyard. 1899. *The Works of Rudyard Kipling*. Century Company.

Kreck, Dick. 2003. *Murder at the Brown Palace: A True Story of Seduction and Betrayal*. Fulcrum Publishing: Golden, Colorado.

Kreck, Dick. 2009. *Smaldone: The Untold Story of an American Crime Family*. Fulcrum Publishing: Golden, CO.

Kreck, Dick. 2016. *Rich People Behaving Badly*. Fulcrum Publishing: Golden, Colorado.

Kutler, Stanley, ed. 1997. *Abuse of Power, The New Nixon Tapes*. The Free Press.

Larsen, Charles. 1972. *The Good Fight: The Life and Times of Ben B. Lindsey*. Quadrangle Books: Chicago, Illinois.

Lawson, Walter. 1910. *Robert Wilbur Steele, Defender of Liberty*. Carson-Harper Company: Denver, Colorado. Chapter 4, Wilder Los Angeles Herald, V 33, N 12, October 1910.

Lay, Shawn, ed. 2004. *The Invisible Empire in the West: Toward a New Historical Appraisal of the Ku Klux Klan in the 1920s*. University of Illinois Press.

Leonard, Stephen J. and Noel, Thomas. 1990. *Denver: Mining Camp to Metropolis*. University Press of Colorado: Niwot, Colorado.

Logan, James K, ed. 1911. *The Federal Courts of the Tenth Circuits: A History*, Volumes 62-63, ed. Wesleyan University (Middletown, Conn.) Alumni Record.

McMechen, Edgar Carlisle. 1919. *Robert W. Speer: A City Builder*. Denver Smith-Brooks Printing.

O'Hare, Sheila and Alphild Dick. 2012. *Wicked Denver: Mile-High Misdeeds and Malfeasance*. Arcadia Publishing: Charleston, South Carolina.

Pettem, Silvia. 2009. *Someone's Daughter: In Search of Justice for Jane Doe*. Taylor Trade Publishing.

Raine, William MacLeod. 1940. *Guns of the Frontier*. Houghton Mifflin Co., the Riverside Press.

Reading, Amy. 2013. *The Mark Inside: A Perfect Swindle, a Cunning Revenge, and a Small History of the Big Con*. Vintage Books.

Smiley, Jerome. 1913. *Semi-Centennial History of the State of Colorado*. Lewis Publishing Company: Chicago/New York.

Smith, Jeff. 2009. *Alias Soapy Smith: The Life and Death of a Scoundrel*. Klondike Research.

Stone, Wilbur Fiske. 1919. *History of Colorado*. S.J. Clarke Publishing Co.: Chicago, Illinois

Tanner, Karen Holiday. 2012. *Doc Holliday: A Family Portrait*. University of Oklahoma Press.

Tooley, Dale. 1985. *I'd Rather Be in Denver: Dale Tooley's Own Story*. Legal Publishing Company.

Van Cise, Philip. 1936. *Fighting the Underworld*, Houghton Mifflin Co.

Wilbanks, William. 2000. *True Heroines: Police Women Killed in the Line of Duty Throughout the United States 1916-1999*. Turner Publishing.

Winstanley, Art. 2009. *Burglars in Blue*. Author House.

Zamonsky, Stanley W., and Teddy Keller. 1961. *The Fifty-Niners: A Denver Diary*. Sage Books.

Made in the USA
Las Vegas, NV
23 October 2024